STERLING

The History of a Currency

STERLING
The History of a Currency

NICHOLAS MAYHEW

JOHN WILEY & SONS, INC.
New York • Chichester • Weinheim • Brisbane • Singapore • Toronto

Copyright © 1999, 2000 by Nicholas Mayhew. All rights reserved.

Published by John Wiley & Sons, Inc.

Published simultaneously in Canada.

This publication is designed to provide accurate and authoritative information
in regard to the subject matter covered. It is sold with the understanding that
the publisher is not engaged in rendering professional services. If professional
advice or other expert assistance is required, the services of a competent
professional person should be sought.

Library of Congress Cataloging-in-Publication Data:
Mayhew, N.J.
    Sterling, the history of a currency/Nicholas Mayhew.
      p. cm.
    Includes index.
    ISBN 0-471-38535-2 (alk. paper)
      1. Money—Great Britain—History. I. Title.
    HG935.M39 2000
    332.4'941 21; aa05 12-02—dc99
                             99-059989

Printed in the United States of America

10 9 8 7 6 5 4 3 2 1

Contents

List of Illustrations

Introduction

Like an underground stream that rarely comes to the surface but that nevertheless irrigates the countryside through which it flows, sterling runs through British history, from the Conquest up to the present day. Occasionally the currency looms large in that history, such as at the time of Henry VIII's debasement of the currency, or when the sterling–Euro dilemma paralyzed the Conservative party after the trauma of Black Wednesday in 1992. We know that similar anguished debate accompanied other medieval and modern devaluations, but between these recurrent crises, throughout Britain's history, the currency has played a less obtrusive though perhaps more fundamental role. For at least a thousand years England's currency has provided a—usually—sound foundation for the development of the national economy. Sterling, like the English landscape, has evolved over the centuries, reflecting and sometimes leading to changes in the nation's history, and also generating a sense of unchanging stability of fundamental importance to the national psyche. This permanent, underlying presence has not often commanded the attention of historians except at moments of rare crisis, but the long centuries of stability need also to be understood, particularly at the moment of possible transition to the Euro.

This is not to pretend that a study of the past will answer questions about the proper monetary policy for the future. But it is important that we understand the history of sterling, so that neither proponents nor opponents of monetary union should misuse that history. Traditionalists must not be allowed to appeal to sterling's unbroken centuries without a full understanding of the extent of evolutionary, and sometimes radical, changes that have occurred over that time. A currency that truly stands still cannot hope to meet the economic needs of the country. Equally, those who favor the change from sterling to Euro must take account of the contribution of sterling to that elusive but significant concept, the national identity. A proper understanding of the past can still inform our decisions, even though it may not simplify them.

Most of the bankers and economists concerned with the fortunes of sterling today are too preoccupied with the daily vicissitudes of the exchanges to spend much time on sterling's history. And most historians nowadays work only on the century or two of "their period," leaving other ages to other scholars. Both these approaches are the product of the increasing specialization that is a hallmark of our times. There is, however, something to be said for a different approach, which looks at a subject with a long perspective down the ages. Historians of money are particularly prone to assume that the workings of the currency only acquired "modern" characteristics at the moment when their own studies began, although as soon as the necessary evidence emerges it shows England's money behaving in essentially the same way from the twelfth century. Equally, contemporary bankers might benefit from a glance at the origins of the English monetary system and the thoughts it provokes about the nature of money. Specifically, the great contrast between historical currencies backed by precious metals and modern ones without such support seems much less significant when it is realized that metal-based currencies were also subject to fluctuations, and that—wittingly or unwittingly—it is governments that set the values of currencies, though these values are always liable to be tested by the markets. In short, the essential characteristics of money are evident in its historical behavior as much as in present times.

Currency problems have brought down ministers and broken whole governments, but more important they can put millions of people in or out of work, can bankrupt businesses, or drive innocent and hardworking families from their homes. Conversely, a successfully managed currency can lay the foundations for the prosperity of generations. Most controversially, the same policy simultaneously can bring wealth to one part of society and ruin to another. However obscure the technicalities of monetary policy may seem, these questions have touched and turned the lives of everybody for at least nine centuries. The victims, beneficiaries, and perpetrators of these policies often have not fully understood what was involved, but their lives were changed by the course of sterling as surely as by Bannockburn or Waterloo.

History has no simple recommendations for the future of sterling, but it can illustrate some of the possible consequences of past policy, and one message is very clear: Monetary policy matters and affects all our lives, as through history it has always done.

The earliest specific reference to sterling dates from the eleventh century, but the idea of the pound as a weight of silver of set monetary value divisible into 20 shillings or 240 pence first occurred in the time of Offa and Charlemagne in the eighth century. The shilling and the old penny were abandoned in 1971, but the pound survives. The pound sterling was a pound weight of silver of sterling fineness (92.5 percent pure silver) as well as a monetary unit, until the mid-fourteenth century, when the pound weight and the pound of money began to diverge. Though still composed of sterling silver, the weight of the monetary pound fell throughout the later Middle Ages. In 1560 its weight was stabilized at a level that hardly changed until the nineteenth century. This long period of stability has contributed significantly to our idea of sterling, but the Middle Ages contain an important lesson: A precious-metal currency is not necessarily an unchanging one, and the value of precious metal also fluctuates. Scholars, economists, and government ministers have for centuries sought a stable currency, and many have put their faith in metal without really grasping that the value of silver and gold will vary in accordance with supply and demand just like any other commodity.

Historians have been particularly prone to imagine that by reducing money to its metal content they could convert it to a constant measure. Even minds of the caliber of Isaac Newton and John Locke were seduced by the dream of a constant and unchanging currency unit with which to measure personal or public obligations. This moral idea of money has been extraordinarily influential and is associated in the public mind with concepts of truth and justice and with the belief that a government's word, like an individual's, should be its bond. A strong currency is like a strong character who walks tall, looking the world in the eye, and dealing fairly and equally with all. The application of such high moral standards in the world of business often has been extremely successful, and in the giving and taking of credit a reputation for fair and honest dealing always has been worth much fine gold—but currencies do vary, and it is a mistake to pretend otherwise. It is curious that although we have come to expect the price of goods to vary, we should be disturbed to see the value of money do so. Yet, of course, since the price of goods is the only reliable measure of the value of money, the two are indivisible. Thus, as every adult wage earner in the twentieth century learned, if prices rise but salaries do not, the value of our money has fallen.

For this reason, a history of the currency is also a history of prices. Here too the long perspective can be important. A study of prices in the twentieth century would suggest that fairly severe inflation was the norm, but if nineteenth-century prices are included in the analysis, one begins to wonder if inflation is the norm at all, or rather an aberration. Yet reliable price data survive from the late twelfth century, and this very long view suggests that rising prices are indeed a constant feature of our history. Such a view, founded on the accumulated evidence of eight centuries, necessarily has a degree of authority, but it needs to be tempered by two considerations. First, in so long a view what appears on the graph as a mere statistical blip may in fact cover the relatively short lives of millions. Second, one has to establish that evidence collected over so long a period is genuinely comparable and that the underlying structures of, say, the fourteenth and the nineteenth centuries are sufficiently similar to permit a meaningful comparison. Does the price of bread matter as much after the introduction of the potato? How do you compare an age when personal possessions might be limited to a brewing vat or a best bed with a time when every household expects to own a television or an automobile? This book will explore these questions and will suggest, without minimizing the differences between historical and contemporary events, that there is more continuity in the monetary history of England than usually is realized.

Consider, for example, the impact of war on the currency. War with France, in every century from the fourteenth to the nineteenth, had monetary consequences as far-reaching as those of the

two world wars of the twentieth century. But many other aspects of
the history of the currency reach across the centuries. For example,
the organization and availability of credit has been fundamental to
the conduct of business since at least the thirteenth century. Similarly linking past and present, sterling's international role always
has influenced its domestic functions, for the Sterling Area has extended far beyond England's borders, since the Middle Ages. The
independent Scottish currency of the twelfth and thirteenth centuries was pegged to sterling until 1367, and both currencies circulated equally in both kingdoms and across most of northern
Europe. In the later Middle Ages Scotland's money diverged from
England's, prompting reflections on the monetary consequences of
an independent Scotland. The accession of the Stuarts in England
brought the Scottish currency once more into line with sterling,
though the process was not formally sealed till the Act of Union in
1707, foreshadowing the years of sterling's global preeminence in
the nineteenth and early twentieth centuries. Again, when medieval
governments experimented with the intrinsic basis of the currency,
they foretold the eventual divorce between money and metal and
introduced us to the problems of managing the money supply. The
difficult path between a hard currency that controls prices but may
inhibit growth and softer money that can promote employment but
also may generate inflation is a path that Plantagenet governments
sought as earnestly as the Bank of England and the Chancellor of
the Exchequer do today.

Nevertheless, it would be foolish to pretend that the sterling
monetary system has not seen great changes. The currency that was
once regarded as a royal perquisite, managed entirely at the
monarch's discretion, gradually became subject to parliamentary
comment and, eventually, control. The silver basis of sterling was
infiltrated and then undermined by gold, and gold itself has been
dethroned by paper, plastic, and the silicon chip. Medieval credit
arrangements were vital to the conduct of business, but they were
revolutionized by eighteenth-century developments in banking, re-
organizing systems to put borrower in touch with lender so as to
improve and widen the provision of credit. Like the great Keynesian
discovery of the twentieth century that the wealth of the few de-

pends on the spending power of the many, this reorganization of credit shows that significant growth is dependent on the successful involvement of the mass of the population in the national economy. If the value of money is protected without sufficient regard for the value of labor, economies stagnate. Yet if the balance between human and money is allowed to shift too far in favor of people, the currency becomes too diluted to serve.

Concern for the effect of the currency on personal lives involves not just the impact of monetary policy on the mass of the population. The lives of the people who took these decisions put flesh on the bare bones of sterling's history. William of Gloucester, the thirteenth-century royal goldsmith, made a fortune from Henry III's money, as surely as George Soros did out of Norman Lamont's, and the story of their lives sheds a different, personal light on monetary policy. The lives of Thomas Gresham or John Maynard Keynes illustrate their times as well as influencing the course of sterling.

The history of sterling is thus in part the history of kings and bankers, but it is also truly popular, since from at least the eleventh century even the lowest peasants used coin and measured their assets and obligations in money terms. When government changed the money, or when it was left untouched, everyone felt the consequences. Now, for the first time in our history, government is likely to consult the people directly and specifically on a major currency question. For the sake of British currency, we really ought to take the subject seriously, since the outcome will certainly influence our future prosperity and may even affect the development of European democracy.

I

English Money from the Domesday Book to Henry VIII

I do not know which makes a man more conservative—to know nothing but the present, or nothing but the past.

—J. M. Keynes

English money was first called sterling in the late eleventh or early twelfth century. Uncertainty about the precise date arises because mentions of the use of sterling in the 1080s occur first in twelfth-century sources. However, we learn from the autobiography of Guibert of Nogent, written in 1115, that in 1107 he bribed a group of cardinals with £20 sterling to secure papal confirmation of the election of Waldric, chancellor of Henry I, as bishop of Laon. The earliest firmly dated use of sterling thus involved papal corruption on behalf of a senior English government minister to help secure a lucrative European post. As we shall see, much else in the medieval history of sterling has a surprisingly modern ring to it.

Such links with the continent were entirely natural in an age when the whole of western Europe was united in its Christian allegiance to Rome, and when the kingdom of England was united under the same lord as the Duchy of Normandy. In monetary terms, although the currencies of Europe already differed significantly from one another, broadly similar accounting conventions were applied from Rome to the Rhine and from Cologne to Carlisle. This system ran from the eighth century in Carolingian France until the Revolution and continued in Britain until 1971; it consisted of a pound made up of 20 shillings, each shilling composed of 12 pennies.

The pound was originally based on a medieval understanding of the Roman pound weight, and the monetary pound was a unit of value equal to a pound weight of silver. In the accounts of the Middle Ages, a pound (or lira or livre) was written in Latin as *libra*, and abbreviated to *li* or *l*. Our modern pound symbol, £, which will be used throughout this book, was introduced in the eighteenth century, and is merely an ornate letter L. When sterling began, around 1080 to 1100, the only coin of any kind was the penny, abbreviated as *d.* from the Latin *denarius* (French = *denier*). There were 240d. (12 × 20) made from each pound of metal. The shilling, abbreviated as *s.* from the Latin *solidus* (French = *sou*), simply meant 12 pennies. A halfpenny or a farthing could be made by cutting a penny into halves or quarters. A mark meant two-thirds of a pound and, like the pound, could be either a unit of weight, or of account in which case it was worth 160d. or 13s. 4d.

one pound (£) = 20 shillings (s.) = 240 pennies (d.)
1 shilling = 12 pennies
one mark = 13.33 shillings = 160 pennies = 13s. 4d.

A sterling meant one English penny, and £5 sterling actually was written as £5 *of sterlings.* Because the earliest references to sterling all relate to English money in France, it may be that the term originated as a foreign word for English pence. We meet the word "sterling" first in its Latin form, *sterlingus,* followed in the twelfth century by versions in French and by German and Italian forms in the thirteenth century. It is not known in Old English but appears in Middle English in the thirteenth century. The etymology of the word remains a mystery, though there has been no shortage of suggestions linking it variously with starlings, easterlings (i.e., merchants of northeastern Europe), and most convincingly with the Middle English root *ster-,* which has connotations of strength and stability. This last theory would fit well with the evidence of the coins themselves, which suggests that in the 1080s William the Conqueror introduced a major reform, raising and stabilizing the weight of the currency.

For almost a century before the Conquest, Anglo-Saxon coins had been struck according to a highly sophisticated and complex system of adjustable weight. This system is still not completely understood, but it is clear that otherwise identical Anglo-Saxon coins were deliberately struck on different weight standards. William I resolved to replace this system with the issue of coins on a single, unchanging heavyweight standard. The essential characteristic of the new coinage was that it was strong and stable, and it would not be surprising if this fixed coinage of William I was soon given an informal name that reflected these qualities. The commonest coins of William I, which were struck in the last few years of the reign, seem to have been struck to a weight of about 1.38 grams, while coins from earlier in the reign are of lighter and much more variable weight. Not enough of the earlier types of William's coinage have survived for us to be certain when the policy of a fixed-weight heavy coinage was introduced, but it may well have been part of William's overall administrative reform package of the 1080s. As well as the currency reform, a very heavy land tax was introduced in 1084, and the infamous survey of national wealth that quickly became known as the Domesday Book was set in hand in 1086.

The Anglo-Saxon people may have hated the Domesday Book, but it provides such a remarkable collection of data that it has permitted historians to make a series of very approximate estimates about the size of the population of England and the wealth it shared. It seems likely that about 2.25 million people lived in England and Wales at the end of the eleventh century, while the national annual income has been estimated at £400,000. Of course, this estimate, like the Domesday Book itself, puts a money value on many goods and services that were not actually paid for in cash. Every schoolchild knows that in medieval England many rents were paid off by working on the landlord's land, and some wages were paid in kind rather than coin. Some trade was conducted by barter. This picture has become so well established that some people are surprised to discover just how much coin was in use in early medieval England. But the Domesday Book in fact presents a picture of a society full of money, and money payments. Although manors sometimes were held for rents paid in kind or in exchange for service, rents paid fully or partly in money are common. There are many references in the Domesday Book to the particular way in which money payments should be made—by counting the coins or weighing them, or by making allowance for poor weight—that make it clear that coins really were involved. Moreover, when valuations are made, and the valuation of land was a principal feature of the Domesday Book, it is clear that such valuations often were closely based on real money rents. This picture is confirmed by the evidence for money rents that comes down to us in early twelfth-century monastic rentals, many of which list rents closely in step with Domesday entries.

If rural rents were so often paid in coin, it seems likely that money played an even greater role in early Norman towns. Although medieval town life was still very rural by modern standards, in towns a significant proportion of the population earned the larger part of their living from nonagricultural work. Townspeople specialized in a particular craft or trade, which led them to buy many of the necessities of life from other specialists. The agricultural belt around the urban settlement prospered from selling its produce to feed the city. Towns, buying and selling, and the use of money all proceed hand in hand.

The Domesday Book gives only a very patchy record of eleventh-century towns. Some major towns, such as London and Winchester, were not properly covered at all, and in other cases towns such as Coventry and Gloucester seem to have been surveyed as rural manors without exploring their urban elements. Markets, on the whole, are more likely to be listed in small places than in the larger towns where their existence seems to have been taken for granted. Nevertheless, enough is said about Norwich, Colchester, and Oxford to get some idea of the nature of eleventh-century towns, and the slightly later surveys of Winchester add to the available evidence. A picture emerges of urban property yielding customary dues and rents of about 12d. per house to a feudal overlord, but in addition there is evidence that these primary tenants then sublet their houses for much larger commercial rents paid by subtenants actually occupying the properties and making a living in trade. London may have had 12,000 inhabitants with York not far behind. Norwich, Lincoln, and Winchester may have had between 5,000 and 8,000 people, and Oxford and Thetford 4,000 or 5,000. The exact figures are less important than the point that these were large populations leading urban lives, and frequently using money.

Royal taxation and the extensive employment of mercenary soldiers also presuppose the kind of monetized society described here. Eleventh-century kings could not have raised the money taxes they did from a society unfamiliar with the regular use of coin. Moreover, it is hard to see why soldiers, for example, would accept payment in coin if at least the whores and innkeepers would not also accept it, and even then it is hard to believe that brewers and brothels alone supported the fiscal foundations of the medieval English state. The sort of model that is sometimes suggested, in which kings tax a subject people to pay their armies, but in which nobody else has much use for coin, simply would not work. By the time that England's money was first called sterling, the habit of buying and selling with coin was already well established, alongside a range of other non-monetary transactions.

A fundamental prerequisite of any precious metal coinage was a ready supply of bullion. No monarch could issue coins unless he had access to the necessary precious metal. Moreover, huge sums were required to provide the country with its means of exchange: A relatively modest sum, say £5,000, would weigh two tons. England never produced significant quantities of gold or silver from its own mines, so bullion had to be earned in foreign trade. This link between Britain's currency and overseas trade is a fundamental feature of the story of sterling that remains of paramount importance from the time of William the Conqueror until the present day.

We have a reasonable idea of how much coin was in circulation in England. It has been estimated that about the time of the death of William the Conqueror, about £37,500 or 9 million sterling pennies were in use. Combined with the estimates of English population, these figures would suggest there was about 4d. per head of the population. Of course, in reality there will have been a huge variation in wealth from person to person and place to place. Moreover, this average per capita figure takes no account of how coin circulated. But this crude coin per capita figure does provide a simple measure of monetization.

This estimate of the degree of monetization that had already occurred by the time of the introduction of sterling around 1080 provides the baseline against which further developments can be measured. For example, by 1300 the per capita supply of coin works out at 36d. for every man, woman, and child in England, and a farm laborer would earn about 1d. per day.

The monetary development of Britain between 1080 and 1300 falls into two periods: the first century to 1180, when currency policy evolved slowly from its Anglo-Saxon origins against a background of dynastic struggle and bullion scarcity, and the period from 1180 to 1300, which was characterized by a huge increase in the supply of bullion, which transformed the economy of Europe and necessitated a reorganization of minting and monetary policies.

William the Conqueror's sterling reform of the coinage in the 1080s may have ended the Anglo-Saxon practice of variable weights for newly struck pennies, but the established custom of altering the designs on the coins every few years, which had been introduced by King Edgar about 973, continued under William Rufus and Henry I. These periodic changes in design would have enabled people to distinguish between new and old coins at a glance.

This recoinage system raises two important points: First, it illustrates the important role of the king's government in validating the money. And second, it raises the issue of old worn coins. Since the coins were made of precious metal, they had an **intrinsic worth*** or value, which would be reduced as the coins became worn. Thus medieval coins had both a face value, usually of one penny, conferred on them by the king, and an intrinsic value derived from the value of the metal in the coin. In an ideal world, the face value and the intrinsic value should be equal or nearly equal. As we shall see, problems could arise if a significant difference grew between the two values, and people often were of two minds about which was the true source of value—the king's authority or the precious metal.

The system of periodic recoinage also had another important effect: It drew silver into the mints. For this reason, recoinage joined international trade in becoming the two most important influences on the level of coin output from the mints. However, there was one important difference between coin attracted to English mints by trade and that brought in for recoinage. While the former was an addition to the existing money supply, the latter merely recycled the nation's existing currency. As we shall see (below, pp. 13–17), the size of the national money supply had an important influence on the national economy, but in the early Middle Ages the crown thought lit-

---

* Terms in bold type are explained in the glossary.

tle about the provision of currency for the kingdom as a whole. The king was, however, very interested in mint output, because he drew a tax, called **seignorage**, from every pound of money coined.

Thus the king had a vested interest in regular recoinage. However, in the twelfth century the output of the mints was generally much smaller than it had been in the eleventh. Even though Henry I (1100–1135) continued the system of periodic recoinage, the levels of mint output fell because less silver was being brought to England in trade. The whole of Europe had less silver because productivity in continental (chiefly German) silver mines was in decline from the very high levels being mined in the late tenth and eleventh centuries. This again is another recurring theme in the history of sterling. Despite a growing appreciation of the importance of the money supply from the Middle Ages onward, the economy of Britain, and indeed of Europe, has been strangely vulnerable to random fluctuations in the output of gold and silver bullion from the mines. In the course of its long history, the value of sterling has been intimately connected with the fortunes of mines as far away as Bohemia, Mexico, and California. Precious-metal currencies made for surprisingly international financial markets.

It sometimes is argued that the whole economy of the western world cannot have been so much at the mercy of mining output. In theory, when precious metals became scarcer, their value would rise, and the rising value of gold and silver would not only make poorer sources of metal viable but also stimulate the search for new mines. This process would increase production once more and restore the equilibrium value of bullion. In practice, however, it never really worked out like that. Even if the theoretical model had operated as described, it would all have taken time, resulting in fluctuations as the forces of supply and demand played themselves out. However, the model also fails to recognize the enormous impact of the fundamentally accidental discovery of new mines. In the history of precious-metal mining, although there is some role for improved techniques, it is above all the discovery of new mines that has transformed bullion supplies, and to that extent supply has been more influenced by chance than by increased demand. Indeed, taking the long view over nine centuries of the history of sterling, increasing demand for money has been an almost constant feature of the developing monetary system, but the major spurts of supply have occurred independently from shifts in demand.

The vulnerability of the whole European economy to the vagaries of bullion supply is thus one of the recurring themes in the history of sterling. Even after the widespread introduction of paper money in the eighteenth century, the relationship between bullion and paper becomes a central theme, and it is not until the twentieth century that money finally frees itself from the chains of gold.

Although government could not control the international availability of bullion, it could influence the share of it coming to England. Most obviously, a healthy balance of payments would result in an influx of silver or gold, while a deficit would result in a national loss of bullion as English coin flowed abroad to pay for foreign imports. Accordingly, later medieval governments devoted a good deal of energy in trying to enhance the inflow of bullion brought by trade and to limit its loss. The resulting legislation seldom was effective and often was positively harmful. However, the governments also discovered the levers of monetary policy, which, when eventually properly understood, would work rather more effectively. This process of blundering discovery was painfully slow, and often attended by as many setbacks as breakthroughs.

For most of the Middle Ages monetary policy meant little more than controlling the intrinsic value of the coinage—in other words, deciding whether to debase or not. One of the most important and well-marked features of the sterling currency was to be its freedom from **debasement**, but it is important to understand what the processes involved, because debasement is the medieval ancestor of **devaluation**. Strictly defined, debasement meant a reduction in the purity of precious metal in the coinage. Sterling traditionally was silver 92.5 percent pure. There were occasional lapses below this figure, but most sterling coins usually were made somewhat better than the minimum purity to be sure of not falling below the required standard. Nonetheless, the basic principle that sterling was almost always at least 92.5 percent pure silver holds good.

However, the term "debasement" is sometimes used more loosely to mean any reduction in the amount of precious metal contained in the pound. Such a reduction could be achieved in other ways besides a reduced purity of metal. For example, the purity of the metal could be left unchanged but the weight of the coinage reduced. This was in fact the chosen method for alterations to the silver content of sterling in the later Middle Ages. (See pp. 28–29.) A reduction in the weight of the coinage was likely to be more open and aboveboard than debasement of the metal purity, but the effect on the intrinsic value of the currency was the same. Reductions in the purity or the weight of the currency both operated in very similar ways to a modern devaluation. Nowadays a reduction in the value of the currency, for that is all a devaluation is, is most obviously revealed by the reduced amounts of other currencies that the devalued currency can buy. This was also true in historical times, but in the past, when information about the foreign exchanges was less constantly available, a devaluation was most apparent in the reduced intrinsic value of the currency. Thus, in the later Middle Ages the pound sterling, which initially had been equal to a pound weight of sterling silver, came to be equal to about half that much silver. (See pp. 28–29.)

The economic effects of a medieval debasement (using the term loosely to mean a reduction in either weight or purity) were just the same as those of a modern devaluation. By reducing the value of the currency, a country made its exports cheaper for other countries to buy. For example, a sterling devaluation or debasement would mean foreign countries would need less silver to buy a pound sterling, enabling them to buy more English goods for any given amount of silver or foreign currency. Conversely, English purchasers abroad would need more sterling to buy goods there. In other words, a devaluation would encourage English exports and discourage imports. A currency of low value relative to the currencies of trading partners is known as a **weak** or **soft** currency, while one that is of high value compared with its neighbors is known as **strong** or **hard**. Countries with a hard or strong currency suffer less from inflation.

In the past, this relative strength or weakness also was revealed by the intrinsic metal content of the coins: Hard currencies contained more silver or gold. Equally, when a medieval currency devalued, it meant that the coins contained less metal. Thus the heavy, pre-devaluation coins could be melted down and made into more, lighter coins. In this way, a devaluation would lead to an increase in the money supply. From the point of view of an early medieval king, a devaluation would allow him to make a larger number of coins from any given supply of metal, and a higher mint output would yield a higher royal seignorage income. This, of course, was the prime motive for most medieval debasement, but its wider economic consequences were the same as those of devaluation today.

There is some evidence that Henry I may have allowed some of his coins to fall below standard. Some suspicion existed about the purity of the metal of some coins, and the weights of certain issues fluctuate. We know that some of the mercenaries paid with his coin complained that it was not up to standard, and Henry allowed his coins to be cut to demonstrate that the metal was good. This sort of snicking, signs of which can be seen on surviving examples, would expose the crudest types of debasement and forgery but would not have been sensitive to a more skillful and measured debasement. Silver 75 percent pure is not visibly distinguishable from 90 percent pure. For this reason the coinage had to be more thoroughly tested by **assay**.

The mint workers responsible for the manufacture of the coins and the purity of the coinage alloy were called moneyers. Although the term is also used to include less skilled laborers in the mint, the most senior and responsible moneyers often were skilled goldsmiths or merchants with substantial experience of international finance and trade. Such moneyers nevertheless had every reason to be careful since they were held personally responsible for the quality of the coins they issued, and every coin bore the name of its moneyer as well as that of the king. At Christmas 1124 Henry ordered all his moneyers to Winchester to attend an inquest into the coinage. It was a very public occasion intended to reestablish confidence in sterling, and at least one chronicle suggests that the coinage had already been judged and found wanting before the moneyers were summoned. It seems that on this occasion 94 out of a total of about 150 moneyers were castrated and had their right hands severed as a punishment for the poor quality of the coins they had made. In the context of early twelfth-century medical expertise, such mutilation probably amounted to a death sentence for many. It was the earliest, and certainly the bloodiest, of a series of attempts that were to take place over the centuries to restore confidence in sterling.

A modern public has learned to be skeptical of attempts to reassure the markets about sterling, but Henry I's purge of the moneyers was a much more dramatic statement intended to demonstrate both his commitment to the sterling standard and the consequences of any attempt to cheat the crown. At one time historians were suspicious about Henry's actions, believing that many of the mutilated moneyers in fact escaped punishment and were allowed to continue in office, but the most recent interpretation of these bloody events suggests that many moneyers were indeed gruesomely punished, and most were replaced in 1124. One or two moneyers, like one Brand at Chichester, may have escaped punishment by offering to pay large fines, but most were less fortunate. Moreover, it is by no means clear that they were all guilty. It is hard to see how individual moneyer fraud could have been so widespread and so coordinated. It is at least possible that contemporary complaints that the money was worth less are better explained by the very bad harvest of 1124. Whatever the truth about this gory episode, it does illustrate the importance already attached to the purity of the coinage, and the lengths to which the king would go to guarantee it.

Ever since Anglo-Saxon times there had always been a special link between kingship and the currency. Coinage was one of the special rights and duties of the king. Political sovereignty and the control of the currency have always gone hand in hand. The crown did delegate rights of coinage, most notably to the archbishops of Canterbury and York and the bishop of Durham, but any unauthorized minting constituted a grave threat to royal authority. This point was most clearly illustrated during the civil war between Stephen and Matilda (1139–1153), when both the rival monarchs, and a number of lesser barons, struck coin. In defiance of the king, his rival Matilda and her son Henry both struck coins in the territories they controlled, as did their supporters, most notably Robert and William of Gloucester. A particularly florid issue was produced, probably at York, by the local magnates Eustace Fitzjohn and Robert de Stuteville. The chroniclers complained that any lord with a castle seemed to be setting himself up as king and striking coin. In Scotland

David I took advantage of Stephen's troubles to seize Carlisle and the silver mines of Cumbria. The coins he then struck, together with those of his son Henry, made at Corbridge and Bamburgh, proved to be the beginning of a separate Scottish coinage. Although subsequently struck at mints within Scotland itself, this issue was closely modeled on English sterling. For the next two centuries this independent Scottish coinage voluntarily held fast to the weight and fineness of English sterling, and the two currencies circulated together at equal value. It was an early example of voluntary (and reversible) monetary union.

In medieval France, a weaker monarchy had progressively devolved coinage rights to counts right across the kingdom. One consequence of this relaxation of central control had been the emergence of a wide range of different coinages of varied weight and purity in different parts of the kingdom. In England it is significant that although some baronial and royal issues were of commendably good quality, sterling did lose something of its reputation for reliably high purity and good weight during the brief anarchy. However, the emergence of Henry of Anjou as Henry II (1154–1189) restored the authority of the monarchy, and with it the soundness of the currency. Although the first half century of sterling had been a rather shaky beginning, Henry II inaugurated a period of 200 years of stability that laid the foundations for sterling's reputation for stability and strength.

Henry II's reign also marked the end of the system of periodic recoinage every few years. In fact, it is possible that Henry I took this step toward the end of his reign, but disruption during the civil war makes it difficult to judge whether the failure to organize regular recoinage every two or three years was an administrative oversight caused by the troubled times or a deliberate shift of policy. But when Henry II turned his attention to the coinage in 1158, he seems to have taken a number of policy decisions. He sacked the existing group of moneyers and installed new ones. He reduced the number of mints, probably bringing those that remained under closer royal control. He increased the weight of the penny, stabilizing it at 1.4g, a weight it would hold well into the fourteenth century. Henry also may have introduced the use of French **Troy weight** in England, with a special **Tower pound** used at the mint in the Tower of London for the weight of the monetary pound sterling. He may have standardized and increased the charges for minting at a shilling in the pound. He abandoned the use of frequent recoinage, instead allowing the type introduced in 1158 to circulate for twenty-eight years.

The monetary reforms of the early part of Henry II's reign have the look of a concerned plan to simplify and rationalize the mints, which took place at a time when income from the mints was low, but from the 1170s these conditions of low output were replaced by a surge of mine and mint production that would transform the monetary picture of Europe over the next 150 years.

A major mining discovery took place in Freiberg, Saxony, in 1168, when carters carrying salt noticed lead ore exposed by their wheel tracks. They tested the ore in Goslar, a center of silver mining since the tenth century, and the results sent Goslar miners hurrying to Freiberg to begin a silver boom there that would last well into the second half of the thirteenth century. Of course the mining transformed the region and made the local margrave, Otto of Meissen, enormously rich on the 10 percent royalty he exacted, but the effects of this discovery reached far beyond Saxony. At exactly this time the mint output of Cologne and Flanders began to increase dramatically, and in the 1170s and especially the 1180s English mint production also rose sharply. In the course of the next 100 years other important mines were exploited at Montieri in Tuscany, in Styria and Carinthia and in the southern Tyrol, in Sardinia, and finally in Bohemia.

The effects of the silver mining boom were felt across the whole continent, and were reflected in raised levels of mint output at a host of mints. These increased supplies of coin provided the means of exchange that permitted a greatly increased volume of business in Europe's markets. Put simply, buying and selling became easier when there was more coin about. So marked was the upturn in economic activity that it has been described as a commercial revolution. Rising population in twelfth- and thirteenth-century Europe seems only to have been waiting for the greater availability of coin to permit a huge surge of economic growth. This synchronized monetary and demographic growth, leading to economic development on an utterly transforming and revolutionary scale, has marked parallels with similar events in the sixteenth and seventeenth century. (See pp. 39–76.) In both periods the economy and society of Europe experienced a time of great development and change, and both medieval and early modern historians have disputed whether the primary cause was demographic or monetary. The truth is that the experience of the time was not composed of separable demographic and monetary features but was rather an entity containing both elements, together with a number of others. For example, climatic and technological change may have affected agricultural and industrial productivity, and social developments may have been a cause of change as much as a consequence of it. This history of sterling naturally concentrates on monetary events in Britain, but it should nonetheless be understood that British monetary history took place within the context of European, and ultimately world, economic and political developments. Monetary factors in Britain influenced and were influenced by a much wider range of experience.

The evidence for English monetary growth in the late twelfth century is based on detailed analysis of surviving coins that allows a comparison between the size of Henry II's first coinage, struck between 1158 and 1180, and his second, introduced in 1180. This demonstrates, in the memorable words of one scholar, that English mint production of the later issue was "rising like a rocket" compared with that of the first issue. This impression is confirmed beyond any lingering doubt by the volume of mint output characteristic of the thirteenth century, for which explicit documentary evidence survives. The English mint accounts survive in an almost unbroken run from the 1230s until the present day, and there are in addition some isolated fragments from earlier in the thirteenth and late twelfth centuries. This run of monetary data can be compared with the surviving information on the price of essential goods in southern England, which also begins in the late twelfth century. Thus English historians enjoy a run of monetary and price data from around 1180 up to the present. No one has ever attempted to look at both runs of data together over the entire period, but such an approach is long overdue, as many of the insights of one period are relevant to another.

The early information on prices begins in the 1160s and comes in the form of isolated prices from the records of central government known as the Pipe Rolls. At that time wheat cost under 2s. a **quarter,** an ox about 3s., a cow a little less, and a sheep about 4d. There is almost no evidence on prices before this time apart from a few isolated scraps that are difficult to interpret. However, as far as we can tell, it looks as if the prices of the 1160s were very probably little changed from those of Domesday. A century of more or less stable prices also occurred from 1400 to 1500 or from 1650 to 1750, so there is no reason to think roughly level prices over the period 1080 to 1180 improbable. However, the Pipe Roll evidence shows clearly that the prices paid by government rose noticeably in the 1170s and 1180s, flattened in the 1190s, and rose once more in the new century. Thus wheat rose above 3s. a quarter, oxen rose above 5s., and sheep more than doubled in price. A much fuller range of prices survives from the early years of the thirteenth century from the records of the estates of the bishops of Winchester, and this source leaves no doubt that prices rose steadily through the thirteenth century. From the 1260s the now plentiful price data have been collected into a single series illustrating the cost of living in southern England up to 1954 by Henry Phelps Brown and Sheila Hopkins. They collected information on what they called a basket of consumables, which reflected the sort of ordinary, essential purchases of the time, and converted the resulting prices into a **price index.** Prices of the period 1451 to 1475 served as the base period, indexed at 100. This Phelps Brown–Hopkins Index can be married to the modern Retail Price Index to provide a rough indication of the behavior of prices over the whole period from the thirteenth to the end of the twentieth century. This index appears as a table in the appendix.

Any comparison of prices over such a long period is bound to contain distortions. New commodities, for example, potatoes, can alter the normal purchasing practice of the time, and any basket of consumables has to be adjusted to allow for this, but such adjustments obviously affect comparability over time. Moreover, if the price of, for example, meat rises, people economize by eating more cereals. Purchasing habits were not constant, even from year to year. Nor were the sources used always comparable, and no one source extended over the whole period covered. The wholesale prices mostly used would not properly reflect the retail purchases of many people. For these reasons historians have constructed a number of alternative price indexes that better reflect the actual purchases of various groups in particular places for much shorter periods. Nevertheless, so long as its shortcomings are understood, for a long-term general impression of the movement of prices the Phelps Brown–Hopkins Index is invaluable. For a history of sterling some such yardstick is essential, because the value of money can be explored only by examining the price of goods.

Despite the limitations of the price data, they compare very interestingly with the information on mint output. In the late twelfth and thirteenth centuries both rose. Now, the mint output statistics call for careful interpretation, just like the price data. Nevertheless, they do provide important information and, properly interpreted, are an essential guide to any estimates of the money supply. From the thirteenth century a number of estimates of the money supply have been made that can be compared with the level of prices. We also have estimates of the size of the whole economy similar to that made on the basis of the Domesday Book. Step by step we can grope our way toward a series of **macroeconomic** indicators for medieval England.

We have a good idea of how much money there was in circulation by 1300 and how rapidly it was changing hands. We also can estimate how big the economy was and what was happening to prices. We can compare each of these assessments with the figures for 1086 to get an idea of how the use of sterling was changing. The picture that emerges shows that money had already become a central consideration in the lives of even the poorest by the beginning of the fourteenth century. Our best estimates suggest that the money supply had grown between 1086 and 1300 from £37,500 to £900,000. Yet however dramatic the growth in the money supply may have been, in practice it will not have seemed so marked. This is because there were many more people sharing the available coins in 1300, so the amount of coin available per head of the population only rose from about 4d. to something like 36d. It cannot be stressed too much that these sorts of estimates can only be very approximate, chiefly because a good deal of uncertainty still remains about the size of the

English medieval population. In the figures given here, the population around 1300 has been guessed at 6 million, but various scholars have speculated about possible populations approaching as much as 7 million or rather less than 5 million, while a generation ago some estimates as low as about 3 million were current. Nevertheless, despite such uncertainty, and making allowance for the fact that everything cost more in 1300, so each transaction required more coins, coin looks more than twice as plentiful in 1300 than it had been in 1086. The size of the economy had grown from about £400,000 to about £5 million at 1300 prices, but allowing for the rise in prices and population, this works out at a figure of £0.21 for **GDP** per head in 1300 compared with £0.18 in 1086.

Estimates of Economic Variables for 1086 and 1300

	1086	1300
Population	2.25m	6m
GDP	£0.4m	£5m
Money supply	£37,500	£900,000
Relative price level	1	4
Velocity	10.66	5.5
Coins per head	4d.	36d.
Coins per head deflated	4d.	9d.
GDP per head	£0.18	£0.83
GDP per head deflated	£0.18	£0.21

What do these figures mean for the lives of the people? In the first place, they suggest that although the economy as a whole had grown significantly by 1300, most of that growth consisted in feeding a much larger population at about the same standard as in 1086. There is little to suggest that the quality of life for most people had altered much. On the other hand, there was a lot more money about. Even though most of that money was devoted to maintaining a higher price level, the increased amount of coin per head of the population exceeded the rise in prices. In **real terms** people had more money and were using it more in the course of ordinary life. This is why **velocity** was lower in 1300 than in 1086: Because there was more money available, it did not have to circulate so fast to accomplish the required business.

In 1086 people were using coin more than most people realize, but they also organized their lives so as to economize on the use of coin. Alongside money rents, there was much land held by labor services and much work rewarded by payments in kind. Between 1086 and 1300 cash payments became more prevalent. We know, for example, that by the twelfth century the sale of bread in towns was regulated to ensure that bakers' prices were not exorbitant and that the towns could be confident of a reliable supply. The retail price and availability of bread was to be a recurring concern of government and people at least until 1970 (see pp. 242–243), but already in the twelfth century it is important evidence for the frequent use of coin in one of the most fundamental areas of life.

Bread prices were controlled by what was known as the Assize of Bread. Town officials had to inquire into the local price of corn and then set the price of bread, allowing the bakers a reasonable payment for their labor. The calculation provided for a different price for bread for every sixpenny change in the price of wheat. In fact, it was the weight of the loaf that was altered to reflect the price change, since this gave more flexibility to the system, so although the price of a loaf was normally fixed at a farthing or a halfpenny (or later a penny or more), when corn was dear people received a smaller loaf for their money. One of the earliest surviving assizes, dating from the reign of Henry II, ran:

This is the Assize for making and selling Bread which has been proved by the Bakers of our Lord King Henry II. Namely that the Baker can sell as is written below . . . When the Quarter of wheat sells for six shillings, then the loaf must be good and white and weigh 16s . . . When the Quarter of Wheat sells for five shillings and six pence, then it must weigh 20s . . . and so on, by sixpences down to 1s 6d per quarter.

Because a pound sterling also weighed a pound, it was possible to use 16s. as a measure of weight. The assize also provided for different grades of bread. But the most important point of the assize was that it established a sliding scale from which the proper price of bread could be calculated from the price of wheat. Thus money stands at the heart of these twelfth-century market regulations for the staff of life. Moreover, not only was bread regularly bought and sold, but the system also assumes a cash market in wheat, in which prices fluctuate to reflect changes in supply and demand. The use and the value of sterling is inseparable from the price mechanism, and little sense can be made of money or prices if they are not studied together.

Bread and ale were almost as inseparable as money and prices, and throughout the Middle Ages the assize, or fixing, of bread usually was accompanied by an assize of ale. As soon as the earliest village court records begin to survive, in the thirteenth century, they show local lords in the countryside regulating the sale and price of ale. Money transactions are thus to be found at the heart of country life too. In the second half of the thirteenth century the best and strongest ale could be bought at 1d. a gallon, but a penny a day was also a typical unskilled laborer's wage. A more skilled specialist, say a thatcher, might get double that, and a top mason could receive 4d. A farthing would buy between one and two pounds of best white bread, depending on the price of corn. Cheese cost about $1/2$d. a pound. An average price for a cow would be about 8s., and a sheep just over 1s.

Nevertheless, although the monetized economy was more dominant by 1300 than it had been in 1086, labor services and payments in kind were still common. For example, in the 1260s a customary tenant of the abbey of Abbotsbury in Dorset such as Walter Blacche paid a fixed rent for his land of 5s. for a holding of about twenty to thirty acres, but he also had to provide labor for the abbey, especially at the busy times of the farming year. If Walter had enough oxen, each year he would spend one day plowing the abbey's fallow land and three days plowing enclosed abbey land. Because this work was seen in some sense as a favor owed to the lord of the manor, the lord customarily provided food, which was specified as white bread. If he was sent out as a carrier, using his own animal as a packhorse, he also got a white loaf, with a dish of cooked food and a drink. Robert Clac, on the other hand, only had four acres; he paid no money rent but had to do work for the abbey every week. He was too poor to have his own oxen, but when he was set to do heavy digging work for the abbey, he received a plowman's white loaf. The sense of mutual and customary obligations expressing the relationship between lord and master did not prevent the abbot from having the detailed arrangements for each tenant drawn up formally to make it easier to enforce his rights. Such formal lists of local customs regulating tenancies were not uncommon in the thirteenth century, and they reveal a balance between a money-based and a service-and-goods–based relationship. But in an important sense the detailed recording of nonmonetary obligations that had originated in a time of a less formal relationship between lord and man marked a stage in a process that saw customary practice codified, priced, and ultimately acquitted in cash. The list of Abbotsbury customs marks a transitional point in the process of monetization, but it leaves no doubt of the direction in which things are moving.

It should not, however, be imagined that the trend toward increasing monetization was unbroken. In fact, it was punctuated by periods of greater or lesser use of money, and the pattern over the country as a whole was patchy. In the thirteenth century the use of money did become more prevalent, but landowners sometimes preferred to exact labor service from their tenants and sometimes opted for cash rents. The process of monetization was a complex one, and did not advance at a steady pace over the centuries.

Throughout the great thirteenth-century commercial revolution England's money came only in the form of the sterling penny. Under Henry III a very few round halfpennies and farthings were struck, indicating a growing need for small change to meet developing retail trade, but for the most part such needs were met by the traditional expedient of cutting the penny into halfpennies or farthings (i.e., quarter-pennies) as required. Such fractions still can be found on surviving medieval fair and market sites, but for the most part the dominance of the sterling penny was complete. No larger English denomination was generally available before the 1340s, so larger payments involved bags, sacks, and sometimes barrel-loads of pennies. The legend of Robin Hood takes on a new aspect when it is understood that the taxes which paid for good King Richard's crusade or bad King John's disastrous campaigns in Normandy were collected and transported about the country in pennies by highly vulnerable packhorse trains. When Edward I sent his armies into Scotland he had to send cash with them in heavily guarded convoys. Medieval money had a very tangible, physical presence, and large sums were necessarily heavy, bulky, and vulnerable.

Only three different types of sterling penny were struck from 1180 until 1344. The Double Short Cross type, introduced in 1180, was succeeded by the Double Long Cross type in 1247, which in turn gave way to the Single Long Cross type in 1279. The 1180 issue bears the king's name HENRICUS REX, which was unchanged during the reigns of Richard and John. It was common practice in France to leave coin types unchanged for centuries at a time. But although the appearance of the coins and the name of the king were not altered, there was much concern about the wear and tear suffered by coins left so long in circulation. In 1205 John issued weights to the public to check the weight of the coinage, and much lightweight coin was then recoined. In 1247 Henry III organized a public assay of the coinage, which found it so depleted that it was necessary to replace the entire coinage with a new type. The old worn coins were melted and restruck, and the people received fewer, but better, new coins in exchange for the old worn ones they handed in. Given that people also had to pay 6d. in every pound to the king for his seignorage, and a further 10d. per pound for the cost of minting and to make up for the poor quality of the old coin, the entire exercise proved very expensive for the public. The chronicler Matthew Paris complained that "twenty shillings could scarcely be obtained from the money-changer's table for thirty," which was probably an exaggeration but does express popular resentment about the costs of recoinage.

If the general public paid heavily for the new coinage, the king and his moneyers did very well out of it. The term "moneyer" in England in the Middle Ages included a wide range of different types of people employed in the production of the currency. At its most comprehensive it could include both illiterate laborers at the bottom of the scale and at the top very senior civil servants such as Peter des Rivaux, who held high office under Henry III, Gregory de Rokesle,

Lord Mayor of London and defender of City privileges in the face of Edward I, and John Sandale, bishop of Winchester from 1316 to 1319. These distinguished men all served as wardens of the mint and exchange, but theirs was essentially a supervisory post, which could be exercised by deputy, monitoring the work of mint staff and accounting for the king's seignorage. Above the laborers but below the civil servants stood a group whose combination of financial experience and hands-on metallurgical knowledge made them the most important mint staff of this period. The central part played by someone such as Philip Aimer in the recoinage of 1180 was fairly typical. Philip was brought from Tours by the bishop of Winchester, and between August 1180 and May 1181 he was paid 16d. per day, double the rate paid to other senior moneyers. His son was paid 4d. per day. Philip Aimer's exalted salary marks him out from ordinary moneyers at a time when even they could be important City figures. Henry de Frowick (ca. 1247/68), for example, was one of the leading citizens of London of his time. He was made assayer at the London mint in 1247 and promoted moneyer a year later. Henry owned property in various parts of the city and rose to the rank of alderman and sheriff, marrying the daughter of another alderman and sheriff. There were strong family and professional links binding many mint workers together. Radulf de Frowick had been moneyer at London from 1218 until after 1222, and Roger de Frowick, goldsmith and moneyer, was active from 1292. Roger as exchanger at the London mint from 1297 to 1327 and was also active in City politics as an alderman and royal tax assessor.

Not surprisingly, many moneyers were goldsmiths, for many of the skills required in both professions overlapped. Nicholas of St. Albans, who acquired a controlling interest in the mints of London and Canterbury from about 1237 until his death in 1252, was a goldsmith. Nicholas's father, described by Matthew Paris as a goldsmith without equal, made the exterior of the shrine at St. Albans, before taking employment under the king of Denmark. Nicholas succeeded him and ran the Danish mint for many years before returning to England to take up a similar position for Henry III. He seems to have bought out several other moneyers and to have been almost solely responsible for the London and Canterbury mints in the early 1240s when activity continued at a very high level. By this time moneyers received a 6d. fee for each pound struck, rather than a daily wage, so high mint output made for very rich moneyers.

Nicholas's dominant role in the mint was subsequently filled by William of Gloucester, who seems also to have achieved a remarkable concentration of power within the mint and exchange in the 1250s. In addition, he was a citizen of London and king's sergeant by virtue of his work as royal goldsmith. The Great Seal in use from 1259 until 1272 was his work, and he carried out a number of royal commissions at Westminster Abbey, including a golden shrine for St. Edward the Confessor. William owned a goldsmithery in St. Vedast's parish. In May 1255 William received a share of the London mint formerly held by Nicholas of St. Albans. In January 1256 William and his wife Joan sold all their lands and houses in the City parishes of St. Helen and St. Martin Outwich. They were clearly substantial figures but they look to have been raising cash, perhaps for investment in minting. At any rate in 1256 William seems to have been a leading figure in a consortium of moneyers who took control of the London mint. Then in 1257 William also acquired the moneyer Robert's share of the Canterbury mint, launched an unsuccessful gold penny coinage for Henry III, the first English gold coin since before the Conquest, and became warden of the exchanges of London and Canterbury, concurrently with his moneyer role.

The property records of the consortium indicate that they all occupied property within a quarter mile of Old Change. This center for mint, exchange, and goldsmiths in London may be approximately located in the area between the St. Paul's Cathedral and Goldsmiths Hall. Old Change lay east of St. Paul's, running north into West Cheap. On the north of West Cheap lay Foster's Lane. Guthren's Lane, a famous center for good silver, ran immediately parallel to Foster's Lane. It is not too much to regard this little quarter as the cradle of sterling in its early years. Edward I moved the mint farther east into the Tower of London, where it remained until the move to Llantrisant in South Wales in 1975. However, long before then the Bank of England had replaced the mint as the real guardian of sterling. In the course of sterling's long history politicians at Westminster would struggle with the City for control of the currency, but it was usually the marketplace rather than the court that had the upper hand. To that extent the 1997 decision to hand the control of interest rates to the Bank of England (see p. 252) merely recognized one of the long-term realities of British monetary history. From earliest times, the nerve center and the beating heart of sterling have always lain in the City of London.

The group of moneyers led by William of Gloucester seems to have operated successfully until June 1260, when a judicial inquiry was set up to amend errors in the mint. Whatever the details of the problem, the upshot was that William of Gloucester was replaced as warden in January 1262. Merchants were being legally charged about 3d. in the pound more for mintage than it really cost. After 1262 this 3d. was claimed by the crown, but from 1247 till 1262 it had fallen to the moneyers and made them very rich. In this period £1 million was struck at London and Canterbury (though not all of it stayed in the country), making, at 3d. a pound, some £12,500 windfall profits for the moneyers, over and above their customary income. At a time when most men worked for a penny a day, an excess profit of 3 million pennies was a staggering sum. That the moneyers escaped the sort of draconian punishment typical of Norman and Angevin rulers may owe something to the milder temperament of Henry III but is probably better explained by the care with which the moneyers established the legal basis for their charges. Essentially some smart City operators had outthought the Exchequer.

The recoinage of 1247 to 1250 was carried out at a range of mints in towns and cities across the country. About half to three-quarters of the total output was struck in London and Canterbury, with the rest being made in the smaller local mints. The dies for all the mints were prepared centrally, presumably in London, and issued to the mints as required. These dies were made of iron with hardened steel tips engraved with the coin designs. An upper and a lower die were required, and the blank coin flan was sandwiched between the dies, which were then struck with a hammer to impress the designs. Each pair of dies seems to have been capable of producing about 10,000 to 30,000 coins. About 138 million pennies amounting to some £575,000 were struck in the three years from 1247 to 1250. Given that the weight and the metal purity of each coin had to be carefully controlled, this was a very considerable technical achievement, but it also gives a reasonable idea of the size of the English money supply in the middle of the thirteenth century. It looks as if the money supply was growing from around £300,000 at the end of John's reign, to about half a million around 1250. The recoinage of 1279 that introduced the Single Long Cross type of Edward I seems to have produced about £700,000, and the very large output that marked the opening years of the fourteenth century probably brought the money supply to over £1 million sterling around 1310 to 1320. It is hardly surprising that such marked monetary growth over the thirteenth century should have contributed to a commercial and price revolution. All the evidence also suggests that this was a time of very significant population growth. New land was everywhere being taken into cultivation as high prices and booming demand rendered even the least promising land profitable. Nor was the boom restricted to arable expansion. By far the most important English export of the period was top-quality wool required to feed the cloth industry of medieval Flanders, and it was this export that was chiefly responsible for drawing silver into England to feed the mints between domestic recoinages. The period has all the hallmarks of a prolonged export-led boom.

When Flemish merchants came to England in such numbers to buy wool, they were required to change their own Flemish coin and bullion into English sterling. The mint records list the names of scores of foreign merchants selling silver to the mint, where it was melted and then recoined as sterling. Although most European medieval rulers tried to enforce the exclusive use in their territories of their own coin, few were as successful in doing so as the kings of England. All transactions in England had to be in English coin, and the evidence of the coin finds shows that in the overwhelming majority of cases this rule was rigorously observed. Thus the Flemish demand for English wool, and the English demand that it be paid for in English coin, combined to ensure a flow of silver to the mints. The English government also tried to prevent the export of sterling, but this regulation was much less successfully enforced. Hundreds of finds of English sterling pennies have been made across northern Europe from the Baltic to the Bay of Biscay. Continental documentary evidence also leaves no doubt that sterling was popular in France, the Low Countries, and Germany. Its reputation for reliably pure metal and good weight made sterling a good currency in which to record debts and payments, for all parties were confident that the value of sterling would not waver. Yet sterling's popularity as a measure of value was equaled by its usefulness as a means of exchange. In most of mainland Europe in the thirteenth and fourteenth centuries sterling also was readily accepted because the merchants' need of sterling for wool purchases in England was so great.

In these circumstances of heavy continental demand there can be no surprise that continental mints began to make their own coins in imitation of sterling. These imitations, which were made mostly in the Low Countries and Germany, passed into circulation in England because they looked so much like ordinary English coins, but they usually contained slightly less pure silver. British hoards often contain about 5 percent of imitations. At times, most notably in the 1290s, the foreign imitations in the circulation grew above that figure, and the government took firm steps to drive them out, but for most of the time these imitations were only a minor irritant to the government. They are, however, evidence of the international popularity of sterling at this time, when a de facto sterling area flourished, embracing the British Isles, Scandinavia, and the northern shores of the continent from Riga to La Rochelle.

After almost 150 years of more or less continuous growth, the later medieval economy began to run into difficulties in the second quarter of the fourteenth century. The flow of silver from the mints and mines of Europe began to dry up, while the West's expensive taste for eastern silks and spices continued to send vast quantities of bullion to Egypt, the Levant, and the Black Sea in the galleys of Genoa and Venice. A huge European famine from 1315 to 1317 seems to have stopped the march of population growth in its tracks. In 1337 Edward III laid claim to the throne of France, beginning a period of intermittent but expensive foreign war that in the long term was to last until the middle of the next century and in the short term was to trigger perhaps the earliest recorded sterling crisis. Sterling fell on the exchanges because Edward III seized the profits of English wool sales in the Low Countries, to help him meet the expense of the war. Subsequently he imposed a heavy tax on wool exports for the same purpose, which eventually resulted in a reduction in English wool exports and a growth in the manufacture and export of quality English cloth. In this way cloth replaced raw wool as the prime English export upon which the strength of sterling depended. But by far the most devastating shock to the later medieval economy was the arrival of bubonic plague in 1348–1349. The Black Death was to reduce the total population by something like a third to a half, and recurrent bouts of plague and other diseases would prevent any demographic recovery for at least a century and a half. The available land and the national money supply were, at a stroke, shared among half as many people.

This catalogue of crisis and calamity transformed the economy of later medieval England and had a profound effect on sterling. Prices in England had been rising steadily through the thirteenth and early fourteenth centuries. They dipped noticeably in the 1330s and 1340s, recovered their buoyancy in the third quarter of the century (perhaps because there was suddenly more money per head of the population), and fell back again from the late 1370s to a lower plateau where they remained until the early years of the sixteenth century. Lower prices, of course, equate with a high value for sterling, while higher prices mean a lower value for the currency in terms of the goods it can buy.

The Black Death also transformed the labor market. Until the middle of the fourteenth century labor had been plentiful and land scarce. So many people died in the plague that after 1350 that position was completely reversed. The lords of manors in most parts of England found it increasingly difficult to find laborers or tenants for their lands. Wage earners suddenly found themselves in a much improved position. Parliament legislated to try to restrain rising wages, but nevertheless the building laborer who before the plague might have earned 1½d. a day after the plague could command 3d. By the early fifteenth century that rate rose to 4d., and a building craftsman would receive 6d. a day. These new wage rates, combined with the very flat prices of the period, clearly marked an improvement in the lot of the wage earner. However, sluggish prices also may have been a sign of a sluggish economy. We know that land was left unfarmed, and most towns show signs of an economic depression. Though wages were good, it was not always easy to find work.

At the other end of the social scale, the rich remained very rich. Richard Fitzalan, Earl of Arundel and Surrey (ca. 1306–1376), provides a spectacular example. A frequent lender to kings and queens, to London merchants and to other nobles, his executors found "in the high tower of Arundel on the day of his death in a coffer in various bags, both in silver and in gold, the sum of 44,981 marks and 20 pence" (£29,987 8s. 4d.). His agent in the City had a further 27,150 marks in chests kept at St. Paul's, and there were another 16,471 marks on the estates on the Welsh borders. This makes over £60,000 in cash, at a time when a typical manor might yield about £100 a year.

However, discussion of sterling prices and incomes is further complicated by changes in the metal content of the currency that took place at this time. The weight of the penny, which had been stabilized by Henry II at about 1.4g, was maintained unchanged until the 1340s, when a series of adjustments between 1344 and 1351 brought the penny down to 1.17g. Similar reductions in the weight of the penny took place again in 1413 (to 0.97g) and in 1464 (to 0.78g).

Weight and Value of the English Silver Coinage

Date	Weight of 1d.		Value of Tower pound
	grams	grains	
1200–1300	1.44	22.2	243d.
1346	1.3	20	270d.
1351	1.17	18	300d.
1413	0.97	15	360d.
1464	0.78	12	450d.

To put the same information in another way, the pound of 5,400 grains used in the Tower for minting purposes (92.5 percent pure silver) was struck into about 240 to 243 pennies until the 1340s, when it made 270d., 1351 when it made 300d., 1413 when 360d. were made from the pound weight of silver, and 1464 when it produced 450d.

The trend is unmistakable: In the later Middle Ages the pound sterling gradually came to contain less and less silver. However, this information needs to be seen in its wider European context, since the intrinsic metal content of every other European currency—in France, Flanders, Italy, Germany—all fell far more. For example, in Lübeck the weight of the pfennig, a much baser coin than the sterling, fell thus:

Weight of the Lübeck Pfennig

Date	Total weight (g)	Silver weight (g)
1255	0.501	0.474
1350	0.405	0.335
1403	0.405	0.227
1422	0.34	0.170
1492	0.27	0.101

The Scottish currency, which began life as the exact equivalent of the sterling in the mid-twelfth century, eventually parted company with sterling in 1367 and thereafter followed a more continental path. Thus from parity in 1357, Scottish money fell to half the intrinsic value of sterling in the 1420s, a third in the 1450s, and a quarter in 1511–1512. Incidentally, this Scottish experience suggests that voluntary monetary union was not irrevocable and did not weaken Scottish sovereignty. In the sixteenth century, however, Scottish debasement further reduced the value of Scottish money to one-twelfth that of sterling by the time James VI became king of England as well, in 1603. For a century thereafter one Scottish shilling was equivalent to one sterling penny, until the 1707 Act of Union once again united the two kingdoms with a sterling currency.

To sum up, although the intrinsic value of sterling fell in the later Middle Ages, that of other currencies fell far more. Sterling contained less silver in 1500 than it had in 1300, but it was still stronger than the currencies of England's trading partners. And, as we have already seen, sterling bought as much in England in 1500 as it had in 1300, despite the reduction in its metal content. This means that the value of silver had risen, the value of sterling (despite its lower silver content) had remained about the same, and the value of other nations' currencies had fallen (resulting in rising prices there).

From our vantage point six or seven centuries later it is easy to be dispassionate about this process of reducing the silver content of sterling, but it all seemed rather more worrying at the time. In later medieval France the debasement was very severe, so concern in England about the reduction in the intrinsic content of the coinage would have been entirely legitimate. There would have been no way of knowing whether the alterations in the period from 1344 to 1351 were the beginning of a series of debasements that would leave the currency very seriously weakened or merely a very modest recognition of the rising value of bullion. There was, moreover, an influential body of opinion that held that any alteration in the money was wrong. Debasement disrupted contracts, rents, and debts by altering the money in which payments were made in ways that those who drew up agreements could have had no way of anticipating. The Parliament held at Westminster in 1351 gave a voice to many of these concerns, and the Statute of Purveyors expressly stated that the coinage should not be reduced further in weight and that sterling should be restored to its ancient state as soon as possible. That Parliament should venture to comment on the coinage, which since Anglo-Saxon times had always been a very special area of royal privilege, marks a milestone in the evolving relationship between king and Parliament. Thereafter, the Commons spoke increasingly freely on the subject. In 1381 they held a long, well-informed debate on monetary policy, and later Henry IV exhibited the insecurity of a usurper by delaying a much-needed adjustment to the coinage for fear of arousing opposition.

Increasing parliamentary involvement in an area so fundamentally royal is noteworthy, but Edward III was probably no more enthusiastic about changing the money than his Parliament. It was essentially a technical decision, made necessary by the rising international value of silver. The main reason for the rise in the value of silver in the later Middle Ages was the reduced output from the mines. Discoveries of fresh silver sources after 1300 became increasingly rare, and compared with the thirteenth-century glut the fifteenth century has been described as a time of silver famine. Especially around 1400, and again around the 1440s, the mints of Europe were striking pitifully small amounts of silver. The English mints, which struck some £2,800,000 in silver in the century up to 1377, struck only about £700,000 in the 100 years that followed. And of course £1 in the earlier period contained more silver than in the century after 1377.

A reduction in the silver content of the currency was an obvious response to the European shortage of silver in the later Middle Ages, but it was not the only monetary policy employed. In England, rather later than on the continent, the decision was taken to augment the silver coinage with gold. Gold coinage became important first in Italy in the course of the thirteenth century. Henry III and Louis IX of France both tried to float a gold currency with little success, but in the 1290s a gold coinage was successfully established in France, and in England the (technically illegal) use of Italian gold florins was becoming more common. This was the time when Italian bankers made themselves indispensable with loans and other financial services rendered to the crown and the church. The inconvenience of a currency of silver pennies for large-scale payments made over long distances has already been noticed, and it must have been hoped that gold might facilitate international trade and high finance, leaving silver for the conduct of domestic trade. In the 1330s exchange arrangements were established at major ports such as Dover and King's Lynn to enable merchants to change their gold for the silver pennies they would require for trade in England.

The exchange at Dover was entrusted to an interesting man named Lapinus Roger (which might perhaps be translated as Roger Rabbit). A Florentine, who succeeded to his uncle's post as assayer and exchanger at Canterbury in 1292, Roger subsequently also worked in the London mint. In addition to, or perhaps as a consequence of, his professional services he also acquired some 300 acres of marsh in Kent. The purchase illustrates both Roger's prosperity and his attachment to Kent. He married a Kentish girl and was admitted a freeman of Canterbury, where he worked for Edward I, II, and III. Roger's conduct seems to have been exemplary, and although he quarreled with the influential treasurer, Walter de Langton, over wages, no charges of misconduct were ever suggested. He was occasionally deprived of office as a consequence of political changes during this period, but he was consistently reinstated and in addition was frequently called on to resolve mint crises in London. His son Robert subsequently also became a moneyer at Canterbury, the third generation of this family to be employed at the mint there. Roger's career illustrates several typical features. For example, family connections were often important in other medieval moneyers' careers. Equally, many other moneyers were of foreign origin but settled permanently in England. And continental experience was especially useful when dealing with foreign gold coin.

In the later Middle Ages gold flowed into Europe from sources in Hungary and from the western Sudan in Africa. In 1344 the English government took the decision that gold coinage had become so important that an English gold coin was required. A new English gold florin worth 6s. was introduced, but with only limited success. It was immediately replaced by the English noble, worth 6s. 8d. (i.e., 80 pennies). Although the weight of the noble was adjusted in 1344 to 1346, 1351, and 1412, its appearance was unchanged and it quickly established itself as the form in which sterling was most often encountered in international trade. Like the sterling silver penny, this beautiful gold coin was much sought after as a coin of reliable weight and purity that was indispensable for those who traveled to England for the wool trade. Like the penny, the noble was also imitated abroad.

The gold coinage unquestionably met a need, but it brought with it a range of completely unforeseen problems, which would complicate English monetary policy until the nineteenth century. In a nutshell, the difficulty was that running a currency composed of gold as well as silver was far more complicated than one consisting only of silver. We have already noticed that the value of silver was liable to change over the middle to long term. This changing value called for corresponding adjustments to the weight of silver in the currency. Gold too fluctuated in value, necessitating adjustments to the coins, doubling the chance that the coins might get out of step with the current market metal values. But bimetallism introduced a further problem. Since sterling payments could now be made in gold or silver, merchants were quick to recognize that they should pay in whichever metal gave them the best deal. If the value set on gold in England was slightly higher than that operating in Flanders, or France, foreign merchants would send gold to England, while the English would choose to make their payments abroad in silver. This phenomenon is known as a **bimetallic flow**.

There were several periods in English monetary history when such flows can be seen to be operating, revealing themselves through a marked imbalance in the metals being brought to the mint. From the 1350s to the 1420s the English mints favored gold. Changes in mint policies abroad made English mints a haven for silver in the 1420s, but thereafter the English preference for gold reestablished itself. As a result, in the 1460s (when a recoinage allows us to make an estimate) it looks as if the circulation in England was made up of about two-thirds in gold coin (by value) and only one-third in silver. Similar periods of imbalance stand out in later periods, for example in the early years of the seventeenth century (see pp. 64–65) and for most of the eighteenth century (pp. 103–104). But the problem was acute in the fifteenth century, when the currency must have been extremely top-heavy. A pound sterling might be represented by only three gold coins or by as many as 240 silver pennies, and there can be no doubt that silver made a much more flexible means of exchange, facilitating far more ordinary transactions. If one imagines a situation today in which £50 notes are readily available but pound coins very scarce, one would get some idea of how the denominational structure of the currency would affect daily business. Undoubtedly the top-heavy nature of the fifteenth-century coinage inhibited business. Although gold might have been planned as an addition to the silver currency, all too often it turned out to be an alternative. Indeed, at certain times it positively contributed to the shortage of silver rather than alleviating it.

A more imaginative response to the monetary problems of international trade was an agreement between Edward IV and Duke Charles the Rash of Burgundy. In 1469 it was agreed that English groats (worth 4d. sterling) and Burgundian **double patards** might pass interchangeably at equal value in England and the Low Countries. Since English coin had always been found plentifully abroad, it is difficult to gauge the immediate effect of the scheme on the mainland, but in England the finds suggest that Burgundian coin was in use alongside English coin for at least forty-five years. This proved to be longer than the double patards lasted in the Netherlands, where their issue was soon discontinued. Such examples of monetary union have an obvious interest for Britain and Europe today, but the lessons they teach are not straightforward. While this instance refutes the notion that monetary and political union are inseparable, it also shows that a successful monetary union requires a degree of economic convergence not achieved in the later fifteenth century.

Some other elements of medieval monetary policy were even less successful. For example, most medieval European governments introduced bullionist legislation designed to oblige merchants to bring precious metal into the country if they wished to trade. The export of coin or bullion was regularly prohibited as part of the same policy. In the 1430s the government of Henry VI required wool to be sold only for cash, as part of the same drive to bring bullion to England. On the whole, most bullionist legislation was ineffective, and when it was successfully enforced it proved to be an impediment to trade rather than a source of precious metal. For example, the 1430s insistence on cash payment brought the wool trade to a standstill, such was the dependence of the trade on credit terms.

The role of credit in the history of sterling was probably as fundamental in the Middle Ages as it is today. Many, perhaps most, sales were made on credit, a bargain being sealed by the payment of an "earnest penny" when the deal was struck, with the balance paid later. We know that the wool and cloth trades involved credit at every stage in the process from sheep to finished cloth, and merchants often carried over debts from fair to fair. But small-scale, local, retail trade also depended on credit sales. The court rolls of scores of manorial courts across England contain hundreds of references to small debts, often dating back years.

For example, in the tiny Dorset village of Gussage All Saints in 1323, William Russell tried to recover a debt of 20s. 11d. from

Joanna, the widow of John Puleyn. William had lent John two quarters of wheat two years earlier. When John died William lent Joanna 11d. cash. Now he sued her in the manorial court to recover his money, offering a **tally** as evidence of the corn transaction, and also claiming 5s. damages. Joanna admitted the 11d. and 7½d. of the 20s. debt but denied the rest, and counterclaimed that William owed her a wool sack. Although it is hard to get to the bottom of a case like this—the court fined both parties in the end—this sort of evidence does give a flavor of small transactions in the heart of the medieval countryside. The tally, the credit sale, the use of real cash, and the exaggerated valuation and claim for damages are all representative of small peasant deals in the fourteenth century.

In another case in the same village in 1347, Robert Bosse admitted owing John Russell and his wife Joanna 18d., outstanding from a sum of 5s. arising from a contract between them for Joanna's marriage. She was presumably Robert Bosse's daughter. Bosse also admitted a further 7d. in marriage expenses, but he denied owing two oxen, priced very cheaply at 2s., or a further 3s. 10½d. for the wedding feast. With a whole sheep costing not more than 1s. 6d., a goose 3d., and ale at eight pints a penny, it was probably a good party.

Such cases offer a glimpse of ordinary life in medieval England and show that money and credit were commonplace even at the lowest levels of society. In more exalted circles, credit might range from the small consumption loans of the wealthy right up to high finance and government borrowing. William Cade, who was lending to a distinguished list of clients in the mid-twelfth century, is among the earliest Christian usurers known to us. In theory at least, the church's prohibition on usury, made at the Council of Tours in 1163, forbade lending at interest, but it is clear that Cade had a number of Christian successors in the twelfth-century merchant community in London in men such as William Fitz Isabel and Gervase and Henry of Cornhill. The Jewish community in London had been established, as a cutting transplanted from the Rouen community, by William the Conqueror, for the Jews had been excluded from Anglo-Saxon England. By the middle of the twelfth century, however, Jewish communities were well established in Norwich, Lincoln, Cambridge,

Winchester, Thetford, Bury St. Edmunds, Northampton, and Oxford. By 1190 they were important enough in York to be massacred, and for much of the thirteenth century they endured the exactions associated with the king's special "protection." Jewish lending was a principal source of cash advances in England until the expulsion of Jews in 1290, and the appearance of Italian financiers in strength about the same time suggests they may have come to fill a vacuum.

Important Italian family banking firms, most famously the Bardi, the Frescobaldi, and the Peruzzi, lent extensively, especially to the king and to monasteries. Edward I secured his loans by allowing the bankers to collect his taxes, and the major religious houses repaid their debts with wool. The Italian firms, however, which often had branches established elsewhere in the centers of European trade, were also well placed to offer exchange and remittance facilities to a range of international merchants. An English merchant needing to make a payment in Bruges could buy a **bill of exchange** from an Italian financier in London, which would enable him or his agent to collect local Flemish coin in Bruges in a few days' time. The system was initially devised to spare the English merchant the trouble and expense of sending English silver out of the country and paying a foreign mint to convert it into local coin. It all worked particularly well if the Italian financier had an agent in Bruges with customers who wanted English coin in London. However, financiers soon recognized that as well as the advantages of easy remittance and foreign exchange, the delay between the purchase of the bill and its presentation for payment amounted to a temporary cash loan. In due course the credit aspects of the transaction grew in importance, especially since medieval laws against usury could be circumvented since interest payments could be concealed easily in the other charges for exchange and remittance. Sometimes the exchange element became notional in what had become essentially a credit transaction. Bills of this sort, though medieval in origin, were to remain important credit instruments into modern times.

Some idea of the scale of credit in medieval England can be gauged from the scheme established by Edward I in 1283 and 1285 to try to improve the recovery of debts. Creditors could send a certificate of the debt from the local court where the debt was first recorded to Chancery. The officials there would instruct the sheriff in the debtor's county to pursue the debt. Over 30,000 such certificates from the 1280s to the 1460s survive, leaving a remarkable nation-wide record of debt. Thus we know, for example, that Lapinus Roger lent Henry de la More, goldsmith, citizen, and merchant, £80 in 1317, which he was due to repay at £20 a year. Such lending was certainly not restricted to the merchant community. The chaplain Henry de Grantham, who lent Ralph Fitz William, knight, £49 13s. 4d. in York in 1294, was one of scores of churchmen who made loans. Ralph's brother, William, was also a borrower, getting 60s. from Juliana Fitz Lawrence of Bootham.

The body of credit revealed by these certificates is impressive evidence of the extent of lending in medieval England, but of course it speaks only of debts that had to be pursued because they had not been repaid as due. The certificates probably represent only about 20 percent of the loans being entered in the town courts. Borrowing and lending were clearly an established part of medieval life.

The sources of credit, which might be local, Jewish, or Italian, shifted over time. Similarly, the preferred instruments of credit varied. Sometimes the lender received a bond—a sealed document recording the debt, the terms for repayment, and the debtor's acceptance of the obligation. On other occasions the debtor acknowledged the debt in the records of the local court, which would facilitate the process of recovery if necessary. The bill of exchange, however, proved especially popular since it might be transferred to another creditor, beginning itself to circulate in place of the money it represented. Since such bills were later sold on to another creditor at less than their face value (i.e., at a discount arranged between buyer and seller), a transferable bill often is described as being **negotiable**. In fact, these sorts of developments took place only slowly over the centuries. What began tentatively as a personal arrangement between Italian merchants who knew and trusted one another gradually spread as customary practice among the wider merchant community but remained unknown more generally. At first these practices were entirely without the force of law, which sometimes took centuries to catch up with merchant practice. Yet despite the extremely slow evolution of credit arrangements, there can be no doubt that lending played a major part in medieval trade. Credit was not a sixteenth-century innovation. All the evidence suggests that lending, either at interest or to clinch a sale, was an essential, everyday part of medieval life, and business simply could not have been carried on without it.

It is sometimes argued that credit should have prevented any serious medieval shortage of coin. This argument loses much of its force once it is recognized that medieval credit was already at full stretch, yet still money was in short supply. But, more fundamentally, it needs to be understood that the extent of possible credit was in fact limited by the money supply. In the sixteenth century contemporaries fully understood that "credit is always most, when there is most Money to satisfie the same" and that "When there was but little Money, the Credit was also very little." And these maxims were as true in the Middle Ages as they are today. Credit rises and falls with the money supply, rather than supplying its deficiencies.

The behavior of medieval money thus has much in common with modern money. Medieval debasements were much like modern devaluations, and the money supply influenced the rest of the economy in the same way as it does today. Credit was of fundamental importance, then as now, and already in the Middle Ages sterling had become established as a badge and symbol of the English nation. The links between sovereignty and the coinage were already well established. Although starting at parity with sterling, by the later Middle Ages both Scotland and Ireland were exploring the possible advantages of weaker currencies and the help such a policy might give to exports. Of course, the choice of a precious-metal currency imposed restraints on governments, as it would continue to do until the twentieth century, but to a surprising degree many of the fundamental qualities of money remain evident whatever the monetary medium.

2

Inflation: 1515 to 1650

... a change in prices and wages as measured by money is capable of transferring wealth from one class to another, and redistributing fortune in a way which baffles anticipation and upsets design.

—J. M. Keynes, 1920

Some time around 1515 prices in England began to rise. After almost 140 years of stable prices, almost everything gradually became more expensive. Of course, good and bad harvests continued to cause short-term peaks and troughs, but by averaging the effects of harvest fluctuation we can discern a new overall price trend. This new price trend was to continue on its upward course until the middle of the following century. So marked was this new trend that the period 1515 to 1650 has been described by historians as a price revolution. It stands, with the thirteenth and the twentieth centuries, as one of the great inflationary episodes in English price history. The price index, which stood at 107 in 1515, reached 839 in 1650. By late twentieth-century standards such single-digit annual inflation may not seem too bad, but for those living any time between the 1540s and 1650 the great inflation was a subject of much distress and not a little discussion. Inflation redistributes wealth, tending to take from those on fixed money incomes while rewarding those productive groups with goods to sell and the energy to renegotiate commitments regularly in the light of new price levels. New prices called also for new wages and new rents, and changing material values altered social and political values too. This process of renegotiation loosened ancient social bonds and posed new and puzzling political questions. Most obviously, by definition, rising prices meant a fall in the value of sterling.

The price index, which monitors the cost of goods from the late twelfth century to the present day, is an invaluable tool that helps us to compare values over time, but it is necessarily a simplification. It is based on a shopping basket of goods, but the prices of the different items in the basket do not all move equally. Some commodities may have risen in price more than the basket as a whole, others less. In the sixteenth century, necessities rose more than luxuries, because people naturally economized on goods they could do without. In the context of the time, this meant that most people, especially in provincial southern England, began to eat less meat, making up the shortfall in their diet with more cereals. As a consequence, grain prices rose more than animal products, and food prices as a whole rose more than other goods. This sort of shift in consumption means that the single shopping basket price may tend to overstate the rise in the cost of living that people actually experienced. This does not mean that they were better off than the single price index suggests, merely that they lived less well than before.

There is also some evidence that in cities, especially London, retail prices may not have risen as much as wholesale prices. (This is because the wage element makes up a larger part of a retail price, and wages rose less than prices, though, of course, retail food still cost more than wholesale.) Urban prices also differed from the smaller town and country prices: On one hand the concentration of rich people in the cities maintained the demand for luxury goods, while on the other some city authorities actively tried to restrain the rise in prices of the most basic foodstuffs for the sake of the urban poor. For all these reasons we need to be aware that individual experience varied widely and the extremely useful basic wholesale prices index is no more than an abstraction. Indeed, it is this truth that gives inflation its most socially corrosive bite: Because prices, wages, and rents move differently from place to place and group to group, inflation creates winners and losers whose individual experience cannot be evened out by some universally applicable deflator.

This makes it all the more important to try to get behind the index to see some of the different components involved in any generalization about price levels. Leaving aside the effects of unreliable harvests and regional variation, we can see that during the early years of the reign of Henry VIII (1509–1547) a quarter of wheat cost around 6s., which meant that a penny would buy slightly more than two large (800g) loaves of best white bread or nearly four large loaves of wholemeal. A cow would cost about 13s. 4d., and butter was 1d. per pound, cheese ¹/₂d., and beef ¹/₂d. Of course harvest fluctuations could easily double or halve these prices in any single year, but these general, typical prices would have been recognized as normal by any English man or woman from around 1380 to 1520. From the beginning of the fifteenth century to the middle of the sixteenth, an unskilled building laborer would have been paid about 4d. per day. For over a century up to 1520, in any normal year that 4d. would have easily bought two large loaves, a gallon of ale, and a helping of meat or cheese. In fact, of course, most of the wages and prices we know about come from southern England, and regional differences played a part. Livestock products tended to be cheaper in the north and cereals dearer. Any simple comparison of wages and prices must recognize that work might not be available every day, or, on the other hand, a man might decline work some days, preferring to value his own leisure if he had already earned enough to live on. Individuals were normally part of households, and the household income was perhaps more significant than that of a single wage earner. Moreover, average wage rates necessarily conceal variations; work might or might not sometimes be paid for in food or in food and money. Servants in town and country were particularly likely to be paid in kind with a relatively small cash element. Nevertheless, despite all these variables, at the beginning of the sixteenth century people had a very firm grasp on how much things cost and what they should be paid. They knew, because the normal range of wages and prices had by then been established for over a century. Dick Whittington, three times Lord Mayor of London in the period 1397 to 1420, would not have been surprised by the prices being paid by the young Thomas More 100 years later.

Of course, many people grew at least a part of their own food, which gave them some protection from inflated prices. This was particularly important as wages followed the rise in prices only slowly. However, hardly anyone was truly self-sufficient. Large farmers and smallholders alike were still heavily involved in the market, selling surpluses for money to pay rents and taxes and to buy the goods they did not produce. And many of the population were already landless wage earners. It has been estimated that over the country as a whole 38 percent of the population were members of landless families who therefore worked for wages insofar as they worked at all. Moreover, many smallholders and craftsmen probably also earned their living chiefly by wage-work. On this basis, it has been suggested that already by the early sixteenth century some two-thirds of the population lived in families supported chiefly by wages or craft sales, who had to buy a large part of their subsistence at current prices. For the majority of people, self-sufficiency provided little or no shelter from the great inflationary storm.

Around 1500, however, that inflation still lay in the unforeseen future. Even laborers without land or taxable property were able to make ends meet relatively comfortably so long as they could find work. Compared with either 1300 or 1600, wages were good and prices low. Thorold Rogers, the nineteenth-century historian of English prices, famously described this period as "the Golden Age of the English labourer." The working man's wages would not again buy as much food until the 1880s. The yeoman in early sixteenth-century society stood above this prosperous laborer. Sir Thomas Smith (1550) described the typical yeoman as earning a yearly income from his land of 40s. (i.e., £2) in the early part of the century. They "commonly live wealthily, keep good houses and [work] to get riches," enjoying "a certain pre-eminence, and more estimation than labourers and the common sort of artificers." The merchant freemen of the towns stood well above the yeomen, while the gentry topped the pile. Knights had an income of about £120 a year or more while barons might receive somewhere between £650 and £1,000. The security of such social divisions, however, was being undermined by inflation. As Smith commented, the £2 yeoman of the early part of the century might make "six pounds as money goeth in our time [1550]."

The causes of this great inflation have been much debated. In the sixteenth century the experts of the day were clear that monetary problems were to blame for the inflation. Some blamed government debasements, while others explained inflation in terms of the influx of new bullion from the Americas. The perspective of history enables us to see that prices begin to move before either debasement or New World bullion began to play a major part. Accordingly, some historians have suggested instead that rising population could have been the prime cause of the increased demand that pushed up prices. Others have developed a more sophisticated monetary explanation and drawn attention to new sources of bullion in Europe before the American supplies began to arrive. In fact, of course, the price level was determined by the working out of a number of factors in concert, so looking at monetary or demographic factors in isolation is unlikely to be helpful. However, the **quantity theory** of money, which explores the relationship between the price level and the money supply, can allow monetary and demographic factors to be analyzed together. Although monetarists in particular have been guilty of arguing for a simple causal association between money supply and the price level, if sufficient consideration is given to changes in the velocity of circulation and in the size of the economy and its productivity, a more rounded and balanced assessment is possible within the structures of quantity theory. Prices were influenced, obviously, by the supply of money but also by the demand for it, which will have been affected by the size of the economy and by the way in which money was being used. All these factors will figure in this discussion of the purchasing power of sterling during the price revolution.

As we have seen, English prices seem to turn upward in the years around 1515. Population was probably at about the same level then as in 1470 (2.3 million) but it was to grow markedly thereafter, reaching some 2.9 million by 1546. If population was growing faster than agricultural output, it may have contributed to rising prices from 1520 to 1540. The money supply seems to have shown some signs of growth before 1515; it has been estimated at about £1.4 million in 1526 compared with about £0.9 million in 1470, though at both dates too much of the available money was in gold, which was a much less convenient and flexible medium than silver. This monetary growth first occurred well before the bullion from the Spanish Americas began to arrive in Europe, for the huge silver mine at Potosi was discovered only in 1545, and gold shipments did not exceed an annual average of 1,000 kilograms (kg) before the 1530s. However, the mines of central Europe had begun a period of renewed prosperity in the last quarter of the fifteenth century, and the Portuguese were bringing in large amounts of gold from west Africa at the same time. In other words, any bullion shortage could have begun to ease long before the American bonanza. Thus money supply, prices, and population all grew between 1500 and 1540.

The interplay between these factors and growth in the economy as a whole is too complex to encourage the pursuit of single-factor explanations to the exclusion of others, but in a history of sterling it is perhaps reasonable to concentrate on the money. In the early years of the sixteenth century, the English mint continued to attract more gold than silver, as it had done throughout the previous century. This was to change significantly in 1526. In that year Henry VIII (1509–1547) reduced the metal content of his gold coinage by 10 percent and of his silver coinage by 11 percent. He also introduced a new coinage of gold crowns only 22 carats pure. Reductions of this sort were very much in line with late medieval English mint practice: Counting 1526, there had been four such reductions since 1279, on average about sixty years apart. Coin about half a century old had inevitably become worn, and each of these devaluations did no more than reduce the weight of the new issues to about the same as that of most of the coins already in circulation. In addition, weight reductions in the silver coinages of France and the Burgundian Netherlands in 1519 and 1521 had forced Henry's hand: Continental mints now made more coin from each pound of bullion, enabling them to pay a higher price for the metal than the English mint. Some response was needed from England to restore its competitiveness, and after the adjustments of 1526 silver especially did flow slightly more readily to London. But two points need to be made clearly. As far as we can see, English commodity prices began to rise perhaps a decade before the 1526 coinage changes, which therefore cannot have instigated the price rise. Second, the mint adjustments carried out in 1526 were of an entirely different character from those that took place in the 1540s.

Medieval Europe was all too familiar with debasement of the coinage, but in England it was practically unknown. For 400 years English sterling had maintained its standard of at least 92.5 percent purity, making it the envy of northern Europe. The currency and the standard were inseparably united under a single name, sterling. As we have seen, from the fourteenth century it had become necessary from time to time to reduce the *weight* of the coinage to reflect the rising value of bullion, but changes of this sort had always been made publicly, often after parliamentary discussion. By contrast, Henry's 1540s debasement was introduced secretly, because any public debate would certainly have exposed its fraudulent nature. In 1540 an Irish silver issue was struck only 75.8 percent pure, to be followed in 1542 by a similar English issue. In both cases no public announcement was made, and the new coins were stockpiled by the crown rather than released into circulation. Secrecy was of the essence, and when the experiment was finally launched on an unsuspecting public in May 1544, the actual purity of the coins—75 percent for silver and 23 carats for gold (in place of the almost pure 23 carats 3¹/₂ grains)—was not made public. The mint was less coy about the new price that it was able to offer for bullion. Fine gold was bought at 48s. per ounce and fine silver at just over 52s. per pound (lb), and the mint went to some pains to advertise these rates, which were a significant improvement on what they had previously offered—45s. per ounce for gold and 45s. per pound for silver.

Advertisement of the new mint prices was essential in order to attract bullion to the mint, but once the new coins were released to the public, their true debased nature could not be concealed. Most of those involved in bringing large quantities of bullion to the mint would have quickly discovered what was involved by assaying the coins. A sample of known weight was melted at temperatures that allowed the base metals to be drawn off; by weighing the remaining pure metal, the fineness of the original sample could be determined. This was a process that required both skill and experience, so most ordinary people were not capable of testing the coins. Thus there was no shortage of people willing to accept the price now offered by the mint for bullion, and over £300,000 worth of gold and silver was struck on the reduced standards from metal brought to the mint in 1544–1545. The government was delighted with the scam, because it paid in debased coin for the bullion and it also took a much larger, undisclosed amount of seignorage for itself. But the crown soon discovered that such high levels of mint output and seignorage could not be sustained for long without a further increase in the price the mint could offer for bullion. So long as seignorage remained high, such an increase in the mint price could be financed only by a further reduction in the standard. In 1545, 1546, and 1549 three further alterations were made to the gold coinage, whose fineness was cut to 20 carats, at its lowest, before being partially restored to 22 carats, the crown gold standard. The face value of a pound of gold reached £34 in 1549, the worst gold coins containing only 73 percent of the metal in the predebasement issues.

The gold coinage escaped comparatively lightly compared with the silver. Between 1544 and 1551 the new silver coins contained less and less silver. The pure metal content of these issues fell from 75 percent to 50 percent, to 33 percent and finally to 25 percent. Some improvements to the standard in 1549, which saw a return to 66 percent and 50 percent silver, were exactly offset by reductions in weight, giving both these improved issues the same pure metal content as the 33 percent issue. The worst 1551 issue contained a mere 17 percent of the silver in the predebasement issues. However, it is clear that considerable resistance to the new coins was building up. As early as 1546 Stephen Vaughan, the royal agent in Antwerp, wrote to Lord Cobham:

if ye send me any money, let it not be neither in new crowns nor new **angels**, for I can put neither of both away without great loss. I have much money even now to be paid here for the king, and I would fain have you send it me in such money as I may pay again, or else I must take up so much by exchange here to great loss, the exchange going now very evil.

In fact, Vaughan of all people had few grounds to complain about difficulties getting the base coins accepted abroad, for he was one of those personally involved in the debasement, receiving income as undertreasurer of one of the debasing mints.

The new coins also became unpopular at home. The copper showed up on the face of Henry's base shillings, and the coins were mocked in John Heywood's satirical verse:

These **testons** [shillings] look red: how like you the same?
Tis a token of grace: they blush for shame.

As the public found it more difficult to pass off the bad money, they became less attracted by the higher mint prices offered for silver. Moreover, although the government did offer bullion holders a slightly higher mint price, the lion's share of the profits of debasement was seized by the crown in the form of a vastly enhanced rate of seignorage. From the mid-1540s the crown had pocketed about half of all the base silver coins struck. For the worst 1551 issue, when the mint paid out £6 in base coin for a pound of pure silver, the crown was first seizing £8 8s. in seignorage. Not surprisingly, the general public soon refused to cooperate, and as people declined to bring silver to the mint the government had recourse to other schemes to get bullion. First it ordered the recoinage of the unpopular Henry testons in 1548–1549. Then in 1550 it deliberately engineered a bimetallic flow by setting the English gold to silver ratio at 9.3 : 1 so that it was profitable to export gold and import silver. Finally, it arranged special contracts with people such as the Augsburg bankers and metal dealers, the Fuggers, for the supply of silver. The government paid well over the odds for this silver, planning to debase it heavily and use the bad coin to pay its domestic debts.

Although there is no evidence that Henry VIII personally originated the scheme, there is no doubt that he was the principal beneficiary. His advisors congratulated one another, observing of the debasement "That office hath marvellously served the King's Majesty." Henry's court and government were notoriously extravagant, and the money was quickly spent with little thought for the consequences. Over the whole period from 1544 to 1551 the crown made £1.27 million from the debasement exercise. The scale of this fraud was truly massive, given that the total money supply for the entire nation has been estimated at less than a million in 1542. The Tudor debasement remains the single greatest fraud deliberately carried out by any English government on its own people. The profits probably amounted to about 10 percent of gross domestic product (GDP). This trauma scarred the collective memory for generations to come. Yet perhaps even more significantly, debasement caused huge and damaging fluctuations in the money supply.

Two scholarly estimates of the size of the money supply in this period have been made.

Money Supply in England, 1542 to 1562

Date	Estimate A (£m)	Estimate B (£m)
1542		0.85
Mar. 1546	1.45	
Apr. 1546		1.19
Sept. 1548	1.76	
early 1549		1.75
Sept. 1549	1.92	
early 1551		2.02
July 1551	2.66	2.17
Aug. 1551	1.38	1.19
Sept. 1560	1.71	1.58
Oct. 1561	1.45	
1562		1.39

Though one estimate is consistently a few hundred thousand pounds lower than the other, the overall shape suggested is broadly similar. Things clearly came to a head in the summer of 1551, when the maximum total figure was almost halved by the 50 percent devaluation of the debased coins. Such a reduction in the face value of the coinage was a dreadful blow to the system. The inevitable confusion was compounded by government indecision about the exact rates to apply, for at first shillings were to be cut only to 9d. Henry Machin, citizen and merchant taylor of London, recorded:

The 8 day of July [1551] ... a proclamation that a testoon [shilling] should be but 9d, and a groat 3d; and another proclamation came out the 18 day of August, that testoon [was] cryd at 6d a piece; a groat at 2d; 2d but 1d; and a 1d ½d; and a halfpenny a farthing.

However, we learn from another source that between July 8 and August 18,

on the 25 daye of July ... was a proclamation declaring it was not the king's nor his council's intent to alter or abase any more his coins yet; for hear we great rumors that in all haste, and prively, the king and council was busy about the altering thearof, to be done out of hand, where upon many

48

men wane [reduce] their debts, which else would not have been paid this 7 years.

Thus, the value of the shilling was cut to 9d.; rumors of a further cut were rife but were vigorously denied by the government, which days later did indeed cut the value to 6d. Men scrambled to pay off long-term debts before the value of the coins was cut. In the early seventeenth century Gerard Malynes described the same phenomenon when he spoke of coins "current between man and man running like a post horse, everyman fearing to receive a loss by the fall." This sequence of panic, rumor, government reassurances, and subsequent devaluation exactly corresponds with modern experience. As we shall see later, more than one twentieth-century chancellor was to lose credibility attempting to talk up the pound. As they did so they were following in a long, though scarcely honorable, tradition.

In 1551 the offending coins themselves were not withdrawn from circulation, and they still enjoyed a face value significantly above their true worth. They remained far more plentiful than the good new issues of either Edward VI or Mary. Even when the government policy was finally decided on, information about the new proclaimed values often must have become confused as it was passed by word of mouth. Individual traders imposed their own unofficial values, though whether on the basis of misinformation or cannily to protect themselves from loss is not always clear. We read that in Norwich in 1551,

Thurston of Lammas reported to them at Sloley fair last past and said these words: Away with your shillings for I have say they were proclaimed at Norwich this day for a groat [4d.] a piece; and they answered it was not true, and the said Thurston said again, I fear me it is too true, for Peter Applyard refused to take them for 6 d a piece.

After the government cut the testoon (or shilling) from 12d. to 9d., and then from 9d. to 6d., a further reduction in value to 4d. was widely expected. In these chaotic circumstances it is difficult to know how far sellers respected the assigned face values. Proclamations threatening prolonged imprisonment for those refusing to take the testoon at 6d. suggest that some traders rejected the coin at this value. In 1556 Henry Machin recorded:

The 23 day of December was a proclamation through London, and shall be through the queen [Mary's] realm, that what man so ever they be that does forsake testoons and do not take them for 6d a piece for carne [meat] or vitals or any other things or ware, that they to be taken and brought afore the mayor or sheriff, bailie, justice of the peace, or constable, or other officers, and they to lay them in prison till the queen and her council, and they to remain [at] their pleasure, and to stand both body and goods at her grace's pleasure.

If reluctant merchants were obliged, on pain of a prison sentence, to take coin, one wonders how far they increased their selling prices to take account of the discredited coin they were receiving.

The behavior of prices at this time should give some answers to these questions, but the price data are not easy to read. Prices do rise from the time of the onset of debasement, and Bishop Latimer certainly reflected popular contemporary opinion when he said "the naughtiness of the silver was the occasion of the dearth of all things in the Realm." However, good harvests in the later 1540s tended to lower prices at exactly the moment when debasement was increasing them. Equally, harvest failures in 1555 and 1556 raised prices when currency reform might have tended to lower them. Livestock and livestock product prices tend to be less volatile, and mutton and candle prices, for example, are much more steady than grain prices. Insofar as we can discount annual fluctuations, it seems that prices do rise with the onset of debasement, but do not fall back as might have been expected either when Edward VI halved the value of the base issues in circulation in the summer of 1551 or when Elizabeth drove them out of circulation altogether with her recoinage in 1560–1561.

A number of factors may have prevented prices from falling back. In the first place, there can be no doubt that the whole debasement experience dealt a severe blow to public confidence in money. Continued high prices may have been the result of a flight from generally distrusted money into goods. It also needs to be remembered that after 1551 the fine silver issues of Edward, Mary, and Elizabeth were lighter. Although the old sterling purity was restored by Elizabeth, the overall intrinsic worth of her new coins only equaled that of the 1547 base issues. In other words, some of the inflationary effects of the debasement lingered. Moreover, as we shall see on various other occasions over the centuries, prices always rise much more easily than they fall. If sellers refuse to lower their prices, trade shrinks. As Keynes pointed out in the 1920s, when prices and wages have once risen significantly, they do not easily go down again. While prices remain obstinately high, the volume of business dwindles, resulting in a severe dose of unemployment.

Alterations to the value of the pound sterling not only affected prices at home; they also affected the value of sterling abroad. The foreign exchanges were particularly sensitive to the true intrinsic value of sterling, so when the silver content of sterling was reduced the pound fell sharply on the exchange. For this reason, the effect of debasement is very similar to a modern devaluation: Because foreign currencies suddenly become worth more in terms of devalued sterling, other nations find they can now buy English exports more cheaply. This increased the demand for English cloth substantially, and cloth exports enjoyed a boom that has been directly attributed to the effects of debasement. (The weakening of the pound after the 1992 fall from the Exchange Rate Mechanism (ERM) boosted exports in just the same way; see pp. 250–252.) Moreover, the devaluation was so large that English merchants were able to increase the price of their goods in sterling terms but still achieve a cut in their price in Flemish currency. Thus Ralph Lane wrote to Sir William Cecil: "The fall of the exchange within these 4 days hath caused and will cause to be bought cloths at £56 the pack which before would not have been bought for £52 the pack"; and yet the boom in the cloth industry was not entirely welcome, for Lane deeply regretted its effects on arable farming, going on:

so that you may perceive that the exchange doth engender dear cloth, and dear cloth doth engender dear wool, and dear wool doth engender many sheep, and many sheep doth engender much pasture and dear, and much pasture is the decay of tillage, and out of the decay of tillage springeth 2 evils, scarcity of corn and the people unwrought, and consequently the dearth of all things.

So the success of the cloth trade and pastoral agriculture did not give much satisfaction to those concerned about the decline of arable farming. Sir Thomas More's famous complaint about sheep eating up men, rather than vice versa, had already expressed this widely felt concern earlier in the century, but these trends were all accentuated by the debasement and the midcentury cloth boom.

Nevertheless, when the coinage was restored by Elizabeth, and the exchange rate climbed once more, plummeting cloth exports gave little satisfaction to contemporary commentators either, for the effects of the slump in cloth sales fed through into a general and widespread recession. We are told "infinite numbers of Spynners, Carders, Pickers of woll are turned to begging with no smale store of poor children, who driven with necessity (that hath no law) . . . come idly about to beg to the oppression of the poor husbandmen . . ." Many turned to crime. In other words, the devaluation triggered an unsustainable cloth export boom, and the revaluation caused a severe slump. In 1563 the government stepped into the depressed cloth market, buying cloth with public funds, in an attempt to alleviate the recession. It is significant that this third quarter of the century also saw the introduction of a compulsory poor rate and a system of public relief works. The scale of the problem (together with the dissolution of the monasteries) meant medieval charitable arrangements were simply not able to cope, so a new system was required.

The exchanges also were influenced by government borrowing. This had been true since at least the days of Edward I and was to be a major influence on the fortunes of sterling on numerous occasions right up to the present day, but the mid-sixteenth century does seem to be the point at which an association between borrowing and the exchange rate is first systematically explored. This exploration, accompanied by deliberate attempts to manipulate exchange rates, was an activity in which Thomas Gresham, the royal agent in Antwerp from 1551, was especially prominent.

Gresham was born into an established City family. His father and uncle had both been Lord Mayor. He was admitted to the Mercers Company in 1544, but in October 1551 he embarked on a career as a royal servant, particularly concerned with the crown's financial business overseas. Gresham carried out whatever purchases abroad English foreign policy might dictate; on one occasion he was said to have bought up all the available armaments in Germany. But his chief role was to arrange loans from the bankers of Antwerp for the crown, a job that involved much travel and long periods of residence abroad. It also required a high degree of financial expertise in the operation of the money market and a full understanding of foreign exchange. Where possible, transactions were effected by bills of exchange, but bullion or coin often had to be moved, whether the proceeds of loans raised in Antwerp to be spent in London or English royal revenue needed in Antwerp for the repayment of those loans.

Royal borrowing had really taken off in the latter years of Henry VIII. When Stephen Vaughan was his royal agent in Antwerp, Henry borrowed almost £1 million between 1544 and 1547. By this time, Henry already had squeezed the more limited English sources of funds dry, but his Antwerp borrowing illustrates both the scale of his extravagance and the preeminence of that city in the middle of the sixteenth century. Antwerp stood at the hub of a huge network of international commodity transactions. The credit facilitated the trade and the trade funded the credit. The city was ideally placed to exploit the resources of the most advanced industrialized region in Europe and the newly arriving wealth of the Spanish monarchs who ruled both the Americas and the Low Countries. On this basis Antwerp established the local structures—the bourse and the brokerage networks—necessary to put borrower and lender easily in touch with one another. It was not surprising that not only the Italian houses from Genoa and Florence but also the newer German firms such as the Fuggers, the Welsers, and Schatz came to congregate there. Even the parsimonious Elizabeth had recourse to this pot of gold at the beginning of her reign. In 1558 she owed some £65,000, and by 1560 that figure had risen to £279,000. What is more, though her total requirements were lower than her father's, she often had more outstanding at any one time than Henry. The 1560 debt not only exceeded her annual revenue; £279,000 was the equivalent of one-half to one-third of the value of the Merchant Adventurers' annual cloth shipments to Antwerp.

Gresham helped to reduce the cost of these loans. The prevailing interest rate for royal loans seems to have drifted down from around 14 percent to 12, and though Gresham may not personally have been responsible for the trend, his refusal to accept loans in the form of overvalued goods did save the crown significant losses. But Gresham himself probably would have thought his major achievement was the manipulation of the exchange rate. His work came at a time when sterling was falling on the exchange because of the reduction in its intrinsic content. From a rate of around 26s. Flemish in 1544, sterling fell to about 22s. Fl. in 1547, 20s. Fl. in 1549, to around 16s. Fl. in 1551. At its very lowest that year it briefly touched 13s. Fl., half its 1544 rate. Thereafter it rose steadily, if slowly, to about 21s. Fl. in 1555, stabilizing at 22 to 23s. Fl. in the 1560s. Gresham was not slow to claim personal credit for this recovery, although it more or less corresponds with the restoration of sterling's intrinsic worth. Nevertheless, he did attempt two maneuvers designed to support the pound on the exchanges by manipulating the supply and demand for sterling abroad. The first plan was a scheme for the crown to exploit the cloth sales of the Staplers and the Merchant Adventurers, a royal ruse that harked back to the Middle Ages. The second plan was for a fund of some £1,500 sterling a week provided by government to support the pound on the Antwerp exchange; it was an idea before its time, which was only to become fully operational in the twentieth century. (See pp. 206–207).

Both these mechanisms were essentially concerned with the short-term exchange rate rather than the long-term trend. Moreover, Gresham knew that this was not a simple matter of trying to raise the exchange rate for sterling at all times. When trying to borrow for the crown in Antwerp, a lower rate for the pound yielded more sterling for any given quantity of Flemish money. Conversely, a high rate would be helpful when exchanging sterling for Flemish money to repay debts to Antwerp. It is exactly the same today, when exporters like a low sterling exchange rate to make it easier to sell goods abroad, but British holidaymakers like a strong pound to buy more francs or pesetas. What complicated Gresham's life a good deal was the fact that merely by entering the money market, whether borrowing or repaying, by increasing or reducing demand for sterling the crown would inadvertently tend to move the rates against its own interests.

Gresham certainly won the respect and gratitude of the monarchs he served, and he did not hesitate to tell them what a good job he was doing for them. If his effect on the long-term exchange rate may be doubted, he nevertheless earned his keep—20s. sterling a day—plus any incidental fees, commissions, and expenses that he could get past the auditors of his accounts. Nevertheless, Antwerp's role in English finance, and it must be admitted Elizabeth's inclination to borrow, seems to have begun to fall off from the mid-1560s, leading to a decline in Gresham's importance. Personal misfortune may have contributed to the waning of his career. He suffered a fall riding, which left him lame, and the loss of his only legitimate child, who died aged twenty, must have been a devastating blow. But it seems likely that Gresham's reputation owed more to Antwerp than to his own personal qualities, and as Antwerp declined so did he.

Nevertheless, posterity has treated his memory kindly. "Gresham's Law"—the observation that bad money drives out good—would have struck most moneyers and merchants since the Middle Ages as obvious rather than remarkable, and its attribution to Gresham is a nineteenth-century fiction. In building the Royal Exchange Gresham has a better claim to fame, but his hope of establishing a London equivalent to the Antwerp Bourse was not achieved, for most of the City exchange business remained in and around Lombard Street, leaving the nascent insurance business to colonize the Exchange. On the whole, it appears that the financial events of the age shaped Gresham's life much more than the other way around.

Elizabeth I (1558–1603) had a very healthy respect for the value of money, and she quickly cut back Gresham's expense allowance as she reduced her dependence on foreign loans. Equally, she grasped the nettle of the debased currency with characteristic firmness at the beginning of her reign. A commission consisting of Sir Edmund Peckham and Sir Thomas Stanley, masters of the mint, together with Sir William Cecil and Sir Thomas Smith, began collecting advice and opinions. On September 27, 1560 the queen announced that the debased coins were to be reduced in value, her government proclaiming: "nothing is so grievous nor likely to disturb and decay the state and good order of this realm as the sufferance of the base moneys (being of divers standards and mixtures) to be so abundantly current within this realm . . ." As a result,

all manner of things in this realm necessary for the sustentation of the people grow daily excessive, to the lamentable and manifest hurt and oppression of the state, specially of pensioners, soldiers, and all hired servants and other mean people that live by any kind of wages and not by rents of lands or trade of merchandise.

Accordingly, detailed instructions were released to reduce the value of the better base testoons from 6d. to 4$^{1}/_{2}$d. and the poorer testoons from 6d. to 2$^{1}/_{4}$d. Because people were unable to distinguish the different types of coins, it was soon agreed that the debased testoons were to be countermarked by experts in the marketplaces, the baser issues with a greyhound mark behind the king's head and the better with a portcullis punch in front. From November that year the mint resumed striking on the full sterling standard of 92.5 percent pure silver, and although 12d. now weighed only 96 grains, compared with 126 grains before the debasement began, the replacement of plentiful base coins with fewer better ones involved a marked reduction in money supply. The base testoons were to cease to be current the following spring, and the base groats were demonetized over the summer. By September 1561 the recoinage was complete. It was regarded as one of the principal achievements of Elizabeth's reign, and the restoration of the money "to its just value" is noted on her monument in Westminster Abbey, alongside the defeat of the Spanish Armada and the establishment of religious peace in England as central to her legacy.

The recoinage was, as Elizabeth acknowledged, "bitter medicine," a phrase with marked similarities to John Major's comment "If it isn't hurting, it isn't working." Both remarks express the truth that monetary indiscipline has to be followed by a period of necessary pain to restore good order. Elizabeth probably hoped and believed that prices would fall as a result of this contraction in the means of payment. But prices always have risen far more easily than they have fallen, and the inflexibility of prices in the 1560s probably increased the problems of scarcity of money and unemployment of which contemporary sources speak. Prices did not fall in the 1560s, but they did pause in the course of the upward march that is so characteristic of the sixteenth century. While prices stalled and men were idle, Spanish bullion began to arrive at the English mint in increasing quantities. From July 1567 until the end of the century, the mint coined on average almost £100,000 new sterling every year.

Such a prolonged period of high mint output was entirely un-precedented. Of course, as this bullion flowed into the country some silver also was being carried out as a result of ordinary trade, foreign war, and diplomacy. Nevertheless, it has been estimated that the cir-culating medium that stood at almost £1.5 million at the beginning of Elizabeth's reign may have more than doubled to £3.5 million be-fore the end of it. Not surprisingly, prices too rose to unheard-of lev-els. A quarter of wheat cost around 11s. at the beginning of Elizabeth's reign and over 34s. at the end. A penny in 1560 would buy just over 2 pounds of best white bread or about 5 pounds of wholemeal, but by 1600 the traditional medieval assize that fixed bread prices no longer worked, because corn prices had risen off the top of the scale. The cost of cereals had risen rather more than the cost of livestock and animal products. Thus a cow would cost al-most 40s. in 1560 and about 50s. in 1600. Butter cost 3d. per pound in 1560, 4½d. in 1600; cheese rose from 1½d. to 2¾d. and beef from 1¼d. to 2d. The unskilled laborer, who made 4d. at the begin-ning of the century, received 6d. around 1560 and 8d. in 1600, and though his wages had risen they had noticeably failed to keep up with inflation. His golden age was very definitely over. Indeed, 1597, the year of Shakespeare's rural idyll *A Midsummer Night's Dream*, has been identified as the very worst combination of high prices—there was a dreadful harvest—and poor wages. Food riots broke out through England between 1595 and 1597. Recorded vagrancy in London rose eightfold between 1560–1561 and 1600–1601.

Servants' wages were to some extent sheltered from the rise in prices, because often staff were paid a large part of their wages in food and clothing. At Burton Dassett in Warwickshire, we know that around the late 1530s and early 1540s Thomas Heritage and Peter Temple paid their servants about 20 to 30s. a year, more or less as pocket money, on top of their keep and clothing. The maid got 16s. a year and a kirtle (gown), clothes, and shoes. Women were regularly paid less, on the grounds that they were less strong. At the end of the sixteenth century casual female harvest workers were paid about half the men's rate.

The failure of wages to keep within reach of surging prices argues powerfully that labor was becoming yearly less scarce through the century, and demographic historians suggest that the population, which stood at 2.3 million in the 1520s, may have reached 3 million by 1560 and just over 4 million by 1600. Moreover, the fact that food prices rose more steeply than those of other goods, and that grain rose more than livestock, confirms the picture of a price rise fueled at least in part by the hunger of an increasingly impoverished but growing population. As the century progressed, rising demand for food was met by rising agricultural production and a rising money supply. The rise in agricultural production was illustrated by the work of men such as Peter Temple, who began by leasing newly enclosed fields to farm more intensively for the market. He was fortunate in that his first leases were set before the midcentury price rise, so his land costs were fixed while his income rose with the price level. By the 1560s Temple was able to buy one-third of the manor of Burton Dassett with his profits. The owner of one other third, Sir Anthony Cooke, an equally typical example of the other kind of conservative, old-fashioned country gentleman, was appalled by the success of the parvenu Temple, and fought his rise in the neighborhood. At one stage Cooke used his influence to have Temple jailed, but Temple continued to rise, socially and economically, on the back of the buoyant market.

Historians have expended a good deal of energy trying to identify which groups or social classes did well out of inflation and which fell back. In this debate, inflation and the massive redistribution of crown and church land that took place in the sixteenth century were both seen as possible underlying causes of a shift in social influence and political power. Specifically, the relative fortunes of the gentry and the aristocracy have been examined, and shifting patterns of wealth have been thoroughly explored in an attempt to discover in these social and economic changes the origins of the political revolution of the seventeenth century. The case of Temple and Cooke shows that individuals with energy and enterprise could prosper while landlords of a more traditional frame of mind looked on with mounting resentment, but evidence that whole classes rose or fell is harder to find. On the whole it appears that some of the gentry did adapt successfully to a world of changing costs and shorter leases, but other gentlemen paid for their inflexibility. In the same way some aristocrats rose while others, especially in the sixteenth century, fell. In the first half of the seventeenth century a threefold rise in rents probably bailed out even the least efficient landowners.

However, some family fortunes were more successfully pursued through the law or favor at court rather than by profit-taking in the marketplace. Furthermore, even if rising or falling classes could be identified successfully, it is by no means clear that such classes were consistently loyal to king or Parliament. In short, it appears that although an increasingly vocal and influential House of Commons did reflect the growing prosperity and self-confidence of various gentry, merchants, and lawyers, social and economic changes of the sixteenth and early seventeenth centuries did not feed through into political change in a simple or straightforward way. What is clear is that inflation forced the renegotiation of countless deals and relationships, calling old assumptions into question and requiring new positions to be thought out afresh. The foundations of the old order were shifting, in a way that was perhaps more destabilizing than a clear-cut change of masters might have been.

People such as Sir Anthony Cooke and Peter Temple personify the social tensions caused by inflation, but the economic tensions resulting from the interplay of a rising population, increasing agricultural productivity, and a growing money supply also had to work themselves out through the price rise. It may well be that the booming money supply was hard put to service the needs of a growing population and a higher price level. If this was the case, the available coin must have worked harder in 1600 than in 1500. In the jargon of the economist, the **velocity** of the circulation may have increased.

Increased velocity is not the same as an increase in the use of money. Indeed, when the use of coin becomes more common, it is usually because people have more coin available to them. Increased use of money thus is usually combined with a *fall* in velocity, made possible by the availability of growing amounts of coin. From the Middle Ages until the twentieth century, the velocity of money has consistently fallen, because of the increase in the supply of money, with the sole exception of the sixteenth century. It is only under the Tudors that society's use of money was able to grow faster than its supply. That it had to do so is a measure of the very considerable stress which the Tudor economy experienced. As we have seen in the Middle Ages, a high velocity meant an economy in which people were kept waiting for the arrival of the coin owing to them, and when it did arrive, it was swiftly paid on again. The turnover of goods in such a society is very different from that in a world where most people carry a certain amount of money on them for casual purchases on the spur of the moment. Thus a falling velocity can be seen as a sign of a more liquid society, enjoying greater access to supplies of ready money. On the other hand, a rising velocity suggests a distressed economy in which the demand for money was growing faster than its supply. The rising velocity of the sixteenth century came about because, although money supply was growing, the economy was growing faster. One possible factor that allowed velocity to increase in the sixteenth century may have been the growth of credit permitted by the growing money supply. As noted, in the Middle Ages, although the supply of coin limits the supply of credit, credit could grow if the money supply was growing too. Another factor assisting the growth of credit was the easing of the legal restrictions on money lending.

The change in sixteenth-century attitudes to money lending reached the English Statute Book first in 1545, probably as a direct consequence of debasement. With prices rising, and the new complication that loans might be repaid in coin inferior to that which had been lent, the argument that the lender deserved some compensation became more compelling. The legislation of 1545 reluctantly came to the conclusion that in these circumstances, interest of no more than 10 percent a year would no longer be illegal. In 1552 this decision was reversed in a change of mind perhaps prompted in part by the end of debasement and the return to sound money. In the later Middle Ages social and above all religious thinkers had refined their attitude to **usury** in various ways. Usury, the lending of money for gain, was condemned. Interest, however, was carefully defined and in certain circumstances permitted. This distinction between interest and usury was often a fairly nice one. A usurer took payment solely for making the loan, and had no share or interest in the venture being funded. As Miles Mosse wrote, "The usurer never adventureth or hazardeth the loss of his principal: for he will have all sufficient

security for the repayment and restoring of it back again to himself."
Interest, on the other hand, arose from a genuine *interest* in the investment, or as compensation for incidental costs or fees incurred, for delay in repayment, or for the opportunity of alternative investments forgone. In this way the line between interest and usury was already becoming blurred long before 1545. Moreover, as we have already seen, the religious and legal condemnation of money lending in the Middle Ages did not prevent it, and the courts were always open to creditors to sue for the repayment of principal. The act against usury of 1496 specifically exempted "lawfull penalties for non payment of the same money lent."

In 1563, with the shortage of coin at its worst, an unsuccessful attempt was made to overturn the 1552 law. This attempt was successfully renewed in 1571. Throughout this period the issue was actively debated, and the arguments of merchants and practical businessmen that the time was right for a relaxation of the prohibition were vigorously refuted by churchmen and civil lawyers. Historians have been much exercised exploring possible links between new religious thinking (puritanism) and new ideas about money lending, and economic individualism. The 1571 act was a compromise in which the opinions of those opposed to a relaxation of the law were fully represented. The act began with the observation that the 1552 prohibition had "not done so muche good as was hoped it shoulde, but rather the said vyce of usurye . . . hathe much more exceedingly abounded." It conceded the point that "all usurie being forbydden by the lawe of God is synne and detestable," but went on to permit interest up to 10 percent. Interest up to that figure was not usurious. However, though it was no longer illegal to take interest up to 10 percent, the courts did not allow creditors to sue for interest payments. The opponents of a relaxation in the law may have felt that they had fought a successful rearguard action, but the 1571 act nevertheless marked a turning point, both in men's thinking and in their actions. Moneylenders always had relied more on the willingness of their clients to pay over the odds than on the courts, and the recognition that a reasonable rate of interest was not usurious proved to be the point that mattered. In 1587 William Harrison described the turning tide of opinion well, observing that only the old men of the village condemned moderate usury, which was "now perfectly practised by almost every Christian and so commonly that he is accompted but a fool that doth lend his money for nothing." Subsequent legislation, which cut the maximum rate to 8 percent in 1624, 6 percent in 1651, and 5 percent in 1713, marked an increase in the availability of money rather than any reversal of public opinion. This shift in attitude toward money lending, like perspective in painting and the use of Indo-Arabic numerals, is one of the great transitions that mark the watershed between the medieval and the modern.

The removal of the legal impediment to the growth of credit coincides with the development of a new type of credit instrument. Medieval lending had given rise to a number of forms of credit, and while domestic lending had created various types of bond and recognizance, international trade had developed the bill of exchange. Although these bills originally were created to facilitate the exchange of currencies and the transmission of funds across frontiers, the inevitable delay between the purchase of a bill and its redemption introduced an element of credit to the transaction. In the second half of the sixteenth century, the bill of exchange came to be used for domestic trade. Of course these inland bills did not involve the exchange of one currency for another, but the credit and remittance functions of inland bills proved as useful within the kingdom as exchange bills had done in overseas trade.

At the heart of this emerging system was the almost universal merchant need to make payments to and from London. Thus at the end of Elizabeth's reign the landowner and grazier Sir Thomas Temple of Stowe, Peter Temple's descendant, found it useful to build up an account in London with the merchant Thomas Farrington. Temple then could make such payments as he wished in London more easily, simply by instructing Farrington, but he also could extend this facility, accepting coin in the provinces for others to claim from his account with Farrington. In another case, we know that William Leonard in 1580 sent William Morris a written order to his factor to pay Morris £50. Gradually these informal arrangements between a factor or agent and his master acquired a more formal character. For example, Edward Firth wrote out his bill as follows:

Received the 4th of March 1641 of Mr Edmund Kay the sum of One hundredth pounds which I promise by these presents to pay to Mr John Owen at 3 Anckers in Laurence Lane this first day of April next by Mr Isaac Knipe factor in Blackwell Hall, I say received.

Thus Firth received £100 from Kay, which he instructed his factor Knipe to repay to Owen. Knipe accepted the bill on March 14, though payment was not due until April. Owen's servant, Thomas Walton, made out a receipt on April 6.

In origin these bills were no more than receipts or orders to pay, sent to an agent in another place for execution in a month or so. However, as confidence grew that these orders would be fulfilled, it became possible to buy goods by offering such notes for future payment. As with all forms of credit, the success of the system depends crucially on a cash payment eventually being made to honor the bill when it becomes due. To this extent such bills can only stretch the use of the available coin, not replace it altogether. This sort of arrangement develops best alongside a growing cash supply, which was indeed the situation at the end of the sixteenth century.

The death of Elizabeth brought James VI of Scotland to England as king in 1603. The Scottish currency had parted company with sterling in 1367 and had fallen in value relative to English money by stages, so that in 1603 the pound Scots was worth exactly one-twelfth of the pound sterling. Although the two currencies remained separate until the union of 1707, in fact debasement in Scotland was halted and the 12 : 1 relationship maintained, bringing a new degree of monetary stability north of the border. Though one English penny was worth one Scots shilling, the actual coins were struck with almost identical designs. In effect, the seventeenth century served as an intermediary experimental period of trial monetary union in the two kingdoms. In 1707 the Act of Union specifically guaranteed the continued existence of a mint in Scotland, but no coins were struck there after 1709. In the British experience, political union brought about monetary union, rather than the other way around.

In England, James's money at first followed the Elizabethan pattern and was dominated by huge issues of silver of overwhelmingly Spanish American origin. Indeed, the mint preference for silver had been accentuated by the adjustments of 1601, when the face value of gold was raised from £33 per pound to £33 10s. (1.5 percent) while silver was raised from 60s. to 62s. per pound (3.3 percent). The amount of gold struck was very modest until 1604, when the face value of gold was raised to £37 4s. per pound, while silver was left unaltered. These rates seemed to have struck a reasonable balance, and both gold and silver were brought to the mint in quantity. The cloth trade was booming. James's finance minister, Lionel Cranfield, estimated that the country enjoyed a favorable balance of trade until 1611, although a poor harvest in 1608 led to the purchase of grain from abroad. It was noted at the time that "The dearth of corn in England of late . . . hath been a great cause of transportation of our coin beyond the sea, for the provision thereof." Mint output certainly began to falter at about that time. As the Dutch had in 1610 raised their rate for gold, the Privy Council was inclined to blame the higher rate for gold on the continent for the reduction in gold coming to the mint: "in general this is the mischief: that our gold is not so much allowed as our silver and therefore being worth more than silver is bought and carried away." This analysis might have been more convincing if silver had been coming into the mint in quantity, but, rightly or wrongly, the council put its faith in this diagnosis and in 1611 dramatically increased the face value of gold 10 percent from £37 4s. to £40 18s. per pound. Gold duly poured into the mint, but silver, now markedly undervalued in terms of gold, was noticeably absent. In their eagerness to attract gold, the government had triggered a classic bimetallic flow, in which merchants with debts to settle abroad paid them in silver, which was less appreciated at home, while foreigners knew well to bring gold to England because of its high price there. The English gold–silver ratio (1 : 13 from 1611, and even 1 : 13.5 from 1619) was markedly out of line with that abroad.

Such was the world's demand for bullion that despite the vast quantities being imported from Mexico each year, the value of both gold and silver was still rising. As a consequence most nations were reducing the bullion content of their money. It is an interesting observation that while the Stuart government recognized the need to cut the content of its gold coin to reflect international trends, it remained unwilling to do so for silver. The Master of the Mint, Sir Richard Martin, told the government explicitly:

as the cause of great plenty of gold brought in since [his] Majesty's proclamation was by raising the price of gold, so the cause of the scarcity of silver, whereof little or none hath been brought into his Majesty's Mint since the proclamation, hath been that the silver is not equally valued with the gold in this realm.

Nevertheless, the government could not bring itself to raise the price of silver, which would entail reducing the silver content of the coins. From 1612 to the 1630s some such scheme was repeatedly under consideration but never actually was implemented. In 1620 an advisory committee of merchants commented, "although the abasing of the standard . . . is . . . the only way at this present to draw silver into the kingdom, yet we dare not advise to put it into practice." Or as Cranfield put it, "experience hath taught us that base monies have always been dangerous to our estate." "The loss to all monied men in their debts, gentlemen in their rents, and the king in his customs" made currency manipulation unthinkable. More than half a century after the Tudor debasement, the trauma of a debauched currency still influenced policy, rather as the German inflation of the 1920s still argued powerfully for the utmost monetary restraint in the councils of the Bundesbank through to the 1990s. For James VI and I the memories of a debased currency in Scotland and the inflation that it brought were more painfully recent.

What is more, the arguments against currency manipulation always seemed particularly relevant to silver, because of its dominant role in the money supply. Malynes said that "The silver coins do rule the market in all places, because of the abundance thereof, being 500 to one of gold." Contemporaries were clear that "the whole body of the land doth stand in continual need of silver monies for their daily trafic, without which our commonwealth can hardly subsist." Indeed, it was felt that if the silver were unaltered, the country would be sheltered from the effects of altering the gold. In fact, of course, because silver was indeed the more important currency metal, the failure to adjust its mint price in England in step with alterations abroad was all the more unfortunate. It was not that the silver was no longer coming to England. In 1612 it was reported that

> silver is continually imported and is found stirring amongst the goldsmiths and otherwise much like as in former times, although in respect of the greater price which it hath with the goldsmiths it cannot find the way to the Mint.

The volume of silver hallmarked by the goldsmiths (who despite their name controlled work in both the precious metals) testifies to the continued availability of silver in London at this time. The East India Company regularly bought huge quantities of silver in London, which it shipped to the Indies. Silver could be had if the price was right, but the government dread of the dislocation and inflation associated with debasement prevented even a moderate increase in the price it permitted the mint to offer.

Of course there were some dissenting voices from this majority opinion. Edward Misselden argued like a true Keynesian when he suggested inflation would be a price worth paying for a larger money supply:

> it is much better for the kingdom to have things dear with plenty of money, whereby men live in their several callings, than to have things cheap with want of money, which now makes every man complain.

But his was a lone voice crying in a cash-starved recession. Official monetary policy was frozen by a failure to distinguish between irresponsible profit-taking debasement and a mint-price adjustment that did no more than recognize that the world was still bidding up the price of bullion. The lesson of the Tudor debasement had been learned too well: From Elizabeth to George IV, the English government tried to operate an almost unaltered silver price in a world where everything else was changing. In the long term it was a policy that would destroy the silver basis of sterling.

The early Stuart government knew that a major silver debasement would be a snare and delusion, but failed to recognize that a modest reduction in the intrinsic content of the silver coinage could be necessary and beneficial. Without such a reduction, sterling was left as an extremely **hard currency** compared with its continental competitors.

A hard or strong currency tends to restrain prices, because each pound- or penny-worth still contains more silver than do competing currencies. For the same reason, sterling performs powerfully abroad, encouraging imports that seem cheap but discouraging exports that seem dear. So long as English exports of cloth and wool were able to name their own price, as they had done for the most part since the Middle Ages, the strength of the currency was confirmed by England's trading performance. In the early seventeenth century, however, English exports began to experience new difficulties that affected, and were affected by, the currency.

England's traditional cloth industry, based above all on the export of heavy and durable undyed quality broadcloths, began the century well. The end of the Anglo-Spanish war in 1604 and the truce between Spain and the Netherlands, concluded in 1609, contributed to a boom in European trade in which English cloth played a major part. For England 1614 marks a peak, but in retrospect there were already grounds for concern. Too many traditional English cloth manufacturers were slow to adapt to innnovations in the trade. Growing supplies of cheaper continental wools were supplying new varieties of lighter, cheaper, and colorful cloth, which were collectively described as "new draperies." In due course the success of the new draperies substantially compensated for the decline of the traditional industry; the new draperies required more labor but economized on the wools used; the completed cloths lasted not nearly so long as the traditional cloths, but even this worked to their advantage, since they were cheap enough to buy more often, permitting a growing awareness of changing fashions. The new draperies were also welcome in new markets in southern Europe that had had little interest in the traditional heavy English cloths. In addition, although English new draperies faced more competition from the continent, where the new techniques originated, the new industry proved much more flexible than the traditional English cloth manufacturers whose regulations, apprenticeship schemes, and marketing arrangements made the old trade fatally unadaptable. The very success of the new draperies spelled trouble for old-style manufacturers.

The traditional English cloth industry also suffered from an improbable but devastating self-inflicted wound. Alderman William

Cockayne approached the government, pointing out that the traditional cloth industry customarily exported its cloths undyed for finishing in the Low Countries, and suggested that the national interest would be well served if these cloths were instead dyed at home and exported in their finished state. It was a reasonable enough idea in theory but made no allowance for opposition in the Low Countries or from the vested interests of the Merchant Adventurers, the company enjoying a monopoly over the organization of the existing trade. Indeed, it seems likely that the whole notion of replacing the export of undyed cloth with that of dyed was little more than a ruse to justify removing control of cloth exports from the Merchant Adventurers in favor of Cockayne and his supporters. Nevertheless, the government swallowed the scheme, and Cockayne got his chance in 1614. No very serious attempt was made to export dyed cloths, not least because the new proprietors of the cloth trade proved quite unable to provide sufficient capital to buy up more than a fraction of the nation's cloths for export. The Merchant Adventurers were invited to join Cockayne but remained aloof. A severe depression hit the industry, as cloths were only with difficulty bought and sold in London, let alone exported, and the whole industry stalled for want of cash. (It is a reminder that an industry which always had been heavily dependent on credit could not survive without cash.) Between 1614 and 1615 exports and customs receipts fell some 20 percent. In 1616 the export trade had declined by a third, but Cockayne, the principal architect of the damage, was knighted. At the end of 1616 the Merchant Adventurers were reinstated, though by then serious damage had been done, and the growing foreign industry had been stimulated by the temporary absence of the market leader.

Some export recovery took place in 1618, though to nothing like the levels of 1614. But the outbreak of the Thirty Years War in Germany dealt a further blow to the traditional exports. The heavy cloths always had found most of their market in the Netherlands, Germany, and Poland, areas disrupted not only by the direct effects of war but even more seriously by debasements in Germany and Poland triggered by the war. As the currencies of these regions lost international purchasing power, traditional English cloths, which always had been expensive, were pushed beyond the reach of many customers. In 1622 cloth exports were 40 percent below the levels of the peak year of 1614, and the government was warned that people "were much discouraged in the clothing counties for want of money, [and] the trade of clothing is so much decayed for want of vent [i.e., sales] . . . that many poor people are ready to mutiny for want of work." In 1623, after a bad harvest, it was reported in the north of England that "scarcity and famine be great . . . yet the prices of corn are . . . such . . . as have been in time of indifferent plenty, and this happeneth because of want of monies and want of employment and labour for the poor."

The difficulties experienced by English exports had a clear link with sterling's exchange rate. Because sterling remained hard while England's trading partners were weakening their currencies, the amount of goods England could sell abroad was reduced. However, in due course, the reduction of English exports lessened demand for sterling abroad, which weakened the exchange rate, even though the intrinsic content of sterling remained unchanged. Since much business was conducted by bills of exchange, the rate for sterling would fall if the call for funds abroad exceeded the foreign demand for sterling in London. The process was well understood at the time, and Thomas Mun described it fully in 1623:

The gain or loss which happeneth in merchant's exchange by bills is ruled by the plenty or scarcity of money in the places where it is delivered out and taken up, and this plenty or scarcity of money is caused only by the over or under balance of our commodities in the respective places of our foreign trade. For it is a certain rule that in those countries beyond the seas which send us more of their wares in value than we carry unto them of our commodities, there our monies are undervalued in exchange, and in other countries where the contrary of this is performed, there our money is overvalued: if it be considered according to the par of the respective standards.

Of course, if *coin* was exported, it always could be melted to extract its full intrinsic value; however, because of the expense of recoinage and the risk involved in remitting coin, merchants preferred to use bills of exchange if possible. However, if the exchange rate for sterling bills declined because of an imbalance of trade, merchants might send coin, causing a drain of specie out of England. Gerard Malynes described the whole process succinctly in 1602: "If the exchange with us be low, so that more will be given for our money being carried in specie, than by bill of exchange can be had, then our money is transported . . ."

Modern writers often tend to adopt a rather knowing and patronizing tone when describing the **mercantilist** preoccupation with national bullion supplies. It is certainly true that an obsessive concern with the national money stock blinded people to the insight that wealth consists in the goods and services that money can provide rather than in the money itself. It is also clear that concern about any unfavorable bilateral balance of trade could prevent the recognition that the multilateral balance might be favorable. Bullionists also often failed to appreciate the role of reexport of imported goods. Nevertheless, any understanding of medieval and early modern trade has to come to terms with the absolutely fundamental role played by the nation's **circulating capital**—that is, its currency as means of exchange. As the liquidity crisis in England's trade in the later part of the reign of James I shows clearly, the interruption of the normal cash flow provided by the export trade, together with the substitution of gold for the more flexible silver, could bring about a recession in the wool and cloth trade that reached deep into the English countryside. One member of Parliament (MP) described the situation in 1621, even before the depth of the recession was reached, in these terms:

the trading and commerce among [the king's] subjects is much decayed, and his people . . . so impoverished, that the greater part have not wherewithal left to pay, and those that have money will not disburse it upon land or any other commodity whatsoever . . . all which premises plainly show that as a body cannot move without sinews, so a realm cannot prosper or maintain itself without money.

England's exports still accounted for only a small proportion of its GDP, but the role of foreign trade in attracting bullion to a land without significant gold or silver mines gave it an entirely disproportionate influence on the trade of the whole country. If money grew scarce, all trade slowed, both international and domestic.

Many merchants and exchange experts were resentful that the bill-of-exchange value of sterling could fall though the coins themselves were unchanged, and attributed the phenomenon to some kind of international conspiracy, as in our own times the gnomes of Zurich or other foreign exchange dealers have been blamed. Thomas Mun at least had no time for such conspiracy theories, writing in 1623 that the undervaluation

which these men call the abuse of the exchange . . . is in truth nothing else but the declination of our trade which vents [sells] not half so many cloths and yet spends twice as much lawns, cambrics and the like as in times past.

The merchant and writer Rice Vaughan went further, attributing the negative trade balance and the bimetallic flow to the high silver content of sterling. He wrote in the 1620s that

whatsoever laws are made against transportation of our monies, if our silver be so rich as the merchants by transporting it into the Low Countries, or elsewhere, can make profit by returning it in commodities, or by exchange; or that which is yet more clear and evident, by returning it in gold, must not our silver be inevitably exhausted.

The worst effects of the monetary disturbance on the continent eased after 1623, but England's conflicts with Spain (1625–1630) and with France (1627–1629) delayed complete recovery. However, the situation did improve significantly in the 1630s. The development of the new draperies in England brought exports a degree of competitiveness that the old trade could not achieve. France and the Netherlands raised their mint rates for gold, making the high English rate less extraordinary and so helping to stem the bimetallic flow. But it was the peace with Spain negotiated by Sir Francis Cottington that proved really important. Not only were hostilities suspended, but from 1632 England began to ship Spanish government bullion to Flanders. Some such scheme had been broached as early as 1622, but it was only after the peace with Spain that it became a reality. This was a valuable service to Spain whose shipments were otherwise subject to the raiding of Dutch privateers, but it proved even more valuable to England. The price of England's cooperation was that two-thirds of the bullion shipped should be minted at the

Tower into English coin. (From 1638 the English coining was cut to one-third.)

The seignorage was a welcome subsidy to the king, but the resulting transfusion of silver into the money supply was of much greater significance. Of course, the bullion remained the property of its Spanish owners, but once it was minted into sterling they used it in London to buy bills of exchange from English merchants payable in Antwerp. The English kept the sterling in return for a promise to pay Flemish coin in Antwerp in a month or so. In other words, the profits of the English export trade were appearing in London in English silver, rather than as Flemish coin in Antwerp, which might have been returned to London either in bills or in imports from the continent. As a direct result of these arrangements, silver output at the mint picked up dramatically and other sources were swept into the stream. The London goldsmith Henry Futter, no doubt partly as an agent rather than solely on his own account, brought over £300,000 in silver to the mint between 1632 and 1636. In total £8.4 million in silver was struck at the Tower mint between 1632 and 1647.

What is more, it is clear from the coin hoards of the period that the bulk of this new silver remained in circulation in England. Thus by 1643 the money supply, including gold, stood at about £10 million, an increase of over £6 million from 1600, which permitted prices and wages to go on rising. Wheat, about 34s. a quarter around 1600, fetched about 48s. a quarter in the 1640s. The cow, which cost about 50s. in 1600, in the 1640s cost more like 70s. Butter now cost 6d. a pound (in 1600 it had been 4$\frac{1}{2}$d.), cheese 3d. a pound (in 1600 it had been 2$\frac{3}{4}$d.), and beef 2$\frac{1}{2}$d. (in 1600 it had been 2d.). The skilled carpenter who earned 1s. a day around 1600 got about 1s. 3d. in the 1640s, while the unskilled laborer (who earned, in 1600, 8d. a day) now took home nearly a shilling. If he fought in the civil war as an infantryman, he would expect only 8d. a day, and military wages were notoriously irregularly paid. Perhaps the adventure of war in contrast to the unremitting toil of agricultural labor was some compensation for poor military pay. Women working in agriculture were earning more than in 1600, but their wages had not risen as much as men's; a woman who earned half a man's wages in the 1640s thought herself lucky, for many of her sisters were not doing so well.

Of course, these are average daily or weekly rates, which conceal a fair amount of variation. For example, Robert Loder, farming in early seventeenth-century Berkshire, paid his workers 1d. or 2d. more in summer, and skilled mowers and reapers could command a premium at harvest times when all available labor was much sought after. The pay of farm servants who contracted for a year at a time was also different. Loder paid his shepherd £2 a year, while his carter got £3 6s. 8d. Maids got 30s. and an occasional present, while a lad got £1 4s. a year and once a pair of shoes valued at 2s. 2d. In addition, of course, they all got full board. The cost of food for each member of the household living in has been estimated at about £10 a year. When the carter lived out one year he received £10, plus perks amounting to as much as another £5.

Henry Best, farming at Elmswell in Yorkshire from 1617 to 1642, seemed to pay slightly less than Loder, and his records show little sign of rising wages over this period. However, it is difficult to compare rates over time, for few of his servants stayed with him long. He made little attempt to retain staff, who probably moved on to better wages if they could get them. Best was aware that others sometimes paid more than he did, commenting on the 10d. a day he paid his mowers at harvest, "some there are that will give them 11d, and some againe 12d in a case of necessity." He also paid his threshers less than the going rate elsewhere. Throughout this period Best usually paid his top man about £3: Robert Gibson got "£3 wages an old hat or else 3s. in money" in 1627. Other men got £2 13s. 4d. or £2 6s. 8d. Boys got 10s. or 12s., maids about 18s. to 22s.

Turning from the particular back to the general overall picture, monetary growth probably did permit the alleviation in some small degree—reflected in a rising GDP per head—of the extremely grim conditions of the 1590s. But money supply probably grew faster now than the economy as a whole, which allowed the velocity of circulation to fall. We saw earlier how a fall in velocity represents an easing of the illiquidity problems so characteristic of Elizabeth's reign, but it should be recognized that such estimates of velocity (which have to be based on very approximate guestimates of GDP) are subject to considerable margins of error. Moreover, a national velocity figure cannot hope to do justice to the countless different patterns of circulation taking place for gold and silver, in town and country, agriculture and industry, all over the country.

Direct contemporary evidence for the state of the circulation is difficult to interpret, not least because merchant commentators seem to complain of shortage of coin almost constantly. In the early seventeenth century it becomes more possible to scrutinize these almost perennial complaints more carefully, and it becomes clear that when men spoke of scarcity or want of coin they did not always have the same conditions in mind. For example, when the harvest was poor and prices were high, coin was scarce among the poor, who could not afford bread. If prices were low, it was producers who suffered a lack of cash. Sometimes the want of money meant tightness of credit, which usually occurred as a consequence of monetary shortage but also could be caused by special nonmonetary conditions. Thus in the early 1640s the political situation created a credit squeeze at a time when the English money supply (and prices and wages) stood at record levels.

In the summer of 1640 Charles I's financial difficulties caused him to look at a number of options. His need for cash was intensified as a result of his quarrels with a radically Puritan Scotland, which found his religious policies fundamentally unacceptable. Yet the Scots could not be brought to heel without money for troops. Throughout the 1630s Charles had ruled without the aid of Parliament. Even if he abandoned his attempt to rule without their unacceptable advice, no English Parliament would have voted him the necessary funds to suppress religious opinions with which they sympathized. Charles therefore took a step for which the financial community never forgave him: He seized the merchants' bullion held in the Tower awaiting coining. The outcry was immediate, and even though Charles offered the owners security and interest on the "loan," and most of the bullion was in fact immediately returned, the damage to the confidence of the merchant community was irreparable. It was still remembered by Samuel Pepys in August 1666, when he reported the opinion of the merchant and MP Sir Richard Ford that "it sticks in the memory of most merchants, how the late King . . . was persuaded in a strait by my Lord Cottington, to seize upon the money in the Tower—which, though in a few days the merchants concerned did prevail to get it released, yet the thing will never be forgot." Moreover, Charles's financial embarrassments remained unresolved.

One obvious possible solution to the royal difficulties was debasement. The City and the international financial community might reasonably have feared such a step, even if Charles had never contemplated such an option, but in this case their fears were well founded. Charles authorized the preparation of a plan for a major debasement, involving the issue of coin only 25 percent silver. The king never felt much enthusiasm for the plan, and he would have abandoned the idea readily in return for a large loan from the City. Yet the City called his bluff, refusing the loan, and asserting that the city merchants would not accept the debased coin if it were issued. Again Charles backed down, having alarmed the City without raising a shilling.

These political difficulties thus managed to create a "shortage of money" at a time when the nation's money supply actually stood at an all-time high. Faced with uncertainty, merchants hoarded cash, declining to invest and often refusing to pay what they owed already. We read that "merchants and chapmen do now refuse to make payment for goods long since sold and delivered." They "do not take up our cloth as they used to do, but our stocks lie dead in our hands," because of the conventional wisdom that "this is no time to pay money." Further,

Strangers, who were wont to be lenders, have called in and remitted those monies by exchange into foreign parts. And such of our own nation as were wont to be lenders have called in their monies and stand in expectation of what things may be . . . And by our general fears and distractions the inland trade of this kingdom is so far decayed that country tradesmen cannot pay their debts in London as formerly, and many of them have been ruined.

This is one of the earliest explicit descriptions of a politically induced financial crisis. The phenomenon certainly occurred in the Middle Ages, when it was less well recorded, but we know for example that credit became unobtainable in York when the Scottish incursions of the early fourteenth century were at their worst. Similar financial reactions to political events certainly recur on various occasions in the course of the rest of this history. As far as the 1640s crisis was concerned, when the civil war eventually did break out in 1642, most of the financial interests had already lost sympathy with Charles Stuart. The City's decision to back Parliament was probably a decisive factor in the outcome of the war. Once again financial and monetary history are fundamentally linked with the political development of the nation.

The civil war also left its mark on the coinage. Since London was held by Parliament, the king lost control of his mint in the Tower. There Parliament continued to strike the traditional coinage with Charles I's name and portrait. The king, however, had to set up other mints in the regions he controlled to convert whatever bullion he could find into money to pay his troops. On this coinage Charles proclaimed his manifesto: He was, he claimed, fighting for the Protestant religion, the laws of England, and a free Parliament. This was, of course, a neat summary of what Parliament was fighting for too.

The insecurity of the times caused many people to bury their cash in hoards. Some of these hoards went unrecovered by their owners and are still being discovered today. These finds give us a good idea of the composition of the currency in the 1640s. They show that the proportion of the money supply coming from the royalist mints was pitifully small compared with the output of the London mint, which made up well over 90 percent of the money. Of course, Royalists continued to use the regular coins as well as their own issues, so the comparison is exaggerated, but it does vividly illustrate the importance of Parliament's control of the richer southeast part of the country, which was to prove critical for the outcome of the war and for the subsequent development of British constitutional history.

3

Goldsmiths, Locke, and the Birth of the Bank

> ... to receive and pay other men's money, whereby the owners
> were freed from much trouble, and loss of bad moneys and in-
> stead of going over the town, they might, many of them, meet
> with all their cash in one man's shop, and thus came in banking.
> —J. Houghton, 1683

The inexorable rise in prices discussed in the previous chapter reached its peak between 1648 and 1650. The chill message of the cost-of-living index is confirmed by personal contemporary testimony. Ralph Josselin, vicar of Earls Colne in Essex, commented on the prices of these years as never before:

26 September 1647 ... things are at that rate as never was in our days, wheat 8s [a bushel]; malt 4s; beef 3d [a pound]; butter 6¹/₂d; cheese 4d; candle 7d; currants 9d; sugar 18d; and every other thing whatsoever dear ...

6 February 1648 ... this was a sad dear time for poor people only their work beyond expectation continued plentiful and cheap; money almost out of the country; what I spent now I borrowed ...

12 September 1648 ... this sum [£50 p.a.] cannot at the great price all things now bear maintain us [a family of five with another child expected, plus a maid] in a very low manner ... let any understanding man judge whether £80 [a year] be not as little as a man can live on in these times, and this place ...

8 October 1648 ... things are yet very dear I gave 8s 2d for a bushel of new wheat, the greatest price I ever gave in my time of housekeeping ...

7 January 1649 ... the great dearness of everything, beef at 3¹/₂d per pound; wheat 7s 6d, rye 6s 4d, cheese 4d, butter 6¹/₂d per pound, and men expect it will be dearer and dearer ...

18 March 1649 ... cheese 4¹/₄d or 4¹/₂d per pound ... butter sold by some at 8d; pork 4¹/₄d or 4¹/₂d, beef 3³/₄d ...

15 April 1649 ... a great scarcity of all things ... beef 4d, butter 7d or 8d, cheese 5d, wheat 7s 6d, rye 6s 8d ...

20 May 1649 . . . great scarcity of all things . . . rye 6s 8d, butter 7d, cheese 6d, beef 5d, lamb 7d . . .

7 October 1649 . . . all things very dear . . . wheat 8s 6d, rye 6s, barley 5s, cheese 4¹/₂d, butter 7¹/₂d

25 November 1649 . . . the times are wonderful hard . . . wheat above 9s, rye above 7s

December 1649 . . . all things wonderful dear . . . wheat 9s, malt 4s 8d, rye 7s 6d, oatmeal 8s, cheese 4¹/₂d . . . all things dear yet the season was indifferent warm and dry. beggars many

24 June 1650 cow £6 10s

27 June 1650 cow £6 5s

21 July 1650 . . . corn at a great rate. 11s and 11s 6d a bushel at Colchester . . .

[Until at last, after the harvest of 1650]

3 September 1650 . . . good new wheat 5s 4d . . . a comfortable abatement from 10s and 11s

In fact, the peak prices were not reached again until 1710 and 1711, and in general the cost of living steadied around mid–seventeenth-century levels, not resuming its upward march again until the 1760s. As we shall see, the money supply continued to grow through the eighteenth century, which might have been expected to continue to stoke inflation. That it did not do so reminds us that prices are not determined by money supply alone. Nonmonetary factors of course play a part, but the character of the money in use is also a factor. This period of stable prices corresponds with a marked shift from a predominantly silver coinage to a currency composed chiefly of copper, gold, and ever more readily negotiable paper. This shift in the physical composition of the sterling currency makes up the main theme of this chapter, and the behavior of prices suggests that the quality of money can be influential as well as its quantity.

The period of price stability seems quickly to have blotted out memories of the price rise. By the 1690s Parliament could behave as if the pound were some fixed and unchanging value, and most people could agree with it. But if the price revolution was then forgotten, the political and constitutional revolution, which had seen the execution of Charles I and the deposition of James II, was still very much alive. Not surprisingly, the political developments of the seventeenth century also colored monetary thought, and conflicting ideas about the nature of money and the nature of sovereignty were debated in theory and acted out in practice. The crown's historic rights over the coinage were called into question. The Stuarts were seen to have proven themselves particularly untrustworthy in monetary and financial matters: Charles I had attempted to seize merchants' bullion awaiting coining at the Tower in 1640, causing Pepys to regret "the unsafe condition of a bank under a monarch" even before Charles II stopped payment of his debts at the Exchequer in 1672. At the end of the century, John Locke, philosophical standard-bearer of the English constitutional revolution, declared that the silver content of sterling was fixed by natural law and so must not be changed by king or government. This was demonstrably untrue, as the behavior of the financial markets of the day and the history of prices and the mint all showed clearly, but, not for the first time or the last, practical experience was much less influential than political wishful thinking. In 1696 the English Parliament declared the silver content of the currency fixed, and in doing so it unwittingly destroyed the silver basis of sterling forever.

Lurking behind this issue was the much more fundamental question: What is money? Experience in the second half of the seventeenth century prompted an increasingly complex answer to this question. At the most obvious level, money was silver or gold coin. Yet how far did the value of that coin consist in its intrinsic, metal content, and how far was it conferred by the government that established its face value? This distinction was of much more than merely academic interest, for if a shilling's value was determined by its silver content, a clipped or otherwise worn shilling would not be worth 12d., but in England practical experience showed that all but the most grotesquely butchered money in fact passed at its face value.

Abroad, of course, foreigners demanded full-weight English coin, and this period saw a new awareness of the foreign exchange value of sterling. Pepys recorded one conversation that no doubt exaggerated the strength of sterling relative to the French *livre tournois* but does give a Restoration flavor to the discussion of hard and soft currency:

26.2.1668 Among other merry discourse about spending money and how much more chargeable a man's living is now, more then it was heretofore, Duncum [Sir John Duncombe] did swear that in France he did live off £100 a year, with more plenty and wine and wenches then he believes can be [had] now for £200 . . .

However, just as today when a strong pound gives the British greater purchasing power abroad, it also made exports seem more expensive to foreigners. Steele, the political journalist, devoted number 170 of his journal *The Guardian* (September 25, 1713) to the problem of a severely adverse balance of trade with France, whose weakened currency made exports very cheap.

Our ships went constantly in ballast [i.e., without goods] . . . to St Malo, Morlaix, Nantes, Rochelle, Bourdeaux, Bayonne, &c. and ever came back full of linen, wines, brandy, and paper: and if it was so before the Revolution [1689], when one of our pounds sterling cost the French but thirteen livres, what are they like to take from us . . . now that for each pound sterling they must pay us twenty livres, which enhances the price of all British commodities to the French above Fifty per cent.

But within Britain money passed at its face value as set by government, and even worn coin was readily accepted. As the City merchant and government financier William Hodges wrote in 1696 in a tract evidently not autobiographically entitled *The Groans of the Poor*, "though the old money was exceeding bad yet it served to Trade with, and go to Market: And as many use to say, if it was Leather, if it would pass, it would serve." Moreover, even copper halfpence and farthings were accepted because the market needed them. A royal copper coinage had been first introduced by Charles II in 1672, though the success of various types of copper tokens earlier in the century had demonstrated the growing demand for small change. Bills of exchange, for long essential in international trade, were increasingly used in the domestic market. Government tallies became more current, and exchequer paper began to pass. Proto-bankers, at first based in scriveners' legal firms and goldsmiths' shops, discovered that their handwritten receipts and memos were beginning to be accepted, so long as the users were confident they could convert these convenient notes into coin when they wanted. Thus the half century from the execution of Charles I in 1649 to the establishment of the Bank of England (1694) saw a marked, though gradual, development in what people used as sterling currency. The banks occupied a central place in this development.

Banking in Britain evolved rather slowly from the working practices of two professional groups, the scriveners and the goldsmiths. Scriveners were legal clerks whose expertise extended far beyond the drafting of documents. The poet John Milton's father was a scrivener. They became especially knowledgeable in certain branches of the law, particularly conveyance and mortgages. Their contact with a wide range of people, including both those with spare cash to invest and those urgently in need of funds, brought them naturally into the business of loan broking, introducing one group to the other. The experience and competence that scriveners thus acquired encouraged their clients to place increasing trust in them. Many people chose to deposit valuables with scriveners, who came more and more to act as London agents for the gentry. They provided safe-keeping for clients' cash and organized clients' payments. It was but a short step from arranging loans between two other parties (broking) to lending on the scrivener's own account. The scriveners, or money scriveners as they were sometimes called, soon learned that lending clients' money as if it were their own enabled them to collect the interest on the loan at 6 to 8 percent rather than merely the much smaller brokerage fee of 5s. per £100. Already by the 1620s one of John Milton senior's servants believed that most of Milton's income came from lending. Milton senior, who began life too poor to be apprenticed himself, later took on apprentices in his business for less than half the normal apprenticeship fee; another slice of his profits he spent educating the greatest exponent of the language in his, or perhaps any, century.

The best surviving money-scrivener business records date from somewhat later in the century. Robert Abbott began business in 1636. By 1640 his premises in Cornhill, advertised by the Pegasus sign outside, had made him one of the wealthiest men in that extremely prosperous area of London. Between 1646 and 1652 he received £341,364 on deposit from 186 clients. He was particularly favored by royalists looking for a safe haven for their funds or seeking cash urgently to permit them to pay fines or recover confiscated lands. He began a new ledger at Michaelmas (September 29) 1652, when the permitted level of interest was cut from 8 percent to 6 percent. In the next three years he had over £1 million through his hands. His records show clearly that he lent more cash on his own account than he actually possessed; in other words, he was certainly lending his depositors' money and collecting the interest himself.

Abbott died in 1658, evidently assuming that the business would die with him, but his nephew, Robert Clayton, and another of his apprentices, John Morris, instead seized the chance to step into his place. Within days of the funeral, they lent the bishop of Rochester £3,037 10s. 9d. A year later General Monck opened an account with them with a deposit of just over £5,000, and Lord Fairfax received a £5,000 loan from Monck and a further £4,000 from East India Company interests. Monck and Fairfax were both extremely senior generals on the parliamentary side, who had grown weary of the excesses of both the radical and the dictatorial wings of the commonwealth, and by the time of Cromwell's death they were beginning to explore the possibilities of a Restoration of Charles II. Within months of grasping the opportunity presented by Abbott's death, Clayton and Morris were established at the financial center of a web of high political intrigue. Banking and power have gone hand in hand ever since.

Because of their particular interests in mortgages and landed property, money scriveners became involved in a good deal of work managing estates, and they soon developed a network of agents in the countryside providing services and information. In 1661 a reference list of 107 landowners in Norfolk was drawn up in the Clayton and Morris shop. The creditworthiness of people such as Sir Fulke Lucy in Cheshire and Sir Francis Chokke in Berkshire was being assessed. In 1671 one Christopher Cratford reported to Morris that Sir Gabriel Lowe of Gloucestershire "has always had the repute of a very honest gentleman, and I never heard he was in debt." Alongside reports on the character of these country gentlemen, detailed surveys were carried out on their estates. Another important part of the money scrivener's work concerned the remittance of cash between town and country. The regularity of the gentry's income that revolved around the times of harvest, slaughter, and the wool-clip was a help to their bankers, who knew these funds often were not required until Parliament, the legal sessions, or the London season brought their clients to town. Between the times of deposit and withdrawal the bankers looked to turn a profit from idle cash, but first the money had to be delivered safely to the City. Various methods were employed. Sometimes a bailiff would bring estate cash himself or send an agent. In 1676 Francis Colles, agent of the Duke of Buckingham's trustees at Burleigh in Rutland, sent £320 in four bags by courier. In 1671 Ralph Clinton sent his rents in by the carrier Richard Blagrave who was paid £2 for his trouble. But there was much concern about the safety of money on the roads. Sheep and cattle drovers, who came in convoys, knew the roads well, and were well protected with dogs and staves, might be entrusted with cash as well as selling the herd at Smithfield market, before delivering the profits of the sale to their masters' bankers in London.

Concern about the safety of cash remittance lay behind the developing use of inland bills. Although there was generally a need to send more cash to London than away from it, the provisioning of the capital, and the purchase of agricultural produce and the fruit of provincial industries, above all cloth, did require payments out of London as well. Insofar as payments to London could be offset against payments from the capital, the actual remittance of coin could be reduced to the settlement of the balance. Thus in 1665 George Powell, comptroller of customs at Milford, handed £69 19s. 4d. cash to John Hinton in Bristol. Hinton had a credit with Thomas Andrews in London, so he was able to draw a bill on Andrews for that amount. The bill was sent by Powell to his bankers, Clayton and Morris, for them to collect from Andrews and credit to Powell's account. In the 1670s Daniel Sharpe of Norfolk sent a series of bills to Clayton and Morris to be redeemed by various merchants in cheese, butter, and horses at addresses in London. Sharpe had provided cash for the merchants in the county, which they repaid to his bankers in London. In 1672 Henry Hilliard promised his banker, John Morris, "I do expect to receive some money out of the north by bill of exchange and so soon as it comes you shall not fail to have it and should have had it sooner if my tenants had not failed me . . ."

Clayton and Morris would have been very well placed to assess the reliability of hundreds of promises like this, and their huge success suggests that their judgment was almost always sound. Morris seems to have been the more steady of the two, while Clayton developed a reputation for what the diarist John Evelyn called his "prodigious feasting and magnificence." He became Lord Mayor of London in 1679–1680 and a Whig member of Parliament. He was governor of the Bank of England from 1702 to 1707, and despite some charitable works on behalf of Christ's Hospital, the Brideswell Hospital, and St. Thomas's Hospital, he acquired a reputation as a grasping banker, credited with the ruin of the Duke of Buckingham and Lord Peterborough. Daniel Defoe tells us that Clayton bought up a London plague pit and set about developing the site without giving the bodies time to decompose. In verse he said of Clayton that he "Will sell his wife, his master, or his Friend," for he was "To boundless Avarice a constant slave,/Unsatisfy'd as Death, and Greedy as the Grave." The portrait of Clayton that appears in Defoe's novel *Roxana* is slightly more generous, for he figures there as the courtesan Roxana's "faithful counsellor." Clayton seems to have been almost as ready to broker a marriage as a mortgage: One client in 1671 asked Clayton to look out for a rich bride for his son, noting "you have all the money and women at London."

However, the scriveners did not have a monopoly of banking services, for a number of goldsmiths were being drawn into the business by a slightly different route. As we have already seen, goldsmiths had been closely involved with the mint and the technical business of foreign exchange and assaying since the Middle Ages. Their experience and skill with precious metals naturally gave them an advantage in handling coin, making them obvious candidates as cash-keepers and paying agents for the wealthy. Vast amounts of silver were appearing in the London bullion market as well as the mint in the first half of the seventeenth century, and the goldsmiths were ideally placed to calculate the relative advantage in holding silver as English coin, silver plate, Dutch coin, or ingots for export to the East Indies. As early as 1637 goldsmiths were said to be offering 2 or 3 percent to sift other people's coins, culling the heavy pieces. They were again identified in 1652 as principal culprits, clipping silver from the coins in their care before returning them to the circulation at their original face value. As an Amsterdam correspondent wrote then,

It is the goldsmiths, especially those in Lombard Street, who are the greatest merchants and London cashiers, and who will receive any men's money for nothing, and pay it for them the same or the next day, and meantime keep people in their upper rooms to cull and weigh all they receive, and melt down the weighty and transport it to foreign parts . . .

The goldsmiths' activities were, however, by no means restricted to clipping, for, like the scriveners, they soon discovered that broking loans and then lending themselves, either their own capital or that of their depositors, could also be extremely remunerative. If Clayton was the outstanding money scrivener, the archetypal goldsmith-bankers were people such as Edward Backwell and Sir Thomas Vyner. These two were already major figures by 1656, when they were used by the commonwealth government to cash the £150,000 worth of Spanish bullion captured by Admiral Blake and brought to London. Such was the urgency of the government's need for coin that they accepted £50,000 down from Vyner and Backwell and £10,000 weekly thereafter, to a total calculated at a halfpenny per ounce below the mint price for silver. The government got current coin more quickly than the mint could have supplied new, while the bankers paid out worn coin in exchange for bullion bought at a favorable rate which they could then recoin and, no doubt, clip.

Charles II was equally impatient for coin, and employed these bankers in much the same way to help process the 4.5 million *livres tournois* received from the sale of Dunkirk in 1662. Pepys reckoned Backwell got 100,000 *livres* (about £7,500) for arranging the transport of this windfall in forty-six carts carrying chests, each chest containing 5,000 *écu*, or French crowns. The bankers provided the king with current coin directly, and the chests were distributed around the City to bankers such as Backwell, Thomas Vyner, and Francis Meynell. Pepys was pretty certain that when almost £328,000 worth of the Dunkirk proceeds eventually were coined, the bankers quickly clipped their shares of the new money. The bankers did a similar deal getting 5.25 percent on the recoinage of almost half a million pounds' worth of commonwealth coin in 1662–1663.

In due course, this generation of goldsmith-bankers was to pay a heavy price for lending to the crown. In 1672 Charles II stopped payment of his debts at the Exchequer, starting a run on the banks and a credit crisis throughout the City. Charles promised eventual payment and 6 percent interest, but five years later some £1.3 million was still owing, including over £400,000 to Vyner and nearly £300,000 to Backwell. It was a body blow from which neither these bankers nor the credit rating of the Stuarts ever recovered. Although James II did establish a reputation as a rather better payer, Whig politicians in particular were quick to argue that Charles I's stop on the mint in 1640 and that of his son on the Exchequer in 1672 ensured that no government bank would ever seem safe under the Stuarts. This history remained an important factor in the birth and development of the Bank of England as a privately owned bank that sold its services to the state on terms guaranteed by Parliament.

Despite the damage suffered by Backwell and Vyner in the 1670s, enough records of their operations survive, along with those of the scriveners Clayton and Morris, to demonstrate how their practices gave rise to paper money. Fundamental to both goldsmith and scrivener banking was the client's deposit of cash with his banker. Their business naturally generated a number of written instructions and receipts in the course of ordinary communications between banker and client. When a client deposited coin with his banker for safekeeping, he received a receipt from the banker. Henry Garway, a money scrivener, issued such receipts in the period from 1613 to 1621, and the goldsmith-banker Lawrence Hoare did so too in 1633. Initially the receipt notes were made out as a promise to repay the depositor that which he had handed over, but certain refinements soon developed. It soon became understood that the coins repaid need not be the very same ones that had originally been deposited. Sometimes the note or bill stated that interest was due on the deposit, sometimes not. Sometimes repayment was due at a specific time. Soon depositors found it convenient to have these IOUs made out to themselves or to "the bearer," that is to say, to whoever happened to possess the note. Although it made the bill less secure, if anyone could receive payment on it, the original depositor could pass it on in payment, rather than having to return to the bank himself to cash it. In a word, it had become **negotiable**. So long as the receipt for the original deposit had been drawn up by a reputable banker, third parties could be confident of getting payment on it. Among the earliest surviving goldsmiths' notes known to have been passed in payment is that referred to by Pepys (February 29, 1668), when he sent the goldsmith Colvill's note for £600 to his father for his sister's marriage portion. Pepys's casual passing reference to the note suggests that by this time there was nothing remarkable about notes like this. As a receipt, the original notes naturally had recorded the whole sums deposited, which were often large and irregular amounts. If the depositor wished to cash only a part of the value he might do so, a note of the partial withdrawal being recorded on the back as an endorsement. It was similarly customary to endorse notes to record their transfer to other parties. In due course depositors might ask for several receipts each made out for smaller sums but equal to the whole deposit in total, since this could facilitate spending only a part of the total deposit. As these bank bills became simpler, without accruing interest, being payable without time limit to bearer, they emerge as something we can now recognize as a bank note. However, as well as evolving informally to meet the convenience of users, each development had to pass from the stage of customary and accepted behavior among merchants and bankers, to universally understood practice enforceable at law. It was not until a statute of 1704 that the negotiability of bank bills (i.e., the practice of passing paper money from hand to hand) was formally secured in law.

In the same way, the depositor's informal written instructions to his banker to make a payment to another person developed into something we would recognize as a check. Clayton and Morris called them variously vouchers, discharges, or orders. For example, on February 16, 1659, Nicholas Vanacker instructed Clayton and Morris to pay £400 to "the bearer Mr Delboe or order." This draft was sent to Delboe, who presented it to Clayton and Morris. The record of account was kept in the banker's ledgers, where the depositor might inspect it when he wished. We know Pepys would check his banker's books from time to time.

Of course the terms used for what we now call bills, notes, and checks were varied, and often no firm distinction was intended by the use of one term rather than another. Nevertheless, it is clear that in the course of the second half of the seventeenth century paper obligations were beginning to pass as money; that is to say, they were becoming negotiable beyond the two originators of the recorded transaction. This was a development of very great importance, for if paper agreements were able to function as well as money, the size of the money stock could be greatly increased. Moreover, bankers soon discovered that although their original notes reflected an equal deposit of cash, a business of a reasonable size was, in the ordinary course of events, unlikely to be required to meet all its promises to pay at the same moment; if all its promissory notes did not have to be redeemed at once, the banks could effectively create money, by issuing more notes than they held deposits.

Samuel Lee's *Little London Directory* (1677) lists forty-four "Goldsmiths that keep Running Cashes" (i.e., current accounts), mentioning twenty-nine in Lombard Street and Cornhill; eleven in Fleet Street, the Strand, and Covent Garden; and four in Cheapside. These banks were not, however, universally popular. *The Mystery of the New Fashioned Goldsmiths or Bankers,* an anonymously composed tract published in 1676, complained that bankers lent other men's money and that they charged excessive interest, and there was much truth in the charge. The two issues were closely connected. Theoretically, the bankers either paid interest to their depositors or offered them banking facilities in lieu of interest. In fact, they often had to pay high interest themselves to attract depositors. Pepys could have got 6 percent from Backwell in September 1664, but he hesitated, observing that he was "doubtful of trusting any of these great dealers because of their mortality, but then the convenience of having one's money at an hour's call is very great." At this time Pepys had about £1,000 in his house. Two years later he did deposit £2,000 at Vyner's, getting 7 percent, breaching the legal maximum. The merchant, William Attwood, often deposited money with bankers such as Backwell on behalf of his Hamburg partner George Watson. He usually got $4^1/_2$ to $5^1/_2$ percent, but like Pepys he got more in 1666, writing to Watson "I did speak with Sir Robert Vynor, and told him I did expect he should allow me 6 per cent. My father Pell was then by, to whom he allowed that rate. He said what he allowed others he would allow." The maximum legal rate then permitted by the usury laws was 6 percent, but goldsmiths admitted they sometimes needed 9 percent and claimed scriveners often charged 12. The concealment of interest was an ancient art, and it is clear that borrowers and even bankers sometimes had to pay over the legal maximum rate. Although these loans often were advanced in the bankers' own notes, the tightness of credit suggests that at this stage the banks were not abusing the freedom provided by paper issues. One factor working against overissue was the mutual restraint imposed by the bankers' own network.

In order to promote the acceptability of bankers' notes, numbers of bankers formed informal networks agreeing to accept and pay one another's notes when they were presented by the public. In other words, you could cash one of Backwell's notes with Vyner. Careful daily accounts were kept, and each banker would return for payment the notes of other bankers to their bank of origin within a couple of days of accepting them. Yet for the client, it was a considerable convenience, and no little reassurance, to discover that the notes he received from his own banker were accepted by most London tradesmen and about a dozen banks other than his own. This bankers' club was established on the firm foundation provided by the Goldsmiths Company.

Since the Middle Ages the Goldsmiths had been one of the premier London liveried companies. Just as the quality of their craftsmanship was safeguarded by rules demanding the highest standards and imposing a rigorous apprenticeship scheme on would-be applicants, so the interests of banking in general were safeguarded by the restraint imposed on the new banking goldsmiths. Goldsmiths remained in close contact with the masters who had trained them and with their fellow apprentices. In later years these contacts, going back over decades of mutual respect and shared interests, provided the foundation of the banking network. Edward Backwell's ledgers show that he operated a mutual clearing system with at least nineteen other bankers operating in and around Lombard Street, and even down Fleet Street to the Strand. Backwell originally was apprenticed to Sir Thomas Vyner, along with his contemporary trainees, George Snell and Robert Vyner. Backwell in turn apprenticed Thomas Rowe, who in turn trained Thomas Cooke. All these men are met with in Back-well's ledgers. Whole family trees of masters and apprentices have been constructed, from the days of Cromwell right through to William III, linking Sir Thomas Vyner, to Edward Backwell, to Sir Charles Duncombe.

On an average day in the course of mutual clearing Backwell seems to have accepted about £1,500 more of other men's notes than they his, but so long as the notes were quickly cleared and balances settled, the value of the system to all participants far outweighed the cost of interest not charged. Moreover, this cooperation sometimes went far beyond mutual clearing. After the second Dutch war (1667), Vyner was heavily pressed by his depositors who had grown concerned at the extent of his lending to the crown. Charles II owed Vyner some £1.5 million at this time and wanted more, with the threat of withholding interest if further loans were not forthcoming. Loans from men such as Backwell, who lent him £35,000 in the summer of 1668, helped bail Vyner out. Yet Pepys tells us that Back-well too was under pressure at this time:

13.6.67 [the day Dutch ships on the Thames threatened London, and Pepys sent his wife and father out of town to hide £1,300 in gold] W. Hewer hath been at the banquiers and hath got £500 out of Backwell's hands of his own money; but they are so called upon that they will be all broke, hundreds coming to them for money—and their answer is "It is payable at twenty days; when the days are out, we will pay you;" and those that are not so, they make tell over their money, and make their bags false on purpose to give cause to retell [recount] it and so spend time;

When the Dutch retired, the banking crisis eased, but in 1670 Back-well sought help in the shape of a £30,000 loan from Thomas Rowe. Mutual aid, rather than cutthroat competition, was the seventeenth-century banker's watchword.

Despite this sort of safety net, the big bankers of the Common-wealth and Restoration periods suffered badly in the 1670s as a result of Charles II's default. As a consequence new names come through, such as Charles Duncombe, Francis Child, and Stephen Evance. Dun-combe, who stepped into Backwell's shoes, later became known as "the richest commoner in England," spending £90,000 acquiring an estate in Yorkshire. He teamed up with Thomas Martin at the Grasshopper in Lombard Street, a firm destined to survive into modern times as Martins Bank. Blanchard, Child and Co. at the Marygold in Fleet Street survived as Child's Bank. Evance was to emerge in the 1690s as a major player in the foreign exchange markets.

In an age of precious-metal coinages, the international exchange rate of any currency should reflect its bullion value fairly closely. Nevertheless, various other factors could influence exchange rates. First, the coinage, especially the silver, became extremely worn with age and badly clipped. We have already seen that there were complaints about clipping from much earlier in the century. To some extent the problem was inseparable from any precious-metal coinage, but by all accounts it became particularly severe from the 1670s onward. Hopton Haynes, weigher and teller at the mint, recalled that the problem "began to be discernable in great receipts a little after the Dutch war in 1672," and from 1686, when he noted payments generally some 11 percent light, until 1695 when fully half the intrinsic value of the coinage had been lost, the difficulty grew increasingly severe. Although the intrinsic value of the bulk of the coinage in ordinary use fell so much below its theoretical value, it continued to be accepted at its full nominal face value in Britain. Haynes noted that in the 1690s many clipped shillings and halfcrowns "were received and passed as current, as when they were of full weight and value; this encouraged the clippers who increased their numbers and their diligence, and vended the money they had clipped in all places without any check or fear from the laws."

A second threat to the intrinsic basis of the sterling currency lay in the growth of credit and paper money. In the later seventeenth century, the total volume of credit-created bank notes, though growing, was probably still quite small. It has been estimated at £2 million, with another £2 million in inland bills, at a time when perhaps £9 million was circulating in silver coin. In addition, well over £8 million had been struck in gold between 1660 and 1700, though of course nothing like all that will have remained in the country. More important than bank paper were some £6 million worth of government tallies. Since the Middle Ages the Exchequer had used wooden tallies as records of debt. Notches of different sizes were cut on a long stick to record the sum outstanding; the stick was then split lengthways to provide each party with a copy. When the debt was finally settled, the two parts could be reunited to check that they tallied. Charles II made very extensive use of tallies. They permitted him to make purchases, paying by tally, which was in effect a promise to pay, redeemable later at the Exchequer. Charles managed to make these tallies acceptable by paying interest on them of some 8 to 10 percent, and Pepys was involved with them a good deal. Tallies were negotiable, but they were difficult to endorse clearly, and for a time Exchequer orders began to replace them. Much government purchasing was conducted with these orders, and they became common in circulation. Small denominations of £1, £2, and £5 were issued, as well as larger amounts, but this early government paper money was irrevocably damaged when the Exchequer suddenly stopped meeting its obligations in 1672. Tallies, however, continued in use, though some government departments had increasing difficulty getting them accepted, and the City accepted them only at a very heavy discount.

Government borrowing, whether by tally or by conventional loans raised in the City, grew most sharply in time of war. Just as the Dutch wars had created financial problems for Charles II, the outbreak of war with France in 1689 stretched William III's resources to the limit. By 1694 he was spending £2.5 million a year on the army alone. Three years later the national debt exceeded £15 million. Not for the first time or the last, heavy military expenditure raised prices, reducing the value of sterling at home, for the pound now bought less. High prices in England encouraged imports and discouraged exports, causing a deterioration in the country's balance of payments, leading to a reduction in the value of sterling abroad, which matched its reduced value at home. From around 35 to 36 Dutch *schellingen* to the pound before the war, sterling fell to about 34 in the early 1690s and to its nadir of 27 *schellingen* in 1695.

The weakening of sterling thus can be attributed to heavy government borrowing and expenditure and to the poor quality of the silver coinage. At the time observers were more conscious of the second of these two causes, and pressure grew for the government to take action to address the problem of an old, worn, and clipped silver currency. But reform of the coinage was more likely to add to the government's expenses, and so more urgent attention was first given to a series of schemes to raise money.

Loans were raised in the City wherever possible. The repayment of tallies was already two years in arrears. A **Tontine** produced £1 million at 7 percent: On the death of each lender, his annual repayments were shared among the surviving lenders, so by gambling on one's own longevity one might scoop a healthy profit. A lottery scheme aimed to raise another million; the prizes were much smaller than in a modern lottery, but even losing tickets still paid 10 percent interest. Taxation was raised as far as it was thought possible, but conventional taxation of land bore heavily on the country gentry, confirming them in their distaste for foreign wars and their lingering fondness for the old Stuart cause. There were also literally scores of schemes for banks of various kinds. Banks were proposed based on land, on goods, on commercial credit, and on government's future revenues. Between 1600 and 1697 there were thirty-eight proposals put forward for different kinds of banks that would issue paper credit based on anticipated government tax receipts. A scheme of this type in 1694 gave birth to the Bank of England.

This particular proposal was put forward by the Scots-born William Paterson, who had succeeded in winning both political support, including that of Charles Montagu, the Chancellor of the Exchequer, and City backing, from potential participants such as Michael Godfrey, who was subsequently to serve as the first deputy governor of the Bank. The essentials of the proposal were these. The Bank was to raise cash from some 1,200 subscribers in the City totaling £1.2 million, which was to be lent to the government by the Bank at 8 percent per annum interest. The Bank was to be chartered as a **joint stock company** and would be permitted to accept other private deposits, apart from the subscriptions to the government loan. Godfrey declared, "Those who lodge their money in the Bank have it as much at their disposal as if it were . . . in their cash chest." Of course, as we have seen from the goldsmiths' private banks, deposit banking was intimately connected with the lending of those deposits and the creation of paper currency.

In fact, there was some opposition in Parliament to the idea of the

Bank of England issuing its own paper currency, and after Paterson's initial proposal of 1693 the question of issue seems to have been left deliberately vague. In practice, however, issue was always a fundamental part of the scheme, and it was implicit in the clause that may have attempted to limit the size of the Bank's activities to the original £1.2 million subscription. It seems likely that the less enthusiastic supporters of banking in Parliament believed the Bank's scope was so limited, but the Bank itself quickly drew a distinction between its formally sealed bills and its running cash notes. The former, bearing the seal of the corporation and an engraved figure of Britannia seated on a heap of cash, were limited to a maximum of £1.2 million, but the less formal running cash notes, signed by the cashier Thomas Speed (1694–1699) and named after him, were not so limited. Before the end of 1694 the total of both kinds of notes issued probably already exceeded £1.2 million. Paterson left the Bank in 1695, and by March 1696 the Bank had issued £1,240,000 of sealed bills and £887,000 running cash Speed's notes. Even the sealed bills were not perhaps as comprehensively backed as some members of Parliament may have imagined, for although the Bank's £1.2 million was rapidly subscribed, the Bank in fact only called up £720,000 in cash. This cash, consisting no doubt of drafts on other banks as well as gold, was paid to the government, together with a further £480,000 in sealed Bank bills, to make up the required £1.2 million. The Bank also used its own paper to buy up tallies and bills with some time still to run before maturity at a discount. As Michael Godfrey put it in his advertisement for the Bank, "All who want money and have securities, know where to be supplied . . ." Thus the Bank played its part in the inflation of the currency, both by helping to float the government's loan and by creating additional credit currency.

It has been estimated that as a result of this credit boom, the size of the money supply may have grown some 18 percent between mid-1694 and mid-1695. Moreover, in the autumn of 1695, the silver currency was about 50 percent underweight, and the price of silver bullion on the open market stood at 6s. 5d. an ounce, though the mint was still offering only 5s. 2d. for it. Guineas priced at 21s. 6d. in 1690 now passed at 29s. 6d. William Stout, a tradesman of Lancaster, described the situation in 1695 well:

As there was not then any [silver] milled money [still in circulation], guineas began to advance in payment here [Lancaster] to 22s or 23s apiece, and all goods in the market advanced accordingly . . . At our coming to London, we found the old silver coin much more diminished and counterfeited than in the country, and guineas were advanced to 28s or 30s apiece . . .

The poor quality of the silver was putting a premium on gold. Thus largely credit-financed government spending had soared to provide the necessities of war, and the newly established Bank of England was contributing significantly to that government debt, at the same time as the silver currency was losing intrinsic value. It was hardly surprising that all this should have adversely affected sterling's foreign exchange position.

However, sterling then rose sharply through 1696, reaching 37 *schellingen* at the end of that year and settling comfortably above 35 in 1697. Its sudden recovery was brought about by the very severe shortage of coin caused by the recoinage of the old silver coins begun in 1696 and the credit squeeze this caused. The money supply that had grown so sharply in 1694 and 1695 contracted by some 32 percent in 1696–1697. Once the recoinage was set in hand and large amounts of lightweight coin were withdrawn, to be replaced eventually by smaller quantities of new full-weight pieces, an acute shortage of silver developed. John Evelyn records in his diary for May 13, 1696, "Money still continuing exceeding scarce, so that none was paid in or receiv'd, but all was on trust." The shortage of coin, and the arrangements for the recoinage, led to protests in Norwich and rioting in Halifax and Kendal. There was a fear of insurrection in Derbyshire and Staffordshire. The government acknowledged the "great hardship upon the labourers and poorer sort of people," and instructed the justices to give thought to the operation of the Poor Law, but above all to keep the peace. As money was scarce, so too was credit. In the spring of 1696 interest rates of 16 and 17 percent were being quoted, the legal maximum rate notwithstanding. The credit crisis precipitated a run on the Bank, and the governor, Sir John Houblon, was able to offer only part payment on Bank of England notes, which immediately began to be discounted, soon by as much as 16 percent. By February 1697 they were being discounted by as much as 24 percent.

To understand how all this came about, it is worth looking carefully at the coinage since the Restoration. Two well-intentioned reforms were introduced in the 1660s. First in 1662 and 1663 the medieval method of making coins by hand with a hammer was replaced by machines, or mills, which improved both the preparation of blanks and the striking. The machines, which were introduced to a very traditional and reluctant mint by a Frenchman, Peter Blondeau, produced "milled" coins that were a great improvement on the old "hammered" pieces. Most significantly, Blondeau's coins were marked around the milled edge so that any clipping of the finished piece would be apparent at a glance. Pepys visited the new machines at the mint on May 19, 1663, and was greatly impressed by what he saw.

The second reform was the abolition of the charge for coinage. In 1666, by the Act for Encouraging of Coinage, a series of customs duties on imported wine, beer, cider, and spirits provided the crown with the necessary funds to offer free coinage for mint customers. Instead of deducting a charge for the cost of coining and the royal seignorage, anyone bringing metal to the mint would receive the full weight in new coin without deduction. The abolition of charges meant that the merchant bringing silver to the mint now received 5s. 2d. for every ounce, instead of 5s. as before. This increase enabled the mint to compete more effectively for silver, but the demand from the goldsmiths for silver for their trade and from the East India men who regularly shipped vast quantities of silver bullion to pay for imports of spices, fine textiles, and teas meant the competition for silver remained intense. Figures for the weight of silver hallmarked by the Goldsmiths Company each year survive for most of the seventeenth century. Although the goldsmiths may often have melted unsold stock to remake it in the latest fashion, their consumption of silver was huge.

The mint was thus involved in a three-way contest for bullion, involving domestic goldsmiths as well as merchants looking to export metal. The merchants could claim with justice that they brought great trading wealth to Britain, and the simplistic ideas of earlier mercantilists who had opposed the export of any bullion from Britain were giving place to a more sophisticated understanding of the nature of wealth. The export of bullion could permit the import of trading goods that would in due course earn more than had originally been lost. This was the essence of the case argued by East India Company men such as Thomas Mun. In 1663 these ideas won over Parliament, and the export of bullion and of foreign coin was made legal, so long as the bullion could be shown to have been imported rather than melted from English coin.

These were all reasonable measures, but they had unexpected consequences for the coinage. Britain tended to place a rather higher price on gold than on silver. Moreover, although the value of a silver coin was fixed by law—a halfcrown was always worth 2s. 6d.—the value of gold coins was allowed to find its own level. Thus the guineas which Charles II issued, marked with an elephant as an indication of the African origin of the gold, were struck at the mint and released into circulation with a theoretical value of 20s. but passed at somewhere between 21s. 2d. and 21s. 10d. In the spring of 1694 it reached 22s. and in June the following year guineas were changing hands at 30s., though the refusal of the excise to accept them at this level helped limit their inexorable rise. (A maximum legal value for the guinea was set at 21s. in 1717.) Yet so long as gold was valued so highly in Britain, merchants would prefer to organize their trade so as to pay their bills abroad in silver. Moreover, it was the better milled silver that would be exported, for while foreigners took English coin by weight on the continent, in Britain the worn and clipped silver continued to pass at its face value. Over £3 million of silver milled coins had been struck since 1663, but William Lowndes, secretary to the Treasury, found almost none of it in the circulation of the 1690s. The milled coin was a huge improvement on the hammered coins, but the great mistake had been to allow both types to circulate together. In textbook fashion, the bad money had driven out the good. The decision not to recoin all the old money at the time of the introduction of the new undermined the new milled coinage, but Charles II seems to have been unwilling to accept either the cost of a recoinage himself or the unpopularity of a recoinage at the expense of the people.

Moreover, even the introduction of free coining without charges worked against the coinage. Coin traditionally had enjoyed a premium of about 5 to 10 percent over bullion, partly because of the convenience of having it in ready-made denominations of guaranteed value that everyone would accept but partly also because coin cost more than bullion as a consequence of the mint charges. Since a pound weight of bullion used to buy only rather less than a pound weight of coin, coin enjoyed a premium; with the abolition of charges, the premium on coin was diminished. As bullion could now be turned into coin without cost, and since old poor coins were worth as much as good new ones, the new milled pieces were more readily melted.

By the 1690s, however, it was becoming clear to all that something had now to be done about the state of the silver coin. In the early summer of 1695 Parliament asked Lowndes to prepare a report on the coinage and suggest what steps might be taken to improve it. His report, which is a model of its kind, consisted of a review of the history of the currency, a diagnosis of the present difficulties, and a sensible set of proposals to address the problem. Parliament received the report in September and debated it in November. Lowndes understood that the fundamental problem was that the mint price for silver was too low. So long as England undervalued silver, full-weight coins would flow out of the country. Silver was actually worth more than the government said it was worth, which was one reason why even worn coins were still being accepted at their full face value. On consulting the records of the mint, Lowndes discovered that this situation had arisen before in the later Middle Ages, and a solution had been found then in reducing the official weights of the coinage to bring them more into line with the open-market value of silver. Lowndes accordingly recommended that a reduction in silver content of some 20 or 25 percent would give the coinage a value more in step with the true value of silver. It was an excellent piece of work by a man who really understood the issues involved, but Parliament in its wisdom rejected both the analysis and the recommendations.

That it did so can be attributed chiefly to the influence of one man, the philosopher John Locke. Locke's political opinions stood at the very heart of the English revolution. They provided the justification for the deposition of despotic monarchs, and having executed one monarch and deposed another within the space of forty years, Parliament was duly grateful for such a support. Central to Locke's ideas was a limitation on the rights of the sovereign over the natural rights of the people to hold property, and money played a key part in Locke's ideas about the origins of private property. Thus Locke's ideas on money were part of a political philosophy and owed nothing to practical understanding of how money worked in seventeenth-century England. It was because of his political beliefs that Locke was unable to accept Lowndes's historically accurate statement that it was the king "to whose regality the Power of Coining Money, and determining The Weight, Fineness, Denomination and Extrinsick Value there of doth Solely and Inherently Appertain." Locke would not even transfer these powers to Parliament, but rather asserted that the values of silver and gold were fixed by natural law and could not be changed by king or Parliament. He likened the notion of altering the silver content of the money to a proposal "to lengthen a foot by dividing it into Fifteen parts, instead of Twelve . . . calling them Inches . . ."

In truth, however, silver was not an immutable yardstick. Its value fluctuated, reflecting supply and demand like any other commodity. Even if it were possible to nail the value of the pound to a fixed unit of silver, the value of other commodities—wheat, wool, gold— would still fluctuate, altering the purchasing power of the pound. Even if values in England could be frozen, those in the rest of the world could not. And there was no shortage of men in late seventeenth-century England who understood this very well. "Money is but a medium of Commerce, a Security which we part with, to enjoy the like in Value," wrote an anonymous pamphleteer in 1694. Henry Layton, who was principally a theological writer, tried to tell Locke "nothing that England can do is able to alter the price of silver in other places of Europe, from whence we must acquire and obtain it." The lawyer Rice Vaughan, writing in the 1620s, though not published till 1675, had been trying to drive home the truth, asking "when your Money is richer in substance and lower in price than the silver in the Low Countries, how can you expect that the Merchant, who only seeketh his profit will ever bring hither any silver"? Yet the experience of the City stood for nothing in the face of Locke's enormous prestige and authority.

Nevertheless, there were practical aspects to Locke's argument.

He certainly had a point when he said that if the state, which was then borrowing heavily, should offer repayment in debased currency, it would damage the government's credit as seriously as the stops on the Exchequer and mint had. Locke put it thus:

It will weaken, if not totally destroy the public faith when all that have trusted the public and assisted our present necessities upon Acts of Parliament in the million lottery, Bank Act, and other loans, shall be defrauded of 20 per cent of what those Acts of Parliament were security for.

The same point could be extended to include private debts, for it was clearly understood at the time that deflation helped landlords and creditors, while inflation helped merchants, shopkeepers, and tradesmen who had borrowed to finance their enterprises. Henry Layton was quick to speak up for debtors, complaining that Locke

extends his Care to Creditors and Landlords, not regarding the Cases of Tenants or Debtors; Men for this four or five years last past, have borrow'd many Thousand Pounds in Clipt Money, but he notes no unreasonableness or injustice in compelling them to pay such Debts again in heavy Money, perhaps of twice the weight.

This was an age-old argument, for the same issues, though rarely so clearly expressed, had attended the debates over medieval debasement. Fundamentally it was a debate about the relative value of Men and Money. Those with money, the creditors, consistently tend to line up on one side, while those with little but their own labor, ingenuity, and enterprise line up on the other. If money is not sufficiently valued, inflation takes hold, eroding the foundations of society. If money is excessively valued, the economy stalls, initiative falters, and unemployment soars. It is the battle of hard versus soft money, and the same debate is argued each month today in the Bank's Monetary Policy Committee when it sets interest rates. This issue would also affect sterling's exchange rate. As we shall see in the following chapters, the same principles apply whether the money is of silver and gold, paper, or plastic.

In the Commons debate of November 1695, the Court Party, dominated by the Whigs who had evicted James II and were most heavily committed to the support of William III, the Protestant

cause, and the war, naturally followed Locke whose political thinking had provided the philosophical justification for their Glorious
Revolution. But even the closet Jacobite country gentlemen must
have been sympathetic to arguments that appeared to safeguard the
silver value of their rental income. In the seventeenth-century Commons the commercial interest carried little weight, and Lowndes's arguments were thrown out; those arguments were still the subject of
Macaulay's ill-informed ridicule even 150 years later.

Thus it was agreed that the clipped money should be called in over
the first few months of 1696, to be recoined into full-weight pieces. A
window tax would provide the government with the necessary funds
to bear the considerable costs of this exercise. However, although
coining was now free to the public, it was they who had to bear the
cost of surrendering poor-weight coin with a high face value in exchange for far fewer full-weight coins. Arrangements were made to
permit tax payments and loans to the government to be paid in
clipped coin, accepted at full face value for a while. While this may
have softened the blow for those with large tax obligations or the resources to lend to government, it did nothing for the vast majority of
the people. In 1696 alone as a consequence of the recoinage, £2.3
million face value was lost to the circulation, and as much may have
been lost again in the following year. The consequences of this sort of
deflation, which Lowndes had foreseen, were severe. Edmund Bohun
wrote from Ipswich to John Cary in Bristol in July 1696:

No trade is managed but by trust. Our tenants can pay no rent. Our corn
factors can pay nothing for what they have had and will trade no more, so
all is at a stand. And the people are discontented to the utmost; many self
murders happen in small families for want, and all things look very black,
and should the least accident put the mob in motion no man can tell where
it would end . . .

As we have seen, some rioting did in fact break out, and the shortage
of coin triggered a run on the Bank. What made matters worse,
much newly struck full-weight silver was carried overseas, for the
fundamental difficulty—the undervaluation of silver in sterling, compared with the value of silver in currencies abroad—had not even
been addressed, much less resolved.

In 1697 Isaac Newton, as warden of the mint, had taken a sensible measure designed to try to separate silver for coinage more effectively from silver in the hands of goldsmiths. It had long been felt that the goldsmiths had far too active an interest in the coinage as a source of bullion for their trade. From this time, the smiths were to work to an enhanced Britannia standard of 95 percent pure silver. It was a reasonable attempt to prevent the melting of coin, which remained at the ancient sterling standard of 92.5 percent. If it had been combined with a realistic mint price for silver, which would have been made possible by the devaluation Lowndes proposed, the silver coinage could have been restored. As it was, silver was effectively driven out of circulation in eighteenth-century England, and sterling, despite its link with silver of a fixed and certain fineness, in practice became a gold-based currency.

4

The Age of Daniel Defoe and Adam Smith

It is not by augmenting the capital of the country, but by rendering a greater part of the capital active and productive than would otherwise be so, that the judicious operations of banking can increase the industry of the country.

—Adam Smith, *The Wealth of Nations,* 1776

The two great monetary events of the 1690s, the foundation of the Bank of England and the great recoinage, had far-reaching consequences during the next century. The recoinage, or more specifically the ill-advised values of gold and silver that were then confirmed, meant that Britain's silver coinage would be inadequate for the needs of the growing economy. The price for silver offered by the mint of 5s. 2d. per ounce was simply not enough to attract customers who knew goldsmiths and East India men would pay more. The East India Company alone exported some £5.7 million worth of silver between 1700 and 1717. The failings of the silver coinage were matched by a huge rise in the currency of gold, copper, and paper money, and the Bank of England eventually was to come to play a central role in the management of this increasingly complex money supply.

Throughout the eighteenth century the value of gold coined far exceeded that of silver. Derisory quantities of silver were brought in and were stockpiled until enough had accumulated to make a silver minting worthwhile. Occasional bonanzas from the capture of booty, most significantly the £500,000 in Spanish bullion stolen by Commodore George Anson in 1744–1745 and paraded through the City in triumph, seemed all the more important because the ordinary commercial channels ran dry. In the second half of the century no silver coins at all were struck in twenty-five years, and in a further nineteen the silver output was limited to the tiny amounts needed for the royal maundy distribution. The half-dozen years of significant output during the period 1750 to 1799, which produced some

£150,000 of silver coin, owed much to attempts by the Bank of England to meet its customers' demand for Christmas tips.

The impact of the shortage of silver currency on the economy as a whole was at least partly offset by the extensive use of copper as small change. The mint struck copper on a fairly substantial basis. More than 800 tons, amounting to about £175,000, was struck into something like 100 million copper halfpennies and farthings from 1729 to 1754. In addition, this legitimate copper coinage probably was doubled by the extremely common counterfeits of the time. In 1741 the government recognized the seriousness of the situation, offering £10—when a weaver might have earned about 7s. a week—as a reward for information leading to convictions for counterfeiting. So severe did the counterfeit problem become that official copper issues were halted in 1754 for fear of a glut, though in fact demand for copper coins seems to have remained high. In 1755 the mint estimated that even the best-quality counterfeits yielded a profit of 50 percent, and poorer copies, still passing at face value, yielded correspondingly more. Many unofficial coiners attempted to evade a charge of forgery by striking copies with a superficial resemblance to the real thing but with subtly altered legends. The official overvaluation of the copper coins allowed unauthorized coiners as well as the Royal Mint to enhance the value of copper significantly simply by striking it as coin. Although in theory there was a legal tender limit of 6d. for copper coins, silver was so scarce that copper had to play an increasing role. The poor were paid almost exclusively in copper, and because silver small change was in such short supply, people were ready to take copper coin at a face value above its intrinsic worth and were even ready to accept unofficial issues.

Indeed, toward the end of the century, when the copper counterfeits eventually were effectively suppressed, a new burst of privately issued copper tokens occurred. Many of them make attractive illustrations of the Industrial Revolution they were designed to serve, such as John Wilkinson's tokens, which were still to be found in Birmingham small change in the 1960s. Matthew Boulton struck millions of such tokens on machinery, "the vastness and the contrivance" of which so much impressed Boswell when he visited the Soho works in 1776. Eventually in 1797, when a further attempt was made to restore the official royal copper issues, it was Boulton's mint that took on the work rather than the more conservative Royal Mint.

If copper was doing the work of silver in small transactions in the eighteenth century, in greater transactions silver was replaced by gold. Though sterling was officially still defined by its silver content, John Conduitt, master of the mint, suggested in 1730 that "nine parts in ten, or more, of all payments in England, are now made in gold." Although large sums of money above a few pounds were increasingly represented in various forms of paper currency, golden guineas were more commonly circulating from hand to hand and were becoming more worn. This wear on gold coins involved a more significant loss of intrinsic value because of the high value of the metal. As a response to this problem of wear, in 1733–1734 about £1 million of old handmade (hammered) gold coins, dating from before 1663, were called in and recoined. Of course, all the post-1662 gold coin that remained in circulation was also subject to wear as well, but such was the demand for coin that even lightweight gold coins continued to circulate at their full face value.

In the second half of the century wear and clipping developed into an extremely serious problem, and where the shortage of coin was most severe, in the textile districts of the West Riding and Lancashire, forgers sprang up, offering to strike new lightweight guineas from gold clipped by their customers from genuine guineas. The demand for coin that allowed worn guineas to circulate at full face value also created an indulgent attitude to clipped coin and to forgeries of good metal. As the mint solicitor complained, around Halifax in the 1760s "the want of cash for circulation gave a currency to everything that bore the face of a guinea." In fact, legitimately worn guineas were often about 2s. light, but passed at their full face value, and John Bates, landlord of the Wheatsheaf in Halifax, found he could clip a further 2s. worth of gold from them and still pass them at their full value of 21s. It became difficult to pass guineas only when they weighed less than about 16s. worth of gold. One James Green bought a specially strong pair of scissors from Sheffield for clipping. This "yellow trade," as it was known, worked as a kind of local devaluation, increasing the money supply by popular direct action. Rockingham's government attempted to halt the trade but found the degree of collusion, even among people of the "better sort," a serious obstacle to law enforcement. Respectable merchants who might have been expected to do whatever they could to safeguard the means of exchange cashed the inland bills they earned in legitimate trade at less than their full face value to get guineas specifically to clip. The clippings were then delivered to "the Halifax mint," operated by William Varley at his isolated house on South Owram Bank. Men such as the clock engraver Thomas Sunderland would make and sell coin dies. Despite numerous depositions made before the magistrates, the really hard evidence, such as the capture of the perpetrators with coining equipment and clippings, proved elusive. Although "King David" Hartley, a leading coiner who earned his title for "saving his country from the formidable enemy—Poverty," was hanged, William Varley got a pardon, and popular sympathy and the difficulty of collecting really incriminating evidence ensured that in all surprisingly few convictions were achieved.

Eventually the government recognized that nothing short of a major recoinage could reestablish once more the intended relationship between the intrinsic and face values of the gold coinage. Light gold coin was ordered to the mint, and from 1774 to 1778 some £16.5 million of worn or clipped gold coin (estimated at three-quarters of the total of gold coin in circulation) came in to be restruck at full weight. It cost the government £0.75 million in the process. Thereafter, special weights and scales were produced to check the good weight of gold coins offered in payment. A decade later the rather more conservative country people were still anxious about getting new, shining coin of good weight, rather to the irritation of their bankers. The Newbury bank, Vincent & Co., wrote to their London agents in 1789 for 1,000 guineas, "in the words of our Mr Vincent, such as are call'd Shiners, finding our Customers of late grow more nice than wise, and consequently we are much pestered by their particularity with respect to our weighing . . ."

The gold recoinage of the 1770s, like the silver recoinage of 1696 to 1697, provides a useful benchmark for the amounts of coin in circulation. Silver alone has been estimated at about £9 million for the 1690s plus perhaps another £4 million in gold, and in the 1770s the recoinage plus new gold issues came to about £18.2 million, to which a mere £800,000 may be added for the circulating silver. A coinage of £19 million represents a dramatic increase over the 1690s estimate, but these bald figures tell only a part of the story. Any estimates of eighteenth-century money supply have to recognize that gold, silver, and copper coin together now only represented a shrinking proportion of the total stock of "money" in its wider sense.

Even in the Middle Ages the concept of money was complicated by the role of credit, but in the course of the sixteenth and more especially the seventeenth centuries the development of increasingly sophisticated credit instruments saw the emergence of a range of alternative means of payment. Credit evolved from simple deferred payment or cash advances, to the point where the bills, notes, or letters of credit themselves began to function and circulate as money rather than merely as a record of debt. In the course of the eighteenth century, coin—though still the ultimate foundation for these alternative kinds of money—came to represent less than half of the money stock in its wider sense.

Noncoin money may be divided into two categories: that which emerged from banking and the other expedients that have their origins even before the late seventeenth-century banking developments. For example, the Exchequer continued to use the medieval wooden tally as a record of debt. At the end of the seventeenth century, government tallies still amounted to some £6 million, out of a total of all means of payment that has been estimated at about £20 to £23 million. Bills of exchange, which were to become more important as the use of the tally declined, also had medieval origins. As discussed, ever since the thirteenth century the problems of making overseas payments had been eased by the development of the bill of exchange. In the seventeenth century, however, bills of exchange came to be employed more and more often to ease payments within England. Obviously, there was no element of *exchange* in these inland bills, but they were still extremely convenient for transferring funds between London and the provinces. If a trader in the north had a payment to make in London, he could buy a bill from a banker in his hometown that would entitle him, or anyone to whom he transferred the bill, to collect payment in cash from the banker's agent—usually another bank—in London. Even more important, inland bills worked well as short-term credit instruments. The time lag allowed between the purchase of the bill in one locality and its repayment in another was often set at around three months, which was much longer than was strictly necessary to allow for the remittance of funds to the repaying agent. In the meantime, the banker enjoyed the use of the coin, while the trader enjoyed the convenience of the bill. Moreover, the bills themselves came to circulate, like money, and the holders of bills found they could cash them easily before the due date if they were prepared to accept slightly less than the full face value. Offering a reduced cash sum for a bill before it was due for payment is known as **discounting**. The whole process of drawing (i.e., writing) bills, discounting, and providing funds for eventual repayment was devised to mobilize available cash resources more efficiently, so that those people or regions with money at their disposal could find a use for it with those in need of finance for enterprise. The volume of inland bills has been guessed at £2 million around 1700, £15 million around 1750 and £30 million around 1775. At the end of the century men such as the MP and later Chancellor of the Exchequer Nicholas Vansittart and the Liverpool banker Benjamin Heywood suggested some £200 million was traded daily in bills, but modern estimates suggest a figure more like half that may be nearer to the truth. Nevertheless, the use of inland bills was increasing dramatically.

These inland bills also contributed to the development of paper money in another way. Adam Smith explained, "It is chiefly by discounting bills of exchange, that is by advancing money upon them before they are due, that the greater part of banks and bankers issue their **promissory notes**." When bankers discounted bills, they bought the bill from its owner before it was due for repayment at less than its full face value, making payment in their own banknotes. Developing from their earliest most informal beginnings, by the early eighteenth century these bankers' promissory notes were increasingly filled out by hand on printed forms. They might be payable by the bank on demand, or at some later date, or only a part of their value might be drawn at any one time, and the note endorsed to that effect. Alternatively, endorsement could direct payment to someone else. The terms "bill," "bank bill," "draft," and "note" were used fairly indiscriminately at first, reflecting the flexible practices from which they originated, but gradually "bills" came to mean inland bills of exchange, "drafts" developed into what we would today regard as checks, and "notes" emerged slowly as recognizable banknotes. The *Daily Courant* and the *London Gazette* regularly carried advertisements for lost notes and drafts. In the novel *Tom Jones* Sophia Western lost a "Bank-bill" for £100 in 1745, and Fielding observed that it could readily have been exchanged for £99 15s. cash. This looks too small a discount for an inland bill not yet due for payment, which suggests Sophia's bank bill was what we would now call a banknote payable to the bearer in cash.

Moll Flanders, whose adventures novelist Daniel Defoe described in 1722, explained very well the complexity of early eighteenth-century money and its management:

... I had a little money, and but a little, and was almost distracted for fear of losing it, having no friend in the world to trust with the management of it; that I was going into the north of England to live cheap, that my stock might not waste; that I would willingly lodge my money in the bank, but that I durst not carry the bills about with me ...

... to keep and carry about with me bank bills, tallies, orders, and such things, I looked upon it as unsafe; that if they were lost, my money was lost, and then I was undone; and, on the other hand, I might be robbed and perhaps murdered in a strange place for them. This perplexed me strangely, and what to do I knew not.

It came in my thoughts one morning that I would go to the bank myself, where I had often been to receive the interest of some bills I had, which had interest payable on them, and where I had found the clerk, to whom I applied myself, very honest and just to me ...

He told me I might lodge the money in the bank as an account, and its being entered in the books would entitle me to the money at any time, and if I was in the north I might draw bills on the cashier and receive it when I would; but that then it would be esteemed as running cash, and the bank would give no interest for it; that I might buy stock with it, and so it would lie in store for me, but that then if I wanted to dispose of it, I must come up to town on purpose to transfer it, and even it would be with some difficulty I should receive the half-yearly dividend, unless I was here in person ...

Defoe, who was a political and economic journalist before he wrote novels, knew what he was talking about. Here we read of interest-bearing accounts, of current accounts that bore no interest but on which bills could be drawn, of cash banknotes payable to the bearer. From 1716 Bank of England notes were consistently cash notes, signed by the chief cashier, usually for quite large amounts of £20 and over, but practice remained variable until legislation in 1765, 1775, and 1777 effectively banned notes for less than £5 (£1 in Scotland) and insisted that notes should be payable on demand without conditions. Of course, as well as issuing notes, bankers accepted deposits that were then lent out again at interest. Thus as well as creating paper money, the banks allowed money to work in two places at once, in the accounts of the depositor and in that of the borrower. By acting as a broker between those with cash to lend and those seeking to borrow, the banks also improved the circulation. Banknotes and deposits taken together have been estimated at some £2 million around 1690, £10 million for the middle of the century, £17 million around 1775, and some £30 million by 1800.

This huge increase in the amount of money of all kinds in England and Wales needs to be set in the context of a similar dramatic rise in the national income over the same period. In approximate terms, a GDP of about £50 million around 1700 had doubled by the middle of the century and doubled again by 1800. Of course changes in population and in prices are concealed within this simple comparison of GDP. Population probably almost doubled over the course of the eighteenth century, with most of the growth occurring in the second half of the century. Prices similarly rose dramatically between the 1750s and 1800, though not much between 1650 and 1750. Samuel Johnson seriously overstated inflation when he suggested that the £3 per annum which Sir William Petty had estimated as the cost of an adult's subsistence in the second half of the seventeenth century should be raised to £6 to allow for the cost of living in 1763, but his comment that "times are much altered" since Petty's day was fair enough. In London in the 1750s a 4-pound loaf could be had for about 5$\frac{1}{4}$d., but by the 1780s it would cost 6$\frac{1}{2}$d. and in the 1790s 9$\frac{1}{2}$d. What is more, London wages failed to keep up with those rising prices, though Lancashire workers did much better. Nor were these better northern wages restricted to the new industrial workers; growing demand for labor affected the rural north too, as the effects of indusrialization spread beyond the towns. Agricultural laborers' pay in the six northern counties, which had been lower than pay in other regions around 1760, was by 1795 higher than in all other regions.

The economic and monetary character of the country was indeed totally transformed in the course of the eighteenth century. Coin, which had accounted for over 80 percent of England's money in the 1690s, made up less than half of the money of 1800, even if we exclude inland bills from our concept of money. Banknotes alone exceeded the total of coin in circulation by the end of the century. In these circumstances, the historian of the currency necessarily looks increasingly from 1700 at the banks rather than at the mints.

The development of a sound banking system was of the first importance, but the establishment of such a system was the result of no deliberate or consistent policy. British banking emerged slowly and painfully from the shocks and crises of the next three centuries. That the Bank of England should preside over those centuries of slowly accumulating knowledge, experience, and understanding would have struck observers of the financial scene in the early 1700s as extremely improbable. In 1696 the proposal for a National Land Bank was founded on the assumption that the Bank of England was already practically dead. Moreover, the position of the Bank was secured only by temporary charter, subject to renewal, which was by no means guaranteed. Indeed, the early renewals were the result of much hard bargaining, and concessions and privileges granted to the Bank had to be paid for in loans extended to the government. For example, in 1707–1708 the Bank negotiated an extension of its charter to 1732, in exchange for a loan to the government of £1.5 million at 4.5 percent. Nor was the Bank the only possible source of government finance. Despite legislation designed to allow it a monopoly, a serious rival, the Sword Blade Company, grew increasingly active in banking activities in the 1700s. Two men in particular at the Sword Blade Company, the burly, domineering scrivener John Blunt and the able, charming, and utterly unscrupulous cashier Robert Knight, were to lead the challenge to the dominance of the Bank of England. It was the schemes of Blunt and Knight that were to create the financial and political scandal known as the South Sea Bubble.

Politically, Queen Anne's reign, like William III's, was dominated by the war with France and the question of how to pay for it. Like William, the queen at first put her faith in the Whigs, who were more sympathetic to the war, especially if it were paid for by land taxes, and by loans arranged through the Bank of England. We have already seen how the Bank owed its very existence to its role in the organization of government debt. While the land tax bore more heavily on Tory country gentlemen, funds raised in the City were sometimes quite remunerative for the bankers involved as intermediaries. Gilbert Heathcote, for example, a director and later governor of the Bank of England, was said to have made £50,000 from a 1697 scheme buying up government tallies at less than their face value and reimbursing himself for their full value in Bank of England stock. Thus at its simplest, the Whigs, led by Francis, Earl of Godolphin, may be thought of as the monied party and the Tories as the landed interest, but some City men, finding themselves outside the charmed Bank-government circle, were not unwilling to back the Tories when Robert Harley brought them into power in 1710. The extent of the Bank of England's commitment to the Whigs may be judged from their warning to the queen that no other party could ensure the government's financial security. Equally, the Sword Blade Company was quick to offer Harley's new Tory administration an alternative source of funds, untainted by years of Whig collusion. Thus the financial consequences of Marlborough's adventures, Britain's first major European land-based conflict since the Hundred Years War, set the scene for a struggle for money, power, and influence that was to prove crucial for the Bank of England. The recurring combination of war, government spending, and financial crisis management was to prove central to the history of sterling at the beginning of the eighteenth, nineteenth, and twentieth centuries.

Harley stoked the opposition to Marlborough's expensive foreign war by revealing a daunting catalogue of government debts amounting to over £14 million. Various schemes were devised to meet these obligations, with the Sword Blade Company rather than the Bank in control, and in 1711 Blunt and Knight's South Sea Company, offspring of the Sword Blade, was born. The South Sea trade, which actually centered on South America and its Mexican silver and

Brazilian gold mines, was regarded as a fount of fabulous wealth, but the South Sea Company (SSC) never had much more than a notional interest in it. An unsavory deal supplying African slaves to work in the mines failed to make a profit. Much more to the point, the holders of £9 million of government debt were brought together under the umbrella of the SSC, the government agreeing to pay 6 percent (rather more than £0.5 million) a year to the company. Thus the government's creditors found themselves owning shares in the SSC. The company now received their interest on the government debt, but it anticipated healthy dividends instead, like those usually paid by the Bank of England, together with the hope of a capital gain as the price of company stock rose. This hope was founded largely on the monopoly granted by the government to the company of "the sole trade and traffick" of South America, even though much of the territory involved was "reputed to belong to the Crown of Spain." At first sight the scheme had much in common with the flotation of the Bank of England, which similarly began life as a holding company for government debt. The Bank, however, usually paid dividends to its shareholders, and was well run, on a sound basis by substantial and experienced City men. The men behind the SSC were shrewd and determined, but more concerned to manipulate the price of company stock than to generate business or real profits. This market in stocks gave a further dimension to the growing range of financial assets other than coin in which early eighteenth-century wealth could be held and manipulated.

A fundamental part of the SSC strategy involved the participation of influential members of the government. Harley, for example, was governor of the company at its foundation, and the court of directors was fairly equally divided between other political nominees and Sword Blade personnel. The politicians provided influence and access to the public debt as well as a degree of respectability. The Sword Blade men took care of day-to-day management and provided the company's real leadership. They moved with great skill and assurance when the death of the queen and the arrival of the Hanoverians sealed Harley's fate. Whereas the Whigs had been instrumental in placing William of Orange on the throne in 1689, many Tories, with their High Church sympathies, were more than a little tainted with old Stuart leanings. Accordingly, on Anne's death the SSC quickly removed all Tories from the court of directors and replaced Harley as governor with the Prince of Wales. When in 1717 the king quarreled with the Prince of Wales, the company moved with equal dispatch to install George I as governor. No sooner was their loyalty to the new dynasty established than another deal was hatched with the incoming Whig government. In 1715 they waived outstanding government payments due to them amounting to over £1 million, in exchange for the right to issue that amount of further stock. The company's issued stock came to over £10 million, making it by far the biggest joint stock company in the country.

Again and again the same strategies were employed. Members of the government were brought into the company, such as Craggs, the postmaster-general, in 1715, and Aislabie, the Chancellor of the Exchequer, in 1717. New government debts were sought out for conversion into company stock, and as the price of the stock rose (it only reached par in 1715), people were increasingly ready to accept it, secure in the knowledge that they could sell it at more than the value at which they had received it. The deaths of two experienced bankers on the board, Bateman in 1718 and Shepheard in 1719, left the company still more dominated by Blunt and Knight. Such money as came into the company, from government interest payments and as a result of speculators' purchase of new company stock, was quickly plowed back into the market to pump up the price of SSC stock. While the price of stock rose, the holders of government debts were ever more ready to accept stock in place of the interest due to them. As Blunt himself put it: "The advancing by all means of the price of stock is the only way to promote the good of the Company."

In fact, much of northern Europe was infected with the same speculative madness. Hamburg and Amsterdam were familiar with similar booms. In France John Law's scheme for investment in his Mississippi company and the replacement of French coin with paper money was linked to another similar stampede. In London SSC stock boomed along with hundreds of original and bizarre proposals for making money. Exchange Alley, the complex of streets between Lombard Street and Cornhill, with its coffeehouses, most famously Jonathan's and Garraway's, was buzzing with schemes. Before formal exchanges and offices were established, dealers set themselves up more or less permanently in the booming talk and coffee shops of the day. There companies were launched for insuring seamen's wages, importing broomsticks from Germany, and "settling the country on a desolate river more than seventy miles up the main continent in Acadia." The South Sea Company, jealous of other scams that appeared to profit from schemes to inflate the markets, used its influence with government to promote legislation—the Bubble Act—to prevent companies without charters floating stock. The act, far from restraining the company, was intended to eliminate its lesser, and even more scurrilous, competitors.

The Bank of England, however, as a royal chartered company established by act of Parliament, was too big a player to be set aside by the Bubble Act, and was still actively competing with the company for government debt that could be turned into stock. In January 1720 the House of Commons examined two rival schemes proposed by the SSC and the Bank. The company bid £3.5 million for the right to offer its own stock to holders of the national debt, but the Bank's directors, meeting at Waghorn's coffeehouse, offered £5.5 million. Nevertheless, the carefully cultivated political influence of the company was to prove crucial. Sunderland, a leading government minister, and Charles Stanhope, the Treasury secretary and cousin to the chief government minister Lord Stanhope, worked hand in glove with the company to offer the House of Commons an improved bid of up to £7.5 million. In February this bid carried the day, and SSC stock rose on the exchange from 129 to 160, while Bank of England stock fell. During the formal debate on the fully detailed bill that gave expression to the deal between the government and the company, SSC stock rose further from 218 to 320, while the Bank, which would be required to surrender all its holdings of government debt except its original foundation loan of 1694, saw its stock go down to 130.

Throughout this critical period the support of the great and (not entirely) good was secured by the allocation of parcels of company stock to friends in high places. These allocations were carefully recorded by Knight in a secret green record book. Indeed, they had no other real existence until the recipients chose to sell their holdings back to the company as the price of stock rose. The profits were paid in Sword Blade banknotes, of course Sunderland, Aislabie, and Stanhope all stood to make hundreds of pounds for every point the stock rose. Sunderland and Stanhope personally guided the bill through the House of Lords. The king, who probably also received an allocation, granted the Royal Assent in April. SSC stock moved up to 335.

Of course, the high price of stock now brought more real cash into the company, but this was quickly paid out again or lent, enabling the recipients to invest still further in the SSC. Politicians and holders of government debt received stock on advantageous terms, which guaranteed a profit even at stock prices below those already reached in the market. But others bought in at the market price, confident of further rises. Other shares also enjoyed the boom. Chetwynd's insurance stock rose from 4 to 50 between February and May 1720. The Royal African Company rose from 105 to 190. Early in June SSC stood at 870.

The profitability of the company was so confidently predicted and the demand for the stock so great that new issues, now no longer restricted to holders of government debt, were rapidly subscribed even at the astonishing price of £1,000. In fact, subscribers had a year to pay and handed over only a tenth of the price on subscription, so there was still no shortage of takers. However, Aislabie took his profits and advised the king to do likewise, telling him that "the stock was carried up to an Exorbitant height by the madness of the people and that it was impossible it should stand." George insisted on reinvesting, subscribing secretly as Aislabie's brother-in-law, Vernon. He was in good company, along with half the House of Lords and more than half the Commons. Four-fifths of the subscription was limited to the directors' nominees, including the likes of Pope, Kneller, and Vanbrugh, and the remaining fifth was fully subscribed by the public in a single day. In August Pope urged Lady Mary Wortley Montagu to buy in for a certain profit.

However, the cracks in the structure were beginning to show. As early as June the Sword Blade Company had moved over £1 million into a new and separate company; Charles Stanhope took care to have money owing to him paid by the new company, as opposed to Sword Blade. In August and September the South Sea Company spent increasingly heavily buying its own stock to support the price,

but, significantly, Blunt began to cut back his own subscriptions, preferring to buy land. Of course there had always been profit-takers.
Thomas Guy, MP for Tamworth, had sold out early and honestly,
making over £200,000, which he used to build the London hospital
still named after him. Hoare's bank, despite many ups and downs,
and great difficulty during the winter crisis, ended up some £28,000
to the good. Many People did make money out of the boom. But the
late summer saw a marked downturn in the price of SSC stock. Early
in September Charles Blunt, Sir John's nephew, cut his own throat,
with the price at 750. Within a week it lost another 200 points.

The king and many of the court and government were still abroad
or in the country when a hastily assembled group met on the night of
September 19–20 at the General Post Office to attempt a rescue
package. Postmaster-General Craggs, Aislabie, and Walpole, the last
of whom was not as severely implicated in the scandal, were there.
The company was represented by a group of directors, but Blunt and
the other Sword Blade personnel were not present. The real financial
muscle was provided by the Bank of England, represented by Heathcote, probably the richest commoner in the land, and by John
Hanger, the governor of the day. The company itself could not be allowed to fail completely: That would, after all, amount to a massive
default on the national debt. The credibility of the government, and
of politicians of every persuasion, required that the fundamental
government debt be honored, but there could be no support for the
company's inflated stock values and especially no support for the
Sword Blade bankers. As Heathcote put it, "If the South Sea Company is to be wedded to the Bank [of England], it [SSC] cannot be allowed to keep a mistress." In return for the Bank's help, all SSC
stock was to be handed over to the Bank, at the Bank's valuation,
and all SSC cash was to be kept at the Bank. The Bank exacted a
heavy price for its support, and subsequently had to reduce still further the help it could offer. Vengeance must have been sweet, as the
Bank emasculated its rival. Doubts about its banknotes soon led to a
run on the Sword Blade bank, as holders of the notes tried to get
them paid in coin and depositors tried to withdraw their cash. The
Sword Blade bank paid out, slowly, sometimes only in shillings and
sixpences, for as long as it could, in the hope that the appearance of

normality would stem the loss of confidence, but the Court Book of the Bank of England records laconically on September 24, "Sword Blade Company don't pay." The preeminence of the Bank of England in matters of British public finance was never again to be challenged.

The intimate association of major war, huge public debt, and monetary, financial, and economic crisis was thus spelled out clearly for the first time. The lesson was not lost on Walpole, whose experience of this fallout from the War of the Spanish Succession taught him to avoid conflict at all costs. As Boswell observed in his *Life of Johnson*, "Sir Robert Walpole was a wise and a benevolent minister, who thought that the happiness and prosperity of a commercial country like ours, would be best promoted by peace, which he accordingly maintained, with credit, during a very long period." Walpole also knew where the South Sea bodies were buried, and went to considerable lengths to ensure that they remained hidden. Whigs and Tories, Jacobites and Hanoverians, all were implicated, and all had reason to be grateful for the cover-up, or "screen" as it was called at the time, that Walpole erected. For example, formal attempts were made to extradite Robert Knight, one of the principal South Sea and Sword Blade villains, from Antwerp. Secretly, however, every effort was made to prevent his return to give evidence that might implicate far too many influential figures, and Knight's escape from Hapsburg custody in Antwerp was discreetly arranged behind the scenes.

Of course, the financial losses resulting from the Bubble could not be so easily concealed. Early in 1721 East India Company stock fell to a mere 38 percent of its 1720 high. William Windham wrote, "There never was such distraction. You can't imagine the number of families undone . . . many a £100,000 man not worth a groat . . ." The Duke of Chandos lost £700,000. The Duke of Portland was brought to the point of bankruptcy, and fled the country to take up the governorship of Jamaica. Lord Irvine likewise sought a colonial post, but died before making his escape to Barbados. Lord Belhaven went in his place but was drowned en route off the Scilly Islands. Nor was the damage limited to the aristocracy. Isaac Newton lost £20,000, and the daughter of the rector of Exeter College, Oxford, lost her fortune of £1,200 and had to take employment as a governess. A string of private banks—Atwill & Hammond, Cox &

Cleave, Long & Bland, Mitford & Mertens—followed Sword Blade to the wall in the autumn of 1720. The banking crisis even extended to the Bank of England, as customers hurried to cash their notes and deposits. The Bank in turn called in all debts owed, in order to meet the demands for payment presented to it, exacerbating the general shortage of credit. The Bank was saved by 100,000 guineas, borrowed and imported from Holland, but by January 1721 Bank stock was down to only 59 percent of its peak value. Moreover, the whole structure of credit was badly damaged. A contemporary observer writing in 1720 estimated that three-quarters of the nation's manufacturing business was driven by "money borrowed at interest," and a large number of otherwise solvent businesses were suddenly embarrassed by a collapse of the credit and payments network. As Edward Harley, nephew to the former minister, observed, "As things appear to me I cannot see how people in London will have money to buy necessaries, what that will produce among the handicraft people is easy to guess." The upper classes were seriously concerned about the danger of riot.

Nevertheless, despite such devastation, the Bubble actually caused surprisingly few bankruptcies. In that respect, the more pervasive but less spectacular depressions of 1709–1710 and 1726–1728 were much worse. In a sense, of course, many of the lost fortunes of 1720 were never more than paper profits that had not existed in 1719. As Daniel Pultney wrote, "'Tis ridiculous to tell you what a sum I might have been master of; but since I had not discretion enough to secure that, 'Tis some comfort to me to have put my affairs in such a way that let what will happen I shall be no loser by it." Moreover, the real impact of the crisis was limited to London, to high society, and to public finance, rather than to provincial and private credit. Indeed, it is a measure of the degree to which the credit systems of Britain in the early eighteenth century were still rather poorly integrated that the consequences of the South Sea Bubble were not more far-reaching. As it was, much of the rest of the century would work at the better integration of banking and credit across the whole country—to include industry and agriculture, and merchants and entrepreneurs as well as aristocrats.

However, although the immediate consequences of the 1720 crisis may have been exaggerated, the South Sea Bubble still deserves its place in the financial history of the nation. It was the first British experience of the speculative insanity to which stock markets have been periodically prone ever since. It is a vivid illustration of the phenomenon of boom and bust and a reminder that unregulated market capitalism, whatever its advantages, is not without shortcomings. It also marks the emergence of the Bank of England as the unrivaled guardian of the national debt and as a symbol of sound financial management. As the dust settled, the reputation of the Bank and of its banknotes emerged not only untarnished but enhanced. Less happily, legislation resulting from the crisis restricted the establishment of other joint stock companies and delayed the development of this means of raising capital for industry and for banking.

In consequence, in the aftermath of the South Sea Bubble, business at the grass roots carried on very much as before. The poor harvests of the late 1720s could still increase mortality and drain gold abroad, leading to economic recession and rising bankruptcies. The capital base of most manufacturers, without joint-stock support, remained relatively modest. Abraham Darby's iron works at Coalbrookdale cost about £3,500 to set up in 1709, and the Walker brothers' foundry near Sheffield was started in 1741 on £10, though capital rose sharply to £600 by 1746, £2,500 in 1750, and £11,000 in 1760. Thus starting-up funds were not completely beyond the reach of small tradesmen such as William Stout, who began business in 1688 by taking £120 from Lancaster to London to buy stock, paying 50 percent down in ready money as was the custom and owing the rest till he returned to restock the following year. Moderate credit of this sort remained central to the system. Daniel Defoe realized that "Credit next to real stock, is the foundation, the life and soul, of business in a private tradesman; it is his prosperity; it is his support in the substance of his whole trade; even in public matters, it is the strength and fund of a nation." Credit, Defoe went on, "makes trade, and makes the whole kingdom trade for many millions more than the national specie can amount to." Credit was the foundation of trade, and "Trade is the Wealth of the World . . . Trade nourishes Industry and Industry begets Trade; Trade dispenses the natural Wealth of the World, and Trade raises new Species of Wealth, which

Nature knew nothing of." Half a century before Adam Smith's *Wealth of Nations*, Defoe was clear that national wealth did not lie in a stock of metal and that properly organized credit structures could liberate the world from its enslavement to bullion.

Yet at the same time, the confidence on which such credit was founded was easily shattered. The Jacobite invasion of 1745 could still trigger a run on the Bank of England. The silver captured by Commodore George Anson, and hastily coined by the Royal Mint, was paid out slowly, in sixpences, to slow the run without having to stop payment. But the Bank did survive, and confidence in the institution continued to grow. There was to be no further major run on the Bank until the 1790s. By 1749 the state owed the Bank £11,686,000, a sum that it gave no further serious thought to repaying, preferring to go on servicing the annual interest charges. It was an arrangement that bound the regime and the Bank together, in a mutually supportive relationship not then fully understood. But the confidence it gave the Bank and its notes, increasingly regarded as good as gold, was a source of great strength.

By the middle of the century the position of the Bank of England was thus increasingly secure, and the embryonic outlines of the rest of the banking structure can just be discerned. A number of private banks developed in London, many growing out of the banking functions of the old goldsmith-bankers of the Restoration era. Jonathan Swift expressed the need that the banks were meeting when he wrote to Alexander Pope in 1727 that he would happily pay £200 or £300 a year to an accountant or cashier who could handle his affairs. West of the City particularly, banks like Hoare's and Coutts's developed their business serving the aristocracy and the country gentry in just this way. They transferred money from country estates, making it available as required in town; they invested in government stock; and they lent to the wealthy, often upon mortgaged property that provided excellent security but usually involved rather long-term loans. Commercial business was rather frowned upon in these West End establishments, but by around 1750 some thirty private banks were operating in the City. Here lending was typically for much shorter periods. Indeed, many loans were repayable immediately on the lender's call, and the bulk of their business was in discounting short-term inland bills. The holder of a bill due for payment in London in a couple of months would surrender it early for slightly less cash than it would later be worth. The holder got the cash he needed, increasingly in Bank of England notes, and the City banker received the bill on which he could claim payment in full typically some sixty days later.

This trade in inland bills necessarily gave City bankers a working knowledge of provincial finance. They had to discern whose bills could be accepted confidently, and the London banks soon began to operate as town agents for the countrymen. In the country towns, farmers flush with the profits of harvest, or government tax collectors, found themselves with cash on their hands, which the wholesalers in the rural centers needed to conduct their business. Local traders could accept farmers' deposits, on which they paid interest, enjoying the liquidity that those deposits could provide for their own business or lending them on again at a slightly higher interest rate. (From 1714 to 1832 the maximum legal rate of interest was 5 percent per annum.) Much of the surplus cash would be remitted to London, for the purchase of stock or luxuries that the capital could provide, or to be lent short-term against good bills. London found itself as the meeting point for surplus funds from the agricultural counties and the borrowing needs of nascent industrial concerns. Gradually a network was taking shape. In London the Bank of England presided over the private banks. It imbued the entire structure with a degree of respectability and confidence. The private bankers often held accounts with the Bank or increasingly used its notes. The City private bankers in turn worked in concert with prominent county-town businesses that found themselves gradually involved in increasing banking activity. By the middle of the century Edmund Burke reckoned that about a dozen provincial banks had completely abandoned their original trades to concentrate full time on banking. Praed's in Truro, Woods of Gloucester, Gurney's in Norwich, and Stevenson & Salt of Stafford may have been the sort of establishments Burke had in mind, but firm evidence from this early date survives only for Smith's in Nottingham. Abel Smith was a draper who drifted into banking activities in the ordinary course of his business as early as 1688. He bequeathed his son a banking and drapery concern, but by 1759 Smith's & Payne concerned itself solely with banking. It soon had offices in London, Lincoln, Hull, and Derby as well. It was unusual, however, for a single bank to operate from so many centers. More typically, country banks were established in one provincial center but worked closely with a particular City bank as their town agent. The dozen country banks and about thirty City banks made up the skeleton banking structure of 1750. It was a skeleton that was to acquire a very great deal of flesh in the next fifty years.

Scotland was not affected by the monopoly of the Bank of England or the restrictive legislation born of the shock of the South Sea Bubble that prevented the development of joint stock companies in England. North of the border a different legal situation prevailed, despite the union of the two kingdoms in 1707, and this system proved a more encouraging environment for the development of banking. Adam Smith was enthusiastic about the benefits it conferred, for, like John Law, Smith was clear "That the industry of Scotland languished for want of money to employ it," but banking developments in Scotland—the Bank of Scotland was founded in 1695 and the Royal Bank of Scotland in 1727—had shown that "The substitution of paper in the room of gold and silver money, replaces a very expensive instrument of commerce with one much less costly" so that "the whole circulation may thus be conducted with a fifth part only of the gold and silver which would otherwise have been required." Banks had sprung up all over Scotland, and the trade of Glasgow was thought to have doubled in fifteen years as a consequence. Smith's passion for Glasgow excited Johnson's mockery, as Boswell remembered: "when Dr Adam Smith was expatiating on the beauty of Glasgow, he [Johnson] had cut him short by saying, 'Pray, Sir, have you ever seen Brentford?'" Indeed the English were prone to such "extravagant sportive raillery upon the supposed poverty of Scotland," thus:

Wilkes "Pray, Boswell, how much may be got in a year by an Advocate at the Scotch bar?"
Boswell "I believe two thousand pounds."
Wilkes "How can it be possible to spend that money in Scotland?"

Johnson "Why, Sir, the money may be spent in England: but there is a harder question. If one man in Scotland gets possession of two thousand pounds, what remains for all the rest of the nation?"

However, such metropolitan wit also concealed a good deal of financial ignorance, and on economic questions there is no doubt we would do better to trust Smith rather than Johnson. Smith had no doubt "That the trade and industry of Scotland . . . have increased very considerably during this period, and that the banks have contributed a good deal to this increase cannot be doubted."

The early development of banking in Scotland, unfettered by restrictive English legislation, encouraged the wider growth of banks and local banknotes there. It is a tradition still alive today in the form of the separate banknotes of, for example, the Bank of Scotland, the Royal Bank of Scotland, and the Clydesdale Bank, and in the continued issue of £1 notes in Scotland after their suppression in England. Adam Smith was justly proud of Scottish banking, but its example was being followed in England increasingly in the second half of the eighteenth century. The dozen or so banks operating outside London in 1750 multiplied tenfold by 1784, doubling again before 1797 when the special arrangements for national finance required by the war (see pp. 135–139) gave another huge stimulus. By 1810 more than 700 local banks were operating in provincial England. Smith spoke as much for English as for Scottish banks when he outlined the fundamental principle of banking and paper money in a famous passage from *The Wealth of Nations* (1776):

That part of his capital which a dealer is obliged to keep by him unemployed, and in ready money, for answering occasional demands, is so much dead stock, which, so long as it remains in this situation, produces nothing either to him or to his country. The judicious operations of banking enable him to convert this dead stock into active and productive stock; into materials to work upon, into tools to work with, and into provisions and subsistence to work for; into stock which produces something both to himself and to his country. The gold and silver money which circulates in any country, and by means of which the produce of its land and labour is annually circulated and distributed to the proper consumers, is, in the same manner as the ready money of the dealer, all dead stock. It is a very valuable part of the capital of the country, which produces nothing to the country. The judicious operations of banking, by substituting paper in the room of a great part of this gold and silver, enables the country to convert a great part of this dead stock into active and productive stock; into stock which produces something to the country.

This was the realization that was to liberate the British economy from the constraints of its metallic money supply. Up to this point the history of sterling has largely been the story of its coined mint output of silver and gold. From the middle of the eighteenth century we are concerned with the delicate balance between paper and coin. However, that balance was by no means easily achieved or sustained. The passage just quoted repeatedly employs the word "judicious." Judgment and discretion on the part of the banker were ever more essential. The *London Chronicle* in the crisis year 1772 took a rather more gloomy view than Adam Smith:

Bills became so universally accepted in lieu of Specie, became almost equal in value; and it being in everyone's power to draw a Bill who could not raise a shilling in specie, hence a door was opened for schemers of every denomination, a knot of whom assuming the external semblance of honesty and fair dealing, could create that capital they never possessed . . . And indeed, when Paper-currency gains such a footing as to be in universal use, it is a matter of no small difficulty so to discriminate as to distinguish the good from the bad . . .

And in June the same year David Hume wrote personally to Adam Smith, "We are here in a very melancholy Situation. Continual Bankruptcies, Universal Loss of Credit, and endless Suspicions."

Thus Smith undoubtedly knew from the daily events all around him that banks which were not most prudently managed were likely to fail and that even the best-run banks or bills were susceptible to a general panic. He argued, reasonably enough, that excess paper issued by a bank would simply return to the bank for cashing, but the central problem of all early banks was that note or bill issues appropriate for the level of business at one time could very quickly become inappropriate if the economic cycle turned or confidence received some unanticipated shock. The rapid expansion of England's provincial banking system and its links with the capital in the second half of the eighteenth century, which were essential structural elements in the industrial transformation of the period, well illustrate the benefits and the problems of expansionary banking. It produced an age of astonishing growth, punctuated by bouts of painful constraint.

By the second half of this century these bouts of periodic expansion and contraction look increasingly like the cyclical boom and bust of the modern business and trade cycle, causing crises of varying degrees of severity in 1763, 1772, 1778, 1783, 1788, 1793, and 1797. Some of these crises originated in the sphere of public, government finance, while others had their origins in private difficulties, with credit networks rapidly transmitting bankruptcies from lender to creditor like a collapsing house of cards or, as Boswell put it in 1772, "like a company connected by an electric wire, the people in every corner of the country have almost instantaneously received the same shock." It was the very efficiency of these networks, so vital for the circulation of trade and credit in good times, that ensured that in bad times later eighteenth-century crises were so much more pervasive than such shocks had been earlier in the century. Thus, whereas the famous Bubble of 1720 was actually of surprisingly limited impact across the country as a whole beyond the most fashionable and powerful circles, by 1772 a more thoroughly integrated system transmitted the fallout of speculative failure much more extensively.

Thus when a partner in the London bank Neale, James, Fordyce & Down disappeared leaving debts arising from stock market speculation amounting to some £300,000, it triggered a crisis that caused runs on banks across the country; Douglas, Heron & Co., bankers as far away as Ayr, stopped payment. The difficulties of that year were all the more severe because of the rapid expansion that had gone before, involving heavy investment in turnpike roads and canals. In 1771 exports to America had boomed; they were down to half the 1771 peak in 1773. The ready credit that facilitated trade and investment all required a steady flow of profits to sustain it. This was particularly true of the developing ruse of drawing and redrawing bills, independently of any genuine trade but merely to create a discountable credit instrument. But even the soundest of trading operations could be jeopardized in times like these. Mrs. Thrale relates in her diary how the 1772 crisis forced them to borrow thousands of pounds from family and friends, to save her husband's brewery. She wrote, for example, "and big as I was with child, I drove down to Brighton to beg of Mr Scrase . . . six thousand pounds more: dear Mr Scrase was an old gouty solicitor, friend and contemporary of my husband's father." Yet despite the success of such emergency fund raising, the brewery's hop and malt suppliers—the principal and involuntary creditors—went unpaid for several years. By 1772 the unraveling of shaky credit systems could have repercussions for even the most well-established businesses and their traditional agricultural contacts. The benefits of a thoroughly integrated system that efficiently put lender in touch with borrower spread credit failures through the network with equal efficiency.

Nevertheless Thrale survived, selling out his firm in 1781 for £135,000. Henry Thrale was a traditional Oxford-educated High Church Tory, but the firm was bought up by a group of Quakers, who relied for the funds on further Quaker banking cousins, including the Barclays, and other family contacts. Historians have been much interested in a possible association between Protestantism and business success, but others have pointed out that minority groups of various kinds—Quakers, Scots, Jews, Asians—often have prospered in trade and commerce, benefiting particularly from close personal and mutually supportive contacts within the group that provided business outlets in good times and greater trust, sympathy, and patience in bad.

In addition, Quakers benefited from a reputation for thrift and for fair and honest dealing, which may have contributed to their very considerable commercial success. By the late eighteenth century many Quaker families had established themselves. Barclays and Lloyds, still famous names in banking, originated as Quaker firms, as did the Norwich country bank, Gurneys. Samuel Gurney's bank was well established in Norwich by the time of his death in 1770. Thomas Bland, Gurney's clerk, later married Samuel's widow, and retained close links with the Norwich firm when he set up with other Quakers in a bank in London. Such links between country and London banks were a vital part of the network that helped bring agricultural savings to London. However, Gurneys' regular London business was conducted through their agents, another Quaker firm, Smith, Bevan &

Benning. At the turn of the century another Samuel Gurney (nephew of the original) learned his banking as a clerk at Fry's, the Quaker banking, tea, and chocolate business, before joining his brother John in the bill-broking firm Richardson, Overend & Co.

Networks of this kind provided invaluable support that was especially important during financial crises. In 1783 a combination of factors put pressure on the Bank of England's gold reserve, which had been run down from over £4 million in 1780 to some £2 million in 1782, largely as a result of military spending in America. The peace of January 1783 brought a marked upturn in trade, resulting in a sharp increase in the numbers of bills looking for discount in London. The government raised another major loan to which the Bank was the principal subscriber, and a crisis in Holland led to the withdrawal of much Dutch gold from London. The combination of an increased Bank note issue and a drain of gold abroad and into the country, where the local banks showed a preference for coin over rather inflated paper, drew further gold from the Bank, whose reserve fell to £673,000 that autumn. However, as Samuel Bosanquet, one of the Bank's directors, later recalled, the critical point was not when the reserves reached their low point but several months earlier, when the Bank felt it had to stop underwriting the most recent government loan, which it did by declining to go on discounting bills to provide the cash for its customers to lend to the government. In retrospect this turned out to have been exactly the right thing to do, since it tightened the supply of money, preventing an overexpansionary boom. The check to the money supply also restored confidence in Bank of England notes, which helped stem the drain of gold and turned the foreign exchanges more favorably for sterling. The Bank's refusal to discount bills *ad infinitum* caused alarm among bankers who had come to rely on this facility but proved an essential bulwark that set limits to the expansion of paper, so that it should not grow too far beyond the coined foundation of the currency or beyond the true needs of the economy.

The relationship between the Bank of England's gold reserve and its note issue was a critical balance. If too little paper was issued, the economy would be constrained for lack of a means of exchange, and a very high exchange rate could hit British exports. If too much paper was released, the economy would grow too fast and prices would rise, gold now undervalued in relation to paper would flow abroad, and domestically people would begin to express a preference for coin rather than too readily available paper. This was essentially the same balance that government had attempted to strike when it settled the mint price for metal in the Middle Ages. In the eighteenth century, now that Locke had so irrevocably fixed the mint price of metal, it was the Bank that came to exercise this crucial adjusting role. In the course of the nineteenth and twentieth centuries, the Bank expressed its willingness to issue paper through the discounting of bills by raising or lowering the interest rate charged for its loans, but the eighteenth-century usury laws deprived the Bank of such flexibility. Instead the Bank could be more or less choosy about which bills it was prepared to accept, or inflexibly turn off the tap almost completely.

Decisions of this sort by the Bank were mirrored in London's private banks and by the country banks, which also had to judge how far they could accommodate their customers, or (in the case of note-issuing banks) what was the appropriate ratio between note issue and the cash reserve. London banks increasingly abandoned their own note issues, preferring to use Bank of England paper, but the rapidly expanding numbers of country banks commonly issued their own paper money, backed by a reserve of Bank notes and gold coin. The relative ease or difficulty of discounting at the Bank encouraged or discouraged smaller banks, and the question of the appropriate ratio between note issue and reserve also was affected by the fluctuations of the economic climate. Too large a reserve in good times involved money lying idle; too small a reserve in bad times left the banks vulnerable to a run on their notes that they might be unable to meet in good Bank paper or gold. Adam Smith's confidence that the system should regulate itself, with too large a note issue simply being returned to the issuing bank, failed to recognize that an entirely reasonable note issue in one year could be far too large six months later. He also seems to have rather underestimated the degree of personal damage that essentially solvent banks and businesses might suffer in a credit crisis visited on them by the failure of other links in the chain.

The ever-changing nature of the underlying economic situation was one reason why the banking experts of the time had so many different opinions about what was the appropriate ratio between issues and reserves. Law and Smith suggested a reserve of one-quarter and one-fifth, while De Pinto (1771) and Boyd (1796) spoke of one-third. Another commentator in 1793, an anonymous one, drew a distinction between London banks, which he thought required a reserve of one-third, and country banks, for which he thought one-eighth enough. In 1797 Henry Thornton, a highly experienced banker, argued the need for flexibility, telling the House of Commons:

It was a mistake to suppose that it required a certain quantity of specie bearing a proportion to the outstanding notes, in order to give security for the punctual payments of a bank. The specie should be proportioned, not to the notes out, but to the probable current demand.

Moreover, even those who were prepared to suggest a theoretical ratio may not always have adhered to it in practice, and the sum was further complicated by some uncertainty as to what might constitute acceptable reserves. Some banks regarded readily marketable London money market assets as reserves as well as specie and Bank of England notes. Nevertheless, despite the difficulty of establishing a fixed rule, this relationship between coin and paper was critical for the stability of the banking system, for the prospects of the whole economy, and for the fortunes of sterling on the foreign exchanges.

Another difficult year, 1788, saw a number of private bankruptcies especially in the textile industry, but thereafter the economy grew strongly until 1793, which brought what was probably the worst crisis of the century. As in 1783, the problems arose after a period of strong growth. William Cobbert remembered 1793 thus:

A spirit of commercial speculation and commerce had been for some time increasing in every part of the kingdom . . . The circulating specie being by no means sufficient to answer the very increased demands of trade, the quantity of paper currency brought into circulation, as a supplying medium was so great and disproportionate, that a scarcity of specie was produced which threatened a general stagnation in the commercial world.

In other words, the boom was met by increased paper issues, which then ran into difficulties as the economic climate changed. The rapidly proliferating country banks and their note issues took much of the blame, but 1793 was a different crisis from that of a decade earlier. In 1793 the paper issues were not excessive, but the system suffered a crisis of confidence, triggered by the very poor harvest of 1792 and the fear of imminent war with France, which eventually did break out in February 1793. As is not unusual in times of uncertainty created by war, people preferred the security of gold to the more chancy opportunities presented by paper, resulting in a run on the country banks. Sir Francis Baring recalled four years later, "What happened in the beginning of 1793 was . . . far beyond anything which preceded or has followed it in magnitude, it pervaded more or less every part or place in both islands and affected every description of property." Other contemporaries recalled that "confidence in their Banks vanished, every creditor was clamorous for payment." Moreover, the subsequent effects of a panic of this sort meant that even fundamentally sound institutions failed, reducing "many respectable, prudent, and, ultimately, very solvent persons to the mortifying necessity of stopping payment." Whereas in 1783 the Bank had to restrict credit to pull the system back into line, in 1793 it went on lending, and was additionally helped by a government scheme based on the release of interest-bearing Exchequer bills, the proceeds of which—some £2.2 million—were lent to 238 leading men in trouble. These additional measures restored confidence, and the government even got its loans repaid. When in 1797 an abortive French invasion in south Wales triggered a very similar panic, the recent memory of 1793 must have contributed powerfully to the case for early and dramatic action. It was little dreamed that the suspension of cash payments—the withdrawal of the right to cash one's notes into gold—which was then decreed as a short-term emergency measure was to last until the end of the Napoleonic wars and beyond.

5

From Pitt to Peel: 1797 to 1847

> That the augmentation of the quantity of money or paper performing the function of money in a country has a tendency to depreciate that money or paper is a principle universally recognised.
>
> —Walter Boyd, MP, 1801

Walter Boyd's "principle universally recognised," like Jane Austen's "truth universally acknowledged" in *Pride and Prejudice* (1813), was in fact much less universally appreciated than Boyd imagined. The observation that an increase in the quantity of money reduces the value of money, like the assumption that a wealthy bachelor must be in want of a wife, are both oversimplifications. Nevertheless, although the truth of Boyd's remark has often been contested, the events of the period 1797 to 1825 tended to support it. These years saw a dramatic increase in the quantity of sterling and an equally dramatic fall in its value, reflected in the rise in the sterling price of goods. The underlying cause of all this was war.

The economic impact of the French war was enormous. The national debt rose from £228 million in 1793 to £876 million in 1815 as a direct consequence of the war. In the first year of the war the annual interest charge on the debt amounted to less than £10 million, and in the last year it was over £30 million, which was more than half of all government expenditure in that year and more than government's whole spending in the last year of peace, 1792. It has been estimated that the government spent some £1,000 to 1,500 million more than it would have spent had there been no war. For comparison, no more than about £20 million was invested in canals over the period 1750 to 1820, and even the huge railway investment boom of 1830 to 1850 committed only about £250 million.

Of course, these war expenditure figures take no account of the sharp rise in prices during the war. The Phelps Brown–Hopkins Index, which had been rising steadily from around 650 in the early 1760s to about 870 in the early 1790s, hit 900 in the first year of war, 1,000 in 1795, 1,500 in 1800, and peaked in 1813 at 1,881. In 1815 it still stood at 1,467. In less abstract terms, the 4-pound loaf, which began the war at about 6d. or 7d., cost somewhere between 9d. and 15d. in the first decade of the nineteenth century and moved decisively to the upper end of that scale in the second decade. Wheat prices, the principal component of the bread price, rose from around 45s. a quarter before the war to an average of about 96s. for the period 1810 to 1815. Not surprisingly, given such prices for corn, arable output increased some 50 percent during the war, and farm rents, already rising in the third quarter of the century, rose still more sharply. In Warwickshire the average arable rent rose from 18s. per acre in 1794 to 29s. in 1813. But the price of livestock products also rose. Josiah Easton reported a rise in the price of meat from less than 3d. per pound before the war to over 8d. for the period 1803 to 1812; butter rose from 6d. a pound to 1s. 4d. The rewards of agriculture had never been so great. Rents on the Alnwick estate in Northumberland rose 64 percent between 1790 and 1820. Lord Darnley's estates in Kent doubled their rental income from 1788 to 1820.

However, the profits of farmers and landowners did not lead to buoyant agricultural wages. Although the agricultural boom created by the war did increase the availability of work in the countryside, wages did not keep pace with rising prices. The Berkshire magistrates at Speenhamland recognized the problem in 1795 when they extended the principle of parish relief to those in work on inadequate wages, but this merely confirmed inadequate wage levels. The agricultural laborer was to remain the worst fed of all nineteenth-century workers. Farm workers in the south and west received significantly lower pay than those in the north, whose wages were enhanced by the alternative of better industrial pay in nearby towns.

War also stimulated industry, as military requirements boosted demand for iron and textiles. It has been suggested that during the Napoleonic Wars one civilian worker at home was required to supply every two combatants at war; in the Second World War when the Home Front was more fully developed, it was to take two workers for every soldier, but the early nineteenth-century domestic war effort was for the time unprecedented. Agriculture and industry thrived, and the effects of the stimulus of war spread far beyond those workers directly serving the military. As workers in those sectors directly boosted by the war spent their wages, they spread increased demand through all sectors of the economy. Employment throughout the whole economy rose, as J. Lowe recalled, in the slightly pompous language of the day:

Many, who from deficient activity or mediocrity of parts [skills], would, in a state of peace, have necessarily remained unemployed, were brought by the war into situations attended with income.

Thus wartime expenditure stimulated economic growth. The central question, just as during the War of the Spanish Succession and the First and Second World Wars, was how to pay for this expenditure. The answers that were found for this question were of crucial significance for the value of Britain's money.

William Pitt, Britain's youngest prime minister, was presented with the same choices that confront all spending ministries. The necessary funds can be raised by taxing, borrowing, or depreciating the currency. Pitt did all three. He began the war by borrowing. We have already seen how short-term funds were raised by an issue of Exchequer bills. The money borrowed from the public in this way was relent by the government to the financial community to help it over the 1793 crisis. The scheme worked well, saving many from bankruptcy and even yielding a small profit for the government when they were repaid. But to finance a major European war and subsidize its allies abroad the government had to borrow on its own account. By the end of 1795 the government owed some £13 million in short-term bills. The success of these bill issues depended crucially on the willingness of the Bank to discount government and commercial bills for members of the public. Confidence in and demand for all bills was significantly increased by the knowledge that the Bank would readily buy them (at a discount) should holders need to sell. Directly or indirectly, in effect, Pitt was borrowing from the Bank. In addition, the Bank's gold reserves also suffered from August 1795 when France abandoned its paper "Assignat" currency in favor of a return to gold; much of the gold that had earlier fled from France now flowed back. As a result, the Bank's reserve, which before the war had customarily stood at about £8 million and had fallen in the 1793 crisis to £4 million, was down to about £2.5 million by early in 1796. Although the Bank never actually refused to accommodate the government, its directors' discomfort was becoming increasingly clear. In 1796 Pitt actually reduced his short-term borrowing from the Bank by about £2 million, turning instead to longer loans direct from the public raised through the sale of government stocks. The Bank's gold reserve, however, remained prilously low. This fundamentally difficult situation was brought to a head by the threat of invasion in 1797.

As is common in times of uncertainty and insecurity, people tended to put their trust in gold. This dash for gold already had been running strongly for months when a Saturday market in Newcastle on February 18 saw farmers readily selling cattle at unusually low prices and then taking the proceeds in notes to the banks for payment in gold. They may have been worried by the Edinburgh papers that day, which carried the Lord-Lieutenant of Midlothian's preparations for defense in the event of invasion triggering a panic among Scottish farmers. The following Monday, February 20, the Scots banker Sir William Forbes remembered, farmers and country people "came to our [Edinburgh] counting-house in considerable numbers, evidently under the impression of terror, calling for payment of their notes . . ." The same day the renewed run on the Newcastle banks caused them to stop payment. In London the governor of the Bank with other senior directors, including Samuel Thornton and Samuel Bosanquet, were already in daily contact with Pitt, as the crisis mounted. The Bank was losing reserves at the rate of £100,000 a day. On Thursday news of the Newcastle stoppage reached London, and the price of government stocks fell sharply, forcing the government to pay more for its loans as people preferred to hang on to their cash. On Saturday, February 25, a French invasion force landed at Fishguard.

In reality the "invasion" was never a serious threat to national security; the invaders surrendered immediately. But in the fevered financial atmosphere that already existed, it was enough to intensify the run on the banks. As Baring described it:

The landing of a handful of French troops created an instantaneous general alarm and occasioned a demand for money to which neither gold nor silver in bullion could be applied, as nothing would be accepted but the circulating coin of the country. Persons of every description caught the alarm; tradesmen, mechanics, and particularly women and farmers.

The king was called from Windsor, and on Sunday, February 26, 1797, an Order in Council declared:

it is indispensably necessary for the public service that the Directors of the Bank of England should forbear issuing any cash [i.e., gold] in payment until the sense of Parliament can be taken on that subject and the proper measures adopted thereupon for maintaining the means of circulation and supporting the public and commercial credit of the kingdom at this important conjuncture.

In plain English, the Bank would no longer pay gold for its banknotes. On Monday *The Times* reassured its readers, and the leading London merchants and bankers met at the Mansion House to declare their faith in the Bank and their intention to give and accept its notes. On Wednesday, March 1, Coutts & Co.'s express message to the Bank of Scotland at last informed Edinburgh of the Order in Council. The same day James Gillray published a rather stoical cartoon, recounting various patriotic reasons for accepting paper in lieu of gold. However, the news was not taken entirely calmly by the public. As Forbes recalled in Edinburgh:

Our counting-house, and indeed the offices of all the banks, were instantly crowded to the door with people clamorously demanding payment in gold of their interest-receipts, and vociferating for silver in change of our circulating paper . . . They were deaf to every argument and although no symptom, nor indeed threatening of violence appeared, their noise, and the bustle they made, was intolerable; which may be readily believed when it is considered that they were mostly of the lowest and most ignorant classes, such as fish-women, carmen, street porters and butcher's men, all bawling out at once for change, and jostling one another in their endeavours who should get nearest to the table, behind which were cashiers and ourselves endeavouring to pacify them as well as we could.

Parliament moved with unusual haste to make the issue of banknotes of less than £5 legal. Thus on Thursday, March 2, 1797, the

Bank of England issued its first £1 note, signed by the chief cashier, Abraham Newland. The issue of the first sterling pound note seems in retrospect more momentous than it did at the time; at any rate, no one thought to keep an example from the first day, for the earliest surviving example, now preserved in the bank, is dated March 6. On Friday, a House of Commons Committee reported reassuringly that the Bank's assets comfortably exceeded its liabilities and that the Bank was, in short, sound, despite the suspension of gold payments. The following week Gillray's sense of humor recovered its edge, portraying Pitt as a Midas in reverse, turning gold into paper, and in May he produced his famous picture of The Old Lady of Threadneedle Street in Danger. The same month George III gave the royal assent to what was termed the Restriction Act, which declared that payments in banknotes were now to be "deemed payments in cash if made and accepted as such." In other words, paper was deemed to be gold. The act was renewed periodically until December 1803, when it was extended until six months after the conclusion of a peace. In Scotland, after the initial panic, Forbes noted:

It was a matter of agreeable surprise to see in how short a time after the suspension of paying in specie, the run on us ceased . . . It was remarkable also, after the first surprise and alarm was over, how quietly the country submitted, as they still [1803] do, to transact all business by means of bank notes for which the issuers gave no specie as formerly.

As we have seen earlier, the country was already fully familiar with banknotes, and it seemed to settle down to the withdrawal of its rights to cash them in gold with very little difficulty. In the summer of 1797 guineas reappeared, circulating at par with paper, and the Bank was able to rebuild its gold reserves. From a low point of just over £1 million at the time of the suspension of cash payments, the reserve was back at about £4 million by August 1797 and was double that by the end of the following year. Confidence returned also to the country banks, which grew in number dramatically over the next decade. Sterling's exchange position improved as well, and the Bank felt sufficiently in control to inform Pitt on a number of occasions between 1797 and 1800 of its readiness to resume payment in gold. The government, however, opted to retain the freedoms that the suspension of payments in gold gave it, and the downside of this decision was not yet apparent.

Conditions in 1797 and 1798 were relatively favorable. Harvests were good; government spending abroad, at about £400,000, was modest for wartime; and the sterling exchange position seemed strong. After dipping a little on the Hamburg exchange in 1795 and 1796, when the pound went for as little as 32 schillings, in 1797 and 1798 it was back well above 34 schillings, as it had been at the beginning of the decade before the war. Although not inclined to resume gold payments, the government did feel able to contribute some silver and copper to the currency, to augment the circulation of paper. Some half million pounds' worth of Spanish dollars were countermarked with the king's head and put into circulation, and Matthew Boulton was awarded a contract to strike copper "cartwheel" pennies. However, 1799 was a much more difficult year.

Appalling harvests in 1799 and 1800 sent the cost of wheat soaring. Despite the rapid and continuing industrialization of the time—only 36 percent of the population was dependent for its livelihood on rural agriculture in 1801, compared with some 60 percent in 1670—the harvest still exercised a crucial influence on the whole economy. Over three-quarters of household expenditure was still spent on food and drink, and within that figure bread played the dominant part. Moreover, when bread was dear, the poor economized on other items, so a poor harvest immediately reduced consumption of most other goods. Manufacturers recognized this and cut production (and employment) when a bad harvest was anticipated. Moreover, because the demand for corn was so inelastic, if the English harvest failed, wheat was bought in from abroad, leading to a renewed export of gold and a fall on the exchange. Gold rose to £4 6s. per ounce, silver to 6s. Sterling fell to 31 schillings in Hamburg in 1799, 30 schillings in 1800, and 29 schillings in 1801. Government war expenditure abroad (up to £2.4 million in 1799–1800) also contributed to the weakening of the exchange. Not surprisingly, government borrowing from the Bank rose again in 1800 in the face of this expenditure. The Bank, which had to provide for the ordinary commercial needs of a rapidly developing economy as well as finance its own and the public's lending to the government, had little choice but to increase the note issue. In the absence of the requirement to pay notes in gold on demand, the Bank's note issue was limited only by public willingness to borrow them at 5 percent interest. The circulation of banknotes, which had stood at around £10 or £11 million since before the outbreak of war, rose to about £16 million in 1800. Despite what Walter Boyd regarded as a universal principle, the implications of such monetary growth for the behavior of prices were not widely appreciated.

In later years when the directors of the Bank were taken to task for the inflation of the note issue, they pointed out that they had never "forced" their notes but merely responded to the demand of the public and its government. This revealing defense was true, though limited. Hardly anyone seems to have given much thought to the need to regulate the note issue in the absence of the restraint historically provided by gold. However, one adjustment that Pitt did make around the turn of the century was a fairly clear shift toward taxation, as opposed to borrowing, as the means to finance the war. The income tax was introduced in 1799, and though it took some time to establish an efficient administration, from 1806 until its abolition in 1816, it raised £172 million. On top of that, the traditional customs and excise, which remained much more important, were yielding four times as much at the end of the war as at the beginning. Thus despite heavy dependence on borrowing at the beginning of the war, Pitt's taxation drive meant that over the war as a whole roughly half the cost was paid for out of tax. This was a far better record than the government achieved during the First World War. However, the advantages of paying for the military out of tax, rather than from borrowing in inflated currency, were not immediately appreciated by the taxpayers. Sydney Smith, in a memorable passage addressed to the Americans on the costs of glory, eloquently described the tax burden of the day imposed by war:

Taxes upon every article which enters the mouth, or covers the back, or is placed upon the foot—taxes upon everything which it is pleasant to see, hear, feel, smell, or taste—taxes upon warmth, light, and locomotion—taxes upon every thing on earth, and the waters under the earth—on every thing that comes from abroad, or is grown at home—taxes on the raw material—taxes on every fresh value that is added to it by the industry of man—taxes on the sauce which pampers man's appetite, and the drug that restores him to health—on the ermine which decorates the judge, and the rope which hangs the criminal—on the poor man's salt and the rich man's spice—on the brass nails of the coffin, and the ribands of the bride—at bed or board, couchant or levant, we must pay.—The schoolboy whips his taxed top—the beardless youth manages his taxed horse, with a taxed bridle, on a taxed road:—and the dying Englishman, pouring his medicine, which has paid 7 per cent, into a spoon that has paid 15 per cent—flings himself back on his chintz bed, which has paid 22 per cent—and expires in the arms of an apothecary who has paid a licence of a hundred pounds for the privilege of putting him to death. His whole property is then immediately taxed from 2 to 10 per cent. Besides the probate, large fees are demanded for burying him in the chancel; his virtues are handed down to posterity on taxed marble; and he is gathered to his fathers—to be taxed no more.

However, despite Smith's tirade, Pitt's taxes enabled government debts to fall and the alarming rise of prices and the banknote issue to pause. Better harvests and the temporary suspension of hostilities following the Peace of Amiens also helped sterling to rally above 32 schillings in Hamburg and to bring gold down to £4 1s. and silver to 5s. 6d. Of course this did not restore the prewar levels, but for much of the first decade of the century it appeared that the value of money had stabilized. Pitt may or may not have worried on his deathbed about the state in which he left the country, but few other commentators saw much ground for concern.

In fact, confidence gradually was building into an economic boom. The opening of the Peninsular phase of the war involved a renewed burst of government spending, for the maintenance of a British army in Europe as well as naval control of the seas did not come cheap. In later years the Duke of Wellington bought the necessary gold from Nathan Rothschild, who relied on his continental contacts to ship it safely, despite the war, to Portugal. Rothschild had brothers in Paris, Frankfurt, and Vienna and together they were able to buy up gold discreetly and arrange transport. Their correspondence in German, written out in a cursive Hebrew script, ensured confidentiality, and they maintained a permanent staff of couriers to carry messages. It was Rothschild who informed Lord Liverpool of the outcome of the Battle of Waterloo, one day before the government's messenger arrived in London and three days before *The Times* carried the story. In one year alone the Rothschilds were said to have sent £11 million in subsidies for allies and cash for Wellington's army in the Peninsula. Rothschild subsequently remembered this as "the best business I ever did," but the 2 per cent commission he earned was only part of his remuneration, since he gained also through associated deals and massively enhanced influence in government circles. Rothschild was said to have made a million in 1815 alone from the payment of British and allied troops, but he was by no means the only man to make a fortune out of the war. Government spending boosted the whole economy.

Government borrowing rose again, but the Bank's commercial discounting, which was allowed to expand to meet demand almost unchecked, grew even more as business boomed. Nor was growth restricted to the war industries. British overseas trade expanded almost unaffected by the war. Indeed, because of the much greater impact of the war on the continental mainland, British traders profited from the absence of competition. While it is true that the French and their allies did manage to capture an average of some 500 vessels a year, this only amounted to 3 percent of total British tonnage. The cost of marine insurance actually fell during the war. In 1808 the opening of the Brazil trade to Britain resulted in a speculative mania that sent huge quantities of British manufactured goods to South America, including a celebrated cargo of ice skates to Rio. The total of deposits at the Bank grew from about £6 million before the suspension of cash payments in 1797 to over £12 million in 1810. The Bank's notes in circulation rose from about £16 million in 1800, to £17 million from 1804 to 1808, over £19 million in 1809, and over £21 million by May 1810. The note issues of the country banks were required by law to bear a stamp from 1782, so some idea of the size of their issues can be estimated from figures from the Stamp Office. However, the new issue of stamped notes can be only an uncertain guide to the numbers in circulation, for bankers kept some reserves unissued, and there is no evidence for how long notes usually survived. However, the figures for 1808–1809 are more reliable, since in 1808 almost all the old notes were scrapped by law, so the £14.5 million stamped in 1808–1809 does give some idea of the additional contribution of the country banknote issue to the money supply. In 1810 several contemporaries tried to estimate the country banknote circulation, coming up with figures ranging from £15 million to £32 million for that year. One point seems clear: The number of Bank and country banknotes was growing fast.

Not surprisingly, as the economy boomed and paper became more plentiful, the price of bullion rose. In theory the pound note, worth 20s., should have been able to buy gold at 77s. 10 ½d. an ounce, the rate at which the mint bought gold with guineas. In practice, if guineas could be found at all, they passed at more than their nominal value of 21s., and the price of gold bullion bought with notes rose to 92s. an ounce. Silver, theoretically worth 5s. 2d. an ounce, in fact fetched 5s. 9d. When bankers had promised to exchange notes for gold coin, they had limited the note issue to prevent any such divergence in the values of paper and gold. Freed of the obligation to convert paper on demand, and regulating their issues solely with regard to public demand, the banks, including the Bank of England, had made money more easily available (and therefore cheaper) than gold. This was the subject broached by David Ricardo in a series of letters to the *Morning Chronicle* in 1809 and by Francis Horner's questions in the House of Commons early in 1810. They argued that the premium on gold and sterling's falling exchange rate were the result of an excess note issue. The pound fell on the Hamburg exchange to 29 schillings in 1809, 27 schillings in 1810, and 24 schillings in 1811.

A House of Commons committee was established to look into this bullion question, the leading members being Horner, Henry Thornton, a banker and brother of the Bank director Samuel, and William Huskisson, then a forty-year-old MP, but destined for a distinguished government career. In the 1820s he was to serve as a reforming president of the Board of Trade before meeting an even more distinguished death: He was killed in one of the earliest passenger railway accidents at the opening of the Manchester and Liverpool line in 1830. The Bullion Committee met and interviewed witnesses fairly intensively in February and March, and less often in April and May, before finally submitting its report to Parliament in June 1810. The heart of the committee's findings was that an inconvertible paper currency could retain its proper value, as revealed by the price of bullion and the foreign exchanges, only if the quantity of the circulating medium "is exactly proportioned to the wants and occasions of the Public." The size of the money supply needed to be tailored to the size of the economy. However, as the Bank of England's Monetary Policy Committee can now (1998) confirm, that is easier said than done, even when fully supplied with a wide range of up-to-date economic statistics. In 1810, rather than blame the Bank for allowing the note issue to get out of hand, the committee concluded:

The most detailed knowledge of the actual trade of the country, combined with the profound Science in all the principles of Money and circulation, would not enable any man or set of men to adjust, and keep always adjusted, the right proportion of circulating medium in a country to the wants of trade.

Rather than find fault with the directors of the Bank, the committee took the line that the job could not be done, and only a return to notes convertible into gold could preserve the purchasing power of sterling.

The governor, John Whitmore, and deputy governor, John Pearce, rather obstinately claimed that the inflated note issue and ease of credit had only been a response to public demand, and they saw no reason to consider the foreign exchanges as a guide to the strength of sterling and the optimum size of the money supply. Nowadays we are used to monthly money supply figures and daily quotations for sterling on the foreign exchanges, but in 1810 the governor of the Bank had no interest in such things. In truth, some directors had understood as early as 1783 that lending should be cut back when the exchanges turned unfavorable, so a less complaisant governor ought to have been sensitive to these indicators. Yet on the whole the Bank escaped serious criticism. In the parliamentary debate on the Bullion Committee Report in 1811, the directors were spared any full-blooded assault. Horner did, however, allow himself the rather despairing observation:

It was to have been expected that the Governor of the Bank and the other Directors should be acquainted with the plainest maxim of political economy that the rise in the value of money or currency is equivalent to a fall in the prices of commodities.

Or, more important in the context of the time, the rise in wartime prices constituted a fall in the value of money that could be associated with the growth of the paper money supply. On the whole the Bullion Committee Report diagnosed the problem accurately. The note issue, unrestrained by the link with gold, had grown faster than the needs of the burgeoning economy. The value of this paper money was therefore less, whether measured against gold, other currencies, or the price of goods. Yet this analysis offered no solution other than the restoration of the right to claim payment of notes in gold, and this was a solution unlikely to win the support of Parliament while the war continued. In the debates of 1811 the committee won the theoretical argument but repeatedly lost the vote on practical steps to rectify the situation. The government case put by Vansittart and Castlereagh was not impressive, but a majority was not prepared to face up to the currency problem while the war continued. This was essentially Canning's position. Others may have felt that criticism of the Bank, however muted and however well deserved, was likely to make things worse rather than better. If the Bank really was the sole guardian of the nation's currency, it was necessary to bolster confidence in it, rather than undermine it.

Nevertheless, despite defeat in Parliament in 1811, the Bullion Committee Report remained an important influence throughout the following decade. As the bible of the hard money school, it was even reissued in 1919 and 1925 when the problem of an inconvertible currency severely depreciated by a war-driven boom was again highly topical.

The boom of 1810 burst toward the end of that year, leaving a large number of firms that had boosted production to unsustainable levels in severe difficulties. Cotton was particularly hit, and Lancashire and Glasgow suffered, but confidence and prices picked up again in 1812 and 1813 and the price of gold rose above £5 per ounce. Government spending and the note issue remained high, and with each year that passed the comments of the Bullion Committee appeared more relevant. It was increasingly understood that action would be taken when peace returned, as it finally did after the battle of Waterloo in 1815.

In the early summer of 1816, reforms of the coinage were set in hand and the Bank announced that it was preparing for the resumption of cash payments. Paper money was once again to become payable on demand in gold. Just as the Bullion Committee Report had done much of the groundwork on the gold question, much of the necessary preliminary thinking about the coinage had been done as early as 1798 when Charles Jenkinson, First Earl of Liverpool, had addresssed the issue. Jenkinson had come down firmly in favor of a gold standard, with silver and copper assigned ancillary roles, defined by legal tender limits of 12d. for copper and 40s. for silver. By chance it fell to the second Lord Liverpool, prime minister in the postwar administration, to put his father's ideas into practice in the Coinage Act of 1816.

The weight of the silver coinage was slightly reduced, 66s. now being struck from a Troy pound in place of the traditional 62s. Since sterling was now defined on a gold standard, there could be no objections to abandoning John Locke's almost sacred standard. The gold coinage became formally the standard-bearer for sterling and clung to its traditional eighteenth-century terms of issue, striking £46 14s. 6d. from the Troy pound of 22-carat gold. Though the gold basis of sterling was unaltered, the coins were changed; the 21s. guinea was replaced by a new 20s. coin known as the sovereign. Both the new silver and gold coins were released in 1817, though at first the role of the sovereign was distinctly limited by the continuing existence of an inconvertible paper pound. In the fullness of time the sovereign, with its glorious St. George and the Dragon reverse by Benedetto Pistrucci, would come to symbolize much of the wealth and power of the British Empire, but in the immediate aftermath of the Napoleonic War reestablishing the right to exchange banknotes for gold coins was no easy matter.

The Bank recognized that before it could successfully offer sovereigns for its paper, it had to build up an adequate reserve of gold to meet the expected demand. Moreover, although it was prepared to buy gold on the open market somewhat above its mint price (£46 14s. 6d. per pound = 77s. 10½d. per ounce) and bear the loss on coining, the scheme was doomed to failure if the value of sterling in note form was too far removed from its value in sovereigns. The principles outlined by the Bullion Committee indicated that the value of sterling notes could be raised to that of sovereigns only if the supply of notes was restricted. At first events conspired to bring this about. With the end of the war lucrative government contracts came to an end, but the postwar recession did not limit itself to the directly war-related industries. Just as government cash had boosted the whole economy in the good times, its withdrawal had equally universal effects. The level of the Bank's commercial discounting, which reflected demand, illustrates the contraction well: From wartime levels in excess of £20 million, discounts fell to £11 million in 1816 and to only £4 million in 1817 and 1818. In the contracting postwar world interest rates were falling, and the Bank's failure to lower its rate below 5 percent made its discounting uncompetitive. The severity of the postwar recession was also illustrated by a fall in prices. They fell from the high point in 1813 (index 1,881) to their lowest point in the decade in 1816 (index 1,344). Wheat cost 110s. a quarter in 1813 and 78s. in 1816. The four-pound loaf that cost 16d. in Oxford in 1812 could be had for 9d. in 1815. As Byron put it:

> . . . corn, like every mortal thing, must fall,
> Kings—conquerors—and markets most of all.

In the summer of 1816 the gold price fell below £4 an ounce, and the Bank built up its reserve, enabling it to announce plans to redeem £1 and £2 notes. In the summer of 1817 the gold reserve reached record levels, and customers were returning gold coin to the Bank asking for paper, which they found more convenient. After twenty years the public had got used to living without the option of gold coin.

However, in the middle of 1817, gold turned and began to flow out of the country as quickly as it had so recently flowed in. An ounce of gold once more cost more than £4, and the Bank's reserve drained away to £6.5 million in the summer of 1818 and £4 milllion in February 1819. Alexander Baring believed much of this gold was quickly converted into French coin. Another factor in the foreign drain of gold was a series of loans to France, Russia, Austria, and Prussia, which may have sent as much as £10 million in gold out of the country in 1817–1818. Yet whatever the causes of the hemorrhage, this loss of gold made it clear that the full resumption of gold payments that Vansittart had hoped to achieve in 1818 would have to be postponed until the Bank of England's reserve had been restored. Only then would the Bank be in a position to offer to redeem its notes in gold. The 1797 Restriction Act was therefore renewed again to July 1819. But by the beginning of that year there had been little improvement, and reserves were still low; the gold price obstinately stuck above £4. A new committee was established under the chairmanship of Robert Peel, and included Huskisson from the 1810 committee. Its goal was to consider the question of the resumption of cash payments once more.

Reduced to its simplest elements, the question involved three main points. First, the theoretical case for resumption was essentially still that expressed by the Bullion Committee in 1810. Second, the practical problems presented by the movements of the exchange and the open market gold price had to be recognized. Finally, some financial experts were seriously worried about the further deflationary effects that might be expected from a full resumption of gold payments at a time when the very severe postwar depression was already generating great distress among both the rural and urban poor. Many observers feared for the political stability of the kingdom.

The government's principal response to rural postwar problems was the Corn Law of 1815. During the war the goal of national self-sufficiency and the rising prices of the inflationary boom had together encouraged arable investment and production. Anticipating likely hardship for these farmers in the changed circumstances after 1815, the government legislated to protect them from cheap imported foreign corn, which was to be allowed in only when the domestic wheat price rose to 80s. a quarter. However, this attempt to shore up prices was directly at odds with the plan to return to cash payments, which was expressly designed to restore the value of money. As Sir James Graham commented in 1826, "It is absurd to talk of price without referring to money; and it is impossible to alter the quantity of money without affecting prices." The corn issue, which was to dominate politics in Britain until the repeal of the Corn Laws in 1846, was inextricably bound up with the gold question. Equally the resumption of gold payments had profound economic and political implications.

The ten years after the end of the Napoleonic Wars were a period of acute political, social, and economic difficulty. The condition of the working classes during the Industrial Revolution has been a subject of intense historical controversy. Nevertheless, even those who emphasize the positive aspects of industrialization would probably agree that the benefits did not really begin to reach the poorest urban groups until the 1830s and 1840s, when wages slowly began to catch up with the leap in prices that characterized the first two decades of the century. In addition, even these optimists would recognize that the shift in population from the country to intensely overcrowded cities, where the inadequacies of early nineteenth-century sanitation and public health were immediately exposed, involved a fall in the quality of life. Of course it is impossible to separate quality of life from the hard material calculation of the level of earnings and the price of bread, and it is important not to subscribe to the fiction of some preindustrial rural idyll where a jolly and kind-hearted squire busied himself with the well-being of his fellow parishioners. Nineteenth-century poverty was nowhere worse than in the rural south and west. Yet however skeptical we may be of William Wordsworth's idealized rural families, "Breathing fresh air and treading the green earth," the contrast between their experience and the grim realities of early nineteenth-century city life must still have been harsh. The indications are that the factory hands thrown together in large numbers in British cities did endure great hardship especially in the period 1815 to 1825. At this time, when the post-war decline in economic activity added unemployment to the woes of the poor, the government became seriously concerned for the maintenance of public order.

In the summer of 1819 magistrates in Salford were warning the government of "the deep distress of the manufacturing classes of this extensive population." Their genuinely sympathetic concern was, however, tinged with fear, as they went on, "when the people are oppressed with hunger we do not wonder of their giving ear to any doctrine which they are told will redress their grievance." Fear got the upper hand in August that year when the neighboring Manchester magistrates called out the cavalry to charge down a peaceful meeting in St. Peter's Fields, resulting in the deaths of 11 and the wounding of over 400. The action was memorably condemned by some wag who named the massacre "Peterloo." In contrast, Lord Liverpool's famously repressive government, which had already suspended habeas corpus in 1817, congratulated the Manchester magistrates, passed six new public order "Gag Acts," and increased the peacetime army by 10,000 men. As almost its only urban palliative measure, the government plowed £1 million into church building in 1818.

This was the political situation when Peel's committee met in 1819 to consider the question of the resumption of gold payments. There was now a broad measure of agreement about the technical questions. Most observers accepted that a reduction in the note issue, which seemed to be a likely consequence of restoring gold payment of notes, would result in an improved sterling exchange rate. It was recognized that the gap between the value of the paper pound and the sovereign would be closed only by raising the value of paper money. And a rise in the value of money means a fall in the price of goods. Most also recognized that a contraction of the note issue would restrict the availability of credit, with profound effects on trade. The attraction of restoring the value of sterling to put right the damage of twenty years of war was set against possible damage to trade in industry and agriculture. Huskisson held out a glorious prospect, which was, in the long term at least, borne out by events, in which the return to gold payments would make "London the chief Bullion market of the World." London could become "the settling House of the Money transactions of the World." But Nathan Rothschild, who was more thoroughly acquainted with bullion than most, warned, with equal prescience, that he did not think a return to gold "can be done without very great distress to this country; it would do a great deal of mischief." He prophesied "Money will be so very scarce, every article in this country will fall to such an enormous extent, that many persons will be ruined."

Bankers such as Rothschild were joined by manufacturers such as Thomas Attwood, the ironmaster and banker who spoke for most of Birmingham, and Robert Owen, the philanthropist mill owner. Generally, however, the cotton interest was more sympathetic to a return to gold, probably because a strong pound could reduce the cost of imported raw materials. On the whole those who opposed the restoration of gold payments feared any hardening of sterling at a time when the market was already depressed, and those who favored it saw it almost as a moral question, in Huskisson's phrase, of "simplicity and truth."

A handful of men argued for a return to gold, but on a reduced standard. It is interesting that this moderate position should have failed to find favor except as a steppingstone toward the full standard. A further refinement was David Ricardo's suggestion that notes might be made convertible to gold bullion rather than to gold coins. The effect would have been to withdraw gold coin from the circulation but restrict the note issue with the obligation to pay gold in much larger units. It was, in fact, in this form that Winston Churchill was to restore the gold standard a century later. Though not a notable success in 1925, if introduced in 1819 it might have proved less deflationary than the chosen approach. As it was, Peel's only concessions by way of a reduced standard, or the Ricardo scheme, were of a strictly temporary nature as intermediary stages of the planned return to gold.

Despite the misgivings of many, the recommendations of the Peel committee were accepted without a division. As Liverpool said in the House of Lords, it seemed the only alternative to giving the Bank of England "the power of making money, without any other check or influence to direct them, than their own notion of profit and interest." The Bank for its part pointed out that the resumption of gold payments would require the government to repay much of its debt to the Bank to help it reduce the volume of outstanding paper. The point was well taken by the government, which immediately arranged the repayment of £10 million and passed an act banning Bank loans to the government of more than three months' duration. The deflationary effects of these measures were so dramatic that the price of gold was down to its prewar level by the summer of 1819. Other prices also fell sharply as money became scarce. In other words, the value of sterling rose dramatically. The Bank's gold reserve became so healthy by the spring of 1821 that it was decided to abandon the remaining intermediary stages of the original plan and reestablish full convertibility to gold two years earlier than originally envisaged.

The sharp reduction in the available quantity of paper money that restored its prewar relationship with gold also restricted the supply of money available for trade. Prices fell—the index stood at 1,492 in 1819, 1,029 in 1822—companies cut back their output, and unemployment rose. Agricultural distress was particularly severe, as the farmers' income no longer permitted them to pay rents and debts taken on in the heyday of wartime expansion. William Cobbett's *Rural Rides* chronicled the sorry state of laborers at Uphusband in Hampshire who were trying to feed families on 6s. a week, which even at the depressed prices of 1822 would scarcely buy nine loaves.

At Chertsey in September 1822 Cobbett found

Cart colts, two and three years old, were selling for less than a third of what they sold for in 1813. The cattle were of an inferior description to be sure; but the price was low almost beyond belief. Cows, which would have sold for £15 in 1813, did not get buyers at £3.

At Wheyhill fair in Hampshire in October 1822 Cobbett recalled:

About £300,000 used, some few years ago, to be carried home by the sheep-sellers. Today, less, perhaps, than £70,000 and yet the rents of these sheep-sellers are, perhaps, as high, on an average, as they were then. The countenances of the farmers were descriptive of their ruinous state. I never, in all my life, beheld a more mournful scene.

... In all the really agricultural villages and parts of the kingdom, there is a shocking decay; a great delapidation and constant pulling down or falling down of houses.

What further infuriated Cobbett was that while the productive heart of the nation struggled to repay paper debts in gold, the wealthy subscribers to the government **Funds** had invested paper but could now convert their interest into hard cash. For years after 1815 these holders of the national debt received some £30 million a year from the nation's taxpayers.

Concern for the condition of the agricultural laborer resulted in an investigation by a Parliamentary Select Committee in 1824 that produced revealing and detailed case-studies. For example, Thomas Smart, aged forty-six, had earned 12s. a week in 1812, but only 8s. in 1824. He had seven living children (out of thirteen), and the three eldest made 6s. a week between them. He got 40s. extra at harvest. His rent and fuel cost £5 a year, and shoes for himself and the family

35s. The family lived almost entirely on bread and cheese, with potatoes grown in the garden; they had had no meat for a month. However, Smart did enjoy steady employment and had received parish
relief only for the burial of his children.

The distress of rural workers was a symptom of difficulties in the
whole agricultural sector. Twenty-six country banks failed in the three
years from the harvest of 1819 to that of 1822, despite reducing note
issues and loans in preparation for the resumption of gold payments.
Nor were complaints restricted to agriculture. Thomas Attwood of
Birmingham asserted with rhetorical flourish that Peel's resumption of
gold caused "more misery, more poverty, more discord, more of everything that was calamitous to the nation, except death, than Attila
caused in the Roman Empire." Such pardonable exaggeration aside, it
seems clear that the return to gold was achieved only at a very heavy
price. The parallels with 1925 are striking. (See pp. 212–214).

The experience of wartime inflation associated with the ready availability of cheap money and of postwar deflation accompanied by the
resumption of cash payments was such that few people in 1822
doubted the connection between the supply of money and the prices of
gold, corn, and foreign exchange. Accordingly, when the levels of distress in the country reached a point at which even Liverpool's government could no longer ignore it, it seemed appropriate to allow some
mild monetary growth. The banks were therefore allowed once again
to issue notes in denominations below £5, though of course these were
now payable on demand in gold. By 1825 up to half the total note issue was in small notes. It was hoped that the ready availability of
these small notes might encourage trade, while their convertibility
would prevent any erosion in the value of sterling. Interest rates,
which fell in the recession, eventually would stimulate activity once
more. The government converted its stock to lower rates, and the
Bank cut its rate in June 1822 to 4 percent. This was still above the
going market rate for loans, so the Bank also needed to promote business in other ways; it began to accept bills for discount with a longer
term to run before maturity and also began lending on mortgages.

In the second quarter of the century government and the banks
struggled to establish the optimal relationship between the money

supply and the needs of the economy—or, expressed differently, the question of the ideal relationship between paper money and gold. Getting the answer wrong was to lead to a series of financial crises, in 1825, 1836, 1839, and 1847, but the underlying monetary problems of the age were severely complicated by cyclical fluctuations of an even more fundamental nature. Historians have found evidence of harvest, trade, and business cycles as far back as the Middle Ages, but in the nineteenth century these cycles became more acutely painful and more obvious. Prosperity builds confidence, and investment, employment, and prices rise to the point at which the newly expanded supply outgrows demand. Sales and prices then stall, companies fail, and falling employment reduces demand still further. Foreign trade fits into this scheme, through the medium of the exchange rate. The rate falls when imports exceed exports, leading to the export of bullion and a contraction of domestic money supply and demand, or rises as exports draw more money into the country permitting an increase in demand. It is possible that the very low agricultural prices of which Cobbett complained may have permitted some slight improvement in conditions in the towns even before government and the Bank began to ease monetary conditions. At any rate a perceptible improvement in 1823 developed into a full-fledged boom in 1824 and 1825. The Bank lent almost £1 million on mortgages in 1824, and the figure stood at almost £1.5 million by the middle of 1825. The directors also lent another million against government securities and their own Bank stock. The country banks followed a similar path, and their note issues grew by an estimated 20 to 25 percent, probably peaking in the second quarter of 1825 when over £2.5 million of new notes were stamped. In 1824, £232 million worth of bills of exchange were stamped and £260 million in 1825. The daily circulation of these bills was estimated to have grown from £58 million to £65 million at this time. Some 600 new joint stock companies were launched in 1824–1825, with a total capital of £372 million. And on top of all this, there was a further boom in foreign lending, particularly to South America.

The familiar elements of a speculative boom were there for all to see. At the very beginning of 1825 Samuel Thornton, merchant and Bank director, noted ominously:

The abundance of money has led to a variety of speculation in England, and scarcely a week has passed but some new company was founded to direct a world projected adventure. What must be the cure of this mania only time can show.

Wellington's assessment, as recorded by his confidante Mrs. Arbuthnot, was characteristically more forthright: "He thinks the greatest national calamities will be the consequence of this speculating mania." Lord Liverpool, in March 1825, went so far as to warn the City that no one should look to the government to bail out speculators this time with Exchequer bills as they had done in the past.

Yet despite such warnings early in 1825, the Bank took no action until the autumn. Its complacency may be attributed in part to the size of the gold reserve, which in August 1824 had stood at nearly £12 million. Even in February 1825 it still looked comfortable at £8.8 million, yet the falling reserve, despite its size, and the downward turn on the exchange should have been warning enough. By August 1825 the reserve was below £4 million, so that when in that densely foggy November the Bank did try to restrain commercial lending and the country banks, it was no longer well protected with enough gold to weather the crisis. Nor was Bank restraint applied with any degree of subtlety. An increase in the Bank rate from 4 percent to 5 percent could have restrained the flow of funds without turning off the tap sharply. Instead the Bank simply started refusing to advance money against bills (i.e., discount) for even the most established houses. Starved of resources, the country banks began to struggle. Elford & Co. in Plymouth failed in the last week of November and was soon followed by others in Northampton and in Leicestershire. As the Norfolk banker J. J. Gurney saw it, "The root of the difficulty is in the Bank of England, where they are extremely restricting their discounts with a view to producing a favourable effect on the exchanges, so as to prevent their being run upon for gold." *The Times,* however, had no sympathy for any of these "men of paper," and backed the government's resolve to offer no help to "the speculating people and their great foster-mother in Threadneedle Street."

Marianne Thornton wrote to a friend describing the crisis at her brother Henry's bank, Pole, Thornton, Free, Down & Scott.

On Saturday [December 3, 1825]—that dreadful Saturday I shall never forget—the run increased to a frightful degree, everybody came in to take out their balance, no one brought any in . . . Such a moment of peril completely turned Free's head . . . Old Scott cried like a child of five years old, but could suggest nothing . . . never, he [Henry] says, shall he forget watching the clock to see when five would strike, and end their immediate terror—or whether any one would come in for any more payments.

On his return home late that night Henry was "perfectly white and bloodless with the anxiety and the exertion he had gone through . . ."

Thornton's bank was fundamentally sound—its assets exceeded its liabilities—but in the face of such a run, and despite loans from rival private London banks and from the Bank, it was forced to stop payment on December 12. That month over sixty country banks failed, more than half of them as a consequence of Pole & Thornton's collapse, and five other big London private banks also failed. Faced with a collapse of this magnitude, the Bank did start lending again in December, despite the government's continued refusal to sanction a suspension of gold payments. The government did, however, allow the Bank to resume the issue of £1 notes, whose popularity for the payment of wages helped ease the demand for gold. City folklore, originating with Alexander Baring, has it that it was only the chance discovery of an old box of 1818 notes that enabled the Bank to keep paying through this crisis. In fact, new notes were rapidly printed, and retired cashiers were drafted in to help in signing them. Staff slept at the Bank over Christmas that year, such was the pressure of work, as advances were now readily made against almost any sort of security. Jeremiah Harman, a director and former governor of the Bank (memorably described by a fellow director as "ignorant, pompous, prejudiced and overbearing"), recalled that they had lent "by every possible means consistent with the safety of the Bank; and we were not upon some occasions over nice; seeing the dreadful state in which the public were, we rendered every assistance in our power." Inevitably, such lending put the reserves under a strain, for the notes lent were all payable in gold if requested, and continuing confidence in Bank notes required that they should be so paid. Once again Rothschild saved the day, shipping in hundreds of thousands of sovereigns from the continent and depositing them in the Bank; he also lent sovereigns to private London banks. In total he is said to have lent £10 million to shore up the entire banking system, though some 145 banks still failed at this time.

Rothschild and the Bank thus were credited with the actions that saved the entire banking system. John Overend, the bill broker, described the crisis as "such a one as I never witnessed before in the 36 years I have been in Lombard Street," which included 1793 and 1797. He wrote, "I hope never to see the like of it again, and if the Bank Directors had not seen the thing in its true light and given the prompt and immediate assistance they did, the game would have been up." With the benefit of hindsight, this seems a somewhat over-generous assessment of the Bank, which certainly should have applied the brake to the boom of 1824 earlier, and more gently, than it did late in 1825. Had it done so, the "landing" would almost certainly have been softer, and in any case the Bank's reserve would have been in a better shape to face up to difficulties. As Rothschild told the government, according to Mrs. Arbuthnot, "if he had been applied to sooner, he would have prevented all the difficulty." Rothschild clearly understood the importance of timing, as had Samuel Bosanquet, governor of the Bank from 1791 to 1793, whose principle of restricting discounts when the exchanges are unfavorable and releasing discounts again as soon as the exchange turns, would have served the Bank well. Equally Henry Thornton (senior) saw clearly that the Bank rate could be used to ration discounts by price if the ban on rates in excess of 5 percent were lifted. Yet such insights that pointed the way to the future were not then common knowledge.

In 1826 the conventional wisdom was that the country bank note issue was to blame. Certainly the existence of several hundred separate issuing banks cannot have facilitated control of the national money supply. Cobbett and Parliament were for once in agreement, blaming country banks and "rag money." Thus, in the first place, legislation was introduced that reestablished the ban on small notes in England and Wales. Westminster even considered imposing a similar ban on Scotland, which had had small notes without problems for over a century. Sir Walter Scott warned them off, telling them "let those who are sick take physic." One reason for the success of the small notes in Scotland was that there was no ban on **joint stock banks** there. Consequently Scottish banks were larger and more soundly based than many English country banks, which had been limited to a maximum of six partners since the early days of the Bank of England. As Lord Liverpool complained, in England "Any small tradesman, a cheesemonger, a butcher or a shoemaker, may open a country bank, but a set of persons with a fortune sufficient to carry on the concern with security are not permitted to do so." Parliamentary language is prone to overstatement, and Liverpool did less than justice to some substantial figures involved in English provincial banking, but his basic point, that the ban on joint stock banks had outlived its early eighteenth-century purpose, was true enough. Accordingly in 1826, as the second string of the postcrisis reforms, the ban on joint stock banks was partly lifted, allowing them on condition they were at least sixty-five miles from London, to safeguard the privileged position of the Bank of England. Though some small provincial banks were to survive into the twentieth century, the 1826 legislation was the first of a series of acts designed to clip their wings.

The Act of 1833 admitted joint stock banks to the capital, providing they did not issue their own notes, so the joint stock banks began also to challenge the position of the London private banks. The London and Westminster Bank, established in 1834, led the way, and there were four other joint stock banks in London by 1844 and others outside the capital. The newcomers had to make their way despite the concerted opposition of the banking establishment. The Bank refused to rediscount their bills, and they were excluded from the London Bankers' Clearing House until 1854. The private bankers claimed that they offered an altogether more gentlemanly service, in which a refined and personal relationship between banker and client permitted a good deal more discretion and attention to detail than the rather inflexible rules imposed by a remote head office on distant branches. But in the fullness of time, the larger capital of the joint stock banks not only provided greater security for depositors but also injected a new, competitive spirit into the rather clubbable banking world. The larger sums assembled by the joint stock ventures could not be left idle, so investment opportunities were sought out more vigorously and more doubtful bills accepted for discount. Depositors were offered better rates, as the joint stock banks cut profit margins and cash reserves to boost overall business. Further acts in 1858 and 1862 extended limited liability to bank shareholders, and Barclays and Lloyds both converted to joint stock firms in the 1860s. By the beginning of the twentieth century, private banks were becoming unusual.

The 1825 crisis also had repercussions for the discounting of bills. The history and development of bills of exchange have provided an additional line of harmony to the main monetary tune since the Middle Ages, but because of the rapid expansion of banknotes, some observers forgot about the continued importance of bills. In fact, they remained central to the development of money in Britain, and had a special importance in the northwest, where they commonly circulated in preference to banknotes. Thus Nathan Rothschild paid Mr. Foulde for goods received in Manchester in July 1802 by writing him a bill promising payment of £500 in three months' time. In fact, Foulde did not present the bill for payment himself, for we know it was subsequently accepted by Monsieur Nonnes Lopez the elder of Paris, whose name also appears on the surviving bill. The institutional arrangements for dealing with bills developed considerably in the first half of the century. Around 1800 the bill broker emerged as a specialist dealer. The broker was familiar enough with both the needs of provincial trade and the sources of funds to make a living from supplying reliable bills to those with ready cash or, alternatively, providing cash to sound concerns in need of short-term funds. The most outstanding early example of the bill-broking species was Thomas Richardson, founder of the broking firm Richardson, Overend & Gurney.

During the Napoleonic Wars demand for money was high, but the usury laws imposed a maximum interest rate of 5 percent. The banks, which had been accustomed to discount bills for much of the eighteenth century, found that buying government stock usually yielded more than 5 percent a year quite legally. (Three percent stock bought at less than £60 for a nominal value of £100, paying £3 a year, would yield over 5 percent.) Accordingly, banks increasingly put their money in such stocks, which were generically known as the

"Funds," rather than making it available to discount commercial bills. Men such as Richardson realized that although the city banks were less and less inclined to discount bills, money was still available, especially in the eastern agricultural districts, while commercial bills requiring discount, especially from the northern industrial regions, were also still plentiful. For one-eighth percent paid by the bill holder, Richardson would undertake to find a discounter. It is a measure of the profit in broking that the business was suggested to Pitt as a possible area of new taxation.

During the crisis of 1825, the sudden refusal of the Bank to accept bills confirmed the reluctance of banks to commit themselves to discounting. This reluctance gave a further impetus to the specialist broking firms, which now began to borrow funds themselves to enable them to discount bills on their own account rather than merely act as broking intermediaries. Overend & Gurney (so named after Richardson's death) was still unquestionably the leading firm in this business. Samuel Gurney, whose generosity to the poor of West Ham was well known, seemed to mix shrewdness with benevolence. In John Overend shrewdness evidently had the upper hand: When he finally withdrew support from his fellow Quakers, the Frys, in 1828, he reported, "They say we have just kept them on until we got out and they call me a great rogue and I tell them I care not what they call me if they do not call me a fool . . ." William Morris, father of the artist, was a partner at the smaller bill-broking firm, Sandersons. Alongside these essentially domestic discounting firms, international bills of exchange grew in importance too. In this area it was above all Rothschilds and Barings who led the field.

Reaction to the crisis of 1825 not only opened the way for joint stock banking and the emerging discount houses but also marked a stage in the further development of the Bank of England. Although most of the blame for the panic of 1825–1826 was laid at the door of the provincial banks, the crisis prompted some Bank of England directors to look again at the operation of the banking system. The most important figure involved in this reexamination was John Horsley Palmer, a director of the Bank since 1811, deputy governor from 1828 to 1830, and governor from 1830 to 1833. Palmer was among the growing number of directors who now accepted the link among the quantity of sterling in circulation, the movement of the exchanges, and the flow of bullion. This insight would permit the Bank in future to anticipate a foreign gold drain and help it take action to protect its reserves. In addition, to regulate the supply of sterling and increase public confidence in Bank notes, Palmer established a rule that the Bank should keep a reserve equivalent to the value of one-third of its liabilities. In calculating liabilities he included deposits as well as notes, recognizing that they were interchangeable: Notes became deposits as soon as a client banked them, while deposits became notes when he withdrew them. Under Palmer, the Bank also began to hold back from discounting bills in the money market. Instead of competing for bills with other institutions, the Bank charged interest above the rate generally available. In this way it could provide a source of funds, available at a price, that would be turned to only when the ordinary channels ran dry. Thus the Bank, as a lender of last resort, could help the money market over the occasional liquidity crises to which the system was periodically prone.

In order to allow this higher rate of interest, the Bank Charter Act of 1833 exempted bills of exchange due for payment within three months from the provisions of the usury laws. Until 1854 the maximum legal rate of interest was 5 percent, but the 1833 act meant that even if the market rate of interest rose, the Bank always could offer help at a higher rate. In effect, loans could be rationed by price, which allowed a restriction of credit when necessary without cutting it off altogether. In addition, Bank notes above £5 were made **legal tender**, so in future panics the public should be happy with notes for larger sums, rather than running on the gold reserves.

The whole scheme was to be severely tested in 1836. In that year the slow and steady growth of the early 1830s built into a cyclical boom, fueled largely by rising exports, especially to America, and railway development. Joshua Bates, the rather dour Bostonian who was a partner at Barings, commented, "there is at present great madness abroad in regard to railroads," but Barings went heavily into American business. The growing demand for credit typical of good times was met by rather too easy a supply. The joint stock banks were now in the market in addition to the other existing banks, and the Bank itself, despite the Palmer rule, was lending freely. The Bank allowed cheap discounts to country banks to try to persuade them to give up their note issue rights, lent East India Company money deposited with it, and accepted various government stocks as security for loans. The Bank note issue did not grow excessively, but the securities it held (a sign of its lending) and the level of deposits in it (i.e., money waiting to be spent) did rise. What is more, the Bank was slow to raise its interest rate in 1836, so for some months its funds were available at the open market rate of 4 percent, before the **bank rate** was raised in July to 4.5 and in August to 5 percent. Too easy a supply of credit when the business cycle was at its peak anyway created conditions of overproduction, which left loans tied up in unsaleable goods that led to a rise in bankruptcies. There was no major banking crisis, but the market suffered a sharp shock. At that very moment, July 1836, Rothschild died, and Alexander Baring for one believed that "[t]he variations of all stocks and their wild fluctuations seem to arise much from Nathan's deaths."

Renewed difficulties occurred as well from a drain of gold abroad in 1839, when gold flowed out to buy U.S. securities and to repair the effects of bankruptcies in France and Belgium in 1838. Despite the falling gold reserve, the Bank continued to lend too cheaply for too long. In July 1839 its reserves were down to below £4 million, one-fifth, rather than one-third, of the note circulation. Moreover, with old Nathan dead, his son Lionel did not feel able to perform the almost customary Rothschild rescue. Instead it was Barings who went to Paris on behalf of the Bank, returning with a £2 million loan from the Bank of France.

Neither 1836 nor 1839 were anything like as serious as 1825, but the two later crises did raise questions about the Bank's management and the reliability of Palmer's rules. Despite the bank rate and control of the Bank note issue, there had been two major runs on the Bank, both of which caused an alarming drop in the reserves. Part of the problem was that the timing of bank rate changes was almost as important as an understanding of the principles involved. Management of the bank rate remains an art that a century and a half of practice has improved but not yet perfected. A further difficulty was that although Palmer had included deposits and notes in circulation in his formula, in practice little attention seems to have been paid to the level of bank deposits.

This raises the question, which still exercises bankers and economists today, of what exactly counts as money. By the late 1830s there were two broad schools of thought. The currency school, which descended in a direct line from the principles of the Bullion Committee of 1810 and Peel's Committee of 1819, limited their concept of money to notes, coin, and bullion that could rapidly be made into coin. For them the management of the note issue was essentially a matter of tying it directly to the available supply of gold. Of course, there were various shades of opinion within this hard money school, and individuals' thinking evolved over time, but this relationship between notes and gold lay at the heart of the matter, and this concept of money had little room for checks, bills of exchange, and bank deposits, which usually were considered means of economizing on money rather than as money itself. To the modern eye, and even to an eighteenth-century one, so limited a view of money had obvious shortcomings, but to many of those who lived through the period 1797 to 1826 this rather narrow concentration on gold and notes and the need for a constant and ideally one-to-one relationship between the two seemed well justified by events. When the note issue got out of hand, the value of sterling, in terms of goods, other currencies, and gold, fell.

In opposition to these views, the banking school argued that money was not limited to notes and gold but included bank deposits and the checks drawn on them together with bills of exchange and other forms of circulating paper. Concentrating on the relationship between notes and gold, they argued, was to misunderstand the true nature of money in nineteenth-century England. It also would impose an irrational and unnecessary limitation on the ability of the banking system to meet the needs of trade. Of course the banking school did recognize the need for some restraint: Palmer had favored a gold reserve of one-third of notes and deposits. But this was a long way short of meeting the one-to-one ideal of the currency school, which argued that the Palmer system had proven inadequate in 1836 and 1839.

A parliamentary committee explored this issue in 1839. Its members included Peel, who ever since 1819 had been firmly committed

1 Early coins, showing obverse and reverse. Top left: William the Conqueror, perhaps the first sterling penny. Issues like this from late in his reign were struck at about the time the sources begin to use the term "sterling." Top right: baronial issue from the time of Stephen and Matilda. Loss of control at the time of the civil war allowed unauthorized types to appear. Center: a cut farthing of Henry III. In the Middle Ages halfpennies and farthings often were supplied by cutting up pennies (obv. only). Bottom left: a Low Countries sterling struck in the 1290s at Mons, in direct imitation of the English sterling penny (bottom right) struck in London in the 1280s for Edward I.

2 England's later medieval coinage. Left (reverse below) gold noble of Edward III, mid-fourteenth century, worth 6s. 8d. or one-third of a pound. Center: silver groat or four-penny piece of Henry VI, struck in Calais in the 1420s. Right: gold angel of Edward IV showing St Michael the Archangel slaying a dragon of evil, struck in the 1470s and worth 6s. 8d.

3 Top right: silver and debased groats of the young and aging Henry VIII. Center: the first shilling of Henry VIII; a debased teston or shilling of Edward VI, countermarked with a portcullis at the time of its revaluation by Elizabeth I. Bottom: groat (rev. and obv.) of Henry VII. Portrait coins of these types were a Tudor innovation copying continental developments.

4 Tudor gold: a very gothic, medieval sovereign of Henry VII (obv. and rev.) and a gold pound of Elizabeth I, very much a Renaissance queen.

5 Above and below: the silver coinage of Elizabeth I, with denominations ranging from a crown of 5 shillings (25p.) right down to a halfpenny. The 6d., 4d., 3d., 2d., 1½d., 1d., and ½d. were difficult to distinguish from one another, so alternate values appear with and without the date and a rose behind the queen's head.

6 Royalist issues were struck by Charles I in the towns he controlled, while Parliament held the London mint where they struck Charles's coinage to its original designs right up until the execution of the king. Top: gold £3, Oxford mint, with Charles's war aims in Latin on the reverse. Bottom left: the Oxford crown with the city visible beneath the horse. Bottom right: a Parliament-issued crown with the royal arms.

7 The Hanoverians. Top left: a shilling of George I, 1723, with the initials of the South Sea Company in the angles of the reverse. Top right: a golden guinea of George III, 1765. Below: a copper halfpenny of George III, 1770. In the eighteenth century the coinage became increasingly dominated by gold and copper.

8 Nineteenth-century gold £5 pieces were never common currency, but these designs capture something of the spirit of the age. Pistrucci's George and the Dragon was introduced under George III but was revived to become inseparably linked with the late-Victorian sovereign. William Wyon's "Una and the lion" (bottom left) symbolizes the young queen and her empire, but from 1893 the old queen replaced the earlier portraits.

9 The impact of war.

Top: a 1697 interest-bearing Exchequer bill for £5. The annotation at the foot of the bill reads "A farthing a day interest."

Center: a "Bradbury" emergency £1 note issued by the Treasury on the outbreak of the First World War.

Bottom: a Vale of Aylesbury Bank £1 note of 1812 typical of much of the paper money issued by the country banks during the Napoleonic Wars, when payment in gold was suspended.

10 George V's sovereign was the last British gold coin in common currency; it was replaced by paper money during the First World War. Top right: George V, shilling; in 1920 sterling silver was replaced with silver only 50 percent pure. George V's penny illustrates a design essentially unchanged from Charles II to Elizabeth II.

11 £1,000, and £5 notes of 1925. Bank of England notes from the eighteenth to the mid-twentieth century retained a broadly similar appearance recalling their hand-written origins, with the Britannia top left, and an elaborate "Sum Block" giving the value of the note bottom left.

12 The George VI halfcrown (12½ p.) of 1947 marks the replacement of silver with a coinage of cupro-nickel. The 1949 halfcrown records the loss of the Indian Empire. The old "copper" penny, halfpenny, and farthing were replaced by the decimal 2p., 1p., and ½ p. in 1971.

13 The 1 and 10-shilling notes of 1928. The monarchs portrait was introduced on Bank of England notes only in 1960; the last Bank of England £1 note was issued from 1978 to 1984.

to the hard money men in the currency school. Although the committee did hear evidence from Manchester, where bills of exchange always had had a particular importance, it seems clear that the ideas of the currency school were in the ascendant. Its idea was simpler and promised an end to periodic banking crises and panics. The more complicated banking analysis seemed to hold out no such solutions. The committee published no report, but the Bank itself took up the dominant ideas of the time. The Bank may have judged that by accepting the need for some control of the note issue, it might be able to establish a less restrictive system than that advocated by the currency school. Thus in 1840 the Bank itself proposed to separate its issue department from its banking department, in order to guarantee that the important public function of note issue should be entirely unaffected by, and independent of, the banking policies of a private city institution. In other words, the banker's instinct to lend for a profit should not be able to lead to an inflation of the note issue, which was to be independently controlled. The rules governing the note issue were clearly laid down. A fixed **fiduciary note** issue of £14 million was permitted, which was to be backed by securities, such as government bonds. Beyond this £14 million, the rest of the Bank's note issue was to be backed, pound for pound, by its bullion reserve, and all of its notes were to be payable by the Bank on demand in gold.

The Bank's experience of financial crises also led it to suggest an emergency clause that would permit the government to authorize an increased fiduciary issue in the event of particular difficulties. Peel rejected this last option, despite the entreaties of numerous experienced bankers who foresaw real problems. Palmer was one of many who pointed out that in the absence of some emergency escape clause, the proposed new regulations would prevent the Bank from easing a crisis as it had done in 1825, 1836, and 1839. Nor was it only the old banking establishment that took this view; Henry Bosanquet of the new joint stock London and Westminster Bank had a similar opinion. But Peel, his resolution stiffened by Samuel Jones Loyd, high priest of the currency school, was not to be moved. He remained confident that crises of the old type would not occur if the note issue were controlled, and may have felt that to anticipate problems in this way would weaken the restraint on overissue. In any case, *in extremis,* governments could take such emergency powers when the time came.

In other respects, the Bank proposal was essentially that introduced by Peel in his Bank Chapter Act of 1844. In due course this act was to establish itself as one of the cornerstones of sterling in the high Victorian age, but the rather inflexible dogma it embodied first had to be tempered in the fire of experience. Within three years events were to expose the impracticality of the currency school theory underpinning the 1844 act.

As the economy recovered from the difficulties of 1839, optimism had grown. Trade, especially with India (no longer the monopoly of the East India Company), was buoyant. In addition, railway building picked up again. Very heavy investment in this sector boosted the economy as a whole, as the work put wages in men's pockets. It also greatly improved the transport infrastructure of the whole country, bringing further benefits. The scramble to invest in so patently good an idea caused a boom on the stock market that rapidly assumed the proportions of a mania. As Prescott's Bank noted in October 1845, "The great feature of the present time is the speculation in Railroads, which has reached an awful magnitude . . ."

At the same time, the banking department of the Bank of England, now separated from the responsibilities of note issue, determined to enter the discount market. *Bankers' Magazine* commented in April 1845 that the Bank directors were "now anxious to push their business, as bankers, to an extent hitherto quite unknown to their system of management." Bank discounts rose from £2 million to £12 million between the autumn of 1844 and the spring of 1846. The Bank also invested £2.5 million in railway debentures.

While London thrived, the failure of the potato crop in Ireland in 1845 and 1846 caused famine, death, and emigration on an unprecedented scale. Yet although two parts of a small united kingdom can seldom have been so far apart, the Irish tragedy did not quite pass unnoticed in England. Indeed, the case for cheaper food and the repeal of the Corn Laws was never more terribly illustrated, and Peel and the Anti-Corn Law League finally got their way in 1846. But the failure of the English wheat price to reflect the Irish famine probably owed less to the import of continental grain than to the fact that those who starved as a result of potato blight were far too poor to buy wheat. The dependence of so large a proportion of the Irish population on the potato, together with English attitudes born of ignorance, misconceived free market ideology, or simple bigotry let millions perish unaided. There were, of course, also poor wheat harvests in England, but in the speculative mood of the times a fair amount of the easy credit available there was put speculatively into corn.

In 1847 the Bank became anxious about falling reserves. (The note issue had been held steady throughout.) It raised the bank rate to 5 percent in April and charged even more than that for longer-dated bills. Loans also were called in, £1.25 million worth of **Consols** were sold, and the reserve was restored. But tighter money that summer—Coutts's bills were refused in Lombard Street—coinciding with a better harvest and falling wheat prices caused difficulties for a number of corn merchants and speculators. In August the bank rate went up to 5.5 percent, and India and China merchants, whose long-distance trade involved them in long-dated bills, also got into difficulties. One particular bankruptcy had notable repercussions: The senior partner of Robinson & Co., the failed corn dealers, was William Robinson Robinson, governor of the Bank of England.

Failures continued through the summer. Sanderson, the bill-broking and discount house, failed in October with liabilities of £2.6 million, though the unexpected death of William Morris, a leading partner of the firm, may have contributed to this collapse. The Bank raised its rate to 5.5 percent for bills maturing within a month and 6 percent or more for longer-dated bills, and announced that it would no longer lend against securities. As the Stock Exchange panicked, the crisis spread to the banks. On October 18 two Liverpool banks folded, along with banks in the northeast later that week. The Bank reserve was down to £3 million, and under the terms of the 1844 act it was powerless to help. Throughout the crisis the note issue had been steady and the Issue Department's reserve of about £18 million was untouched, but the problem had been caused by the expansion and contraction of credit. Checks and bank accounts were certainly showing themselves to be money, requiring control as much as notes.

For weeks Peel and his chancellor, Sir Charles Wood, had resisted calls for a relaxation of the act, but eventually, on Saturday, October

23, 1847, they reluctantly gave way, giving the Bank permission to lend and discount as required, at 8 percent. If this caused them to exceed the fiduciary note issue, Parliament would provide the necessary authorization. The news was published the following Monday, and the crisis, which had bankrupted some thirty major London firms and more in the provinces was over. The Bank printed more notes specially but did not need them. Additional loans of almost £1 million were granted, but these were accessed by checks drawn on the Bank. Once it was known that money could be had if necessary, the panic subsided. For example, Gurney applied to the Bank for £200,000, but as soon as the government released the Bank from the previous restrictions, Gurney's clients, many of whom had looked to withdraw their cash only as a precaution, were content to leave their money with him. As he recalled later, "after the notice [from the government] we only required about £100,000 instead of £200,000. From that day we had a market of comparative ease."

A preoccupation with the note issue characterizes the period from the end of the Napoleonic Wars until the 1844 Bank Charter Act. As a consequence, the extraordinary economic growth of the period was achieved against a background of monetary restraint created by anxiety about the size of the note issue in relation to the gold reserve. Nevertheless, the banks and discount houses were also under pressure to create the credit necessary to finance a rapidly expanding economy, although such arrangements were vulnerable to periodic shocks and crises of confidence, especially after bouts of excess speculation and heady growth. This pattern of periods of expansion followed by sharp checks is clearly reflected in the price index. The price of the basket of goods fell after the Napoleonic Wars to a low in 1822 (Phelps Brown–Hopkins Index about 1,000). It recovered to 1,400 in 1825 but fell steadily thereafter for a decade (low point 1834: 1,011). A recovery set in in the late 1830s, peaking in 1839 to 1841 around 1,200 before falling back once more to around 1,000 from 1843 to 1845. The index reached 1,200 again in 1847 but was back below 1,000 from 1850 to 1852.

A parliamentary report of 1843 enables us to convert these abstract index numbers into more tangible examples. It found agricultural wages as low as 8s. a week, though in ideal circumstances a whole family might bring home as much as 18s. A stonemason at Calne earned 15s. a week, of which a shilling a week was spent on meat, while most of the rest went on bread and potatoes. A widow with an eight-year-old son earned 4s. 6d. a week and received 1s. 6d. a week allowance from the poor law guardians for her son. She spent 4s. 4d. a week on food, rent, candles, and soap and the remaining 1s. 8d. on fuel and shoes. Their diet consisted almost solely of bread, butter, and tea, with home-grown potatoes.

There were more opportunities in the towns. Printers and tailors in London could earn 36s. to 40s. a week. Shipwrights and skilled builders—carpenters, plasterers, bricklayers, and masons—often made 30s. a week. A Manchester cotton spinner in the 1830s might earn 27s. a week. However, some trades suffered a marked decline in the first half of the century, and the earnings of cotton handloom weavers and the framework knitters of Notts and Leicestershire fell dramatically. A Bolton handloom weaver who had made 30s. a week in 1797 took home only 5s. or 6s. by 1830. These wages were generally buying bread at about 2d. a pound, cheese at 10d. a pound, meat about 9d. a pound, sugar about 8d. a pound, and tea at around 1s. 4d. a quarter. Beer cost about 2d. or 3d. a pint, and average consumption fell from over 30 gallons per head per year to under 20 between 1800 and 1850. Even the upper figure gives an average daily consumption of only just over one half pint, but of course many people drank much less and others more.

Charles Dickens immortalized the mid-Victorian budget with Micawber's succinct summary—"Annual income twenty pounds, annual expenditure nineteen nineteen and six, result happiness. Annual income twenty pounds, annual expenditure twenty pounds ought and six, result misery"—but the daily reality was more complicated. Full employment at 25s. or 30s. a week, and cheap bread at 1¾d., could only too easily turn into half pay with bread costing 2½d. a pound. Since a working-class family of five might easily buy six 4-pound loaves a week, they might spend up to half their income on bread, even if they were in full employment. Yet in many trades employment could be as variable as the harvest. Alexander Somerville revealed the effect of part-time work on the budget when he investigated Accrington in the bleak year 1842: He found 1,389 full-time workers with an average wage of 8s. 8d. and 1,622 workers on part-time with average earnings of 4s. 10d. Even below this group were 727 unemployed men described as destitute.

Such harrowing evidence of poverty in and out of work in the first half of the nineteenth century, however, tells only part of the story. While some struggled to earn £30 a year, and William Cobbett argued that a family of five should spend £62 6s. 8d. a year on bread, meat, and beer alone, a wealthy man would spend a similar amount each year keeping a couple of horses. Anyone receiving £150 a year would regard himself as a gentleman. A comfortable middle-class family income of £250 a year would permit at least one maidservant living in, who would receive about £14 a year. A household with £1,000 a year probably would include a coachman on £24, a footman on £22, a cook on £16, a maid on £14, and a nursery maid on £10. A million domestic servants in Britain were recorded in the census of 1851. By 1911 there were a million and a half.

6

The Golden Age of Sterling: 1851 to 1914

The world seems very prosperous since the discovery of gold in
California and Australia, and the extension of railways and nav-
igation by steam are working great changes in the world.
—Joshua Bates of Barings, 1852

Six shillings a week does not keep body and soul together very
unitedly. They want to get away from each other when there is
only such a very slight bond as that between them; and one day,
I suppose, the pain and the dull monotony of it all had stood before her eyes plainer than usual . . .
—Jerome K. Jerome on the suicide of a young woman living on
6s. a week at Goring on Thames, *Three Men in a Boat*, 1889

The Great Exhibition of 1851 was a hugely successful demonstra-
tion of British industrial power and prosperity. A Crystal Palace over
600 yards long was erected in Hyde Park to exhibit the world's sci-
entific and technological achievements, and Britain's contribution
loomed particularly large. It was a monument to the confidence and
optimism of the age, and it marked a period of growth that established Britain as the world's leading industrial and financial center.
Sterling, the British currency, both contributed to that international
preeminence and benefited from it, and William Wyon's gold £5 coin
combining the young queen with a magnificent British lion symbolizes much of the strength and optimism of the age. The last half of
the nineteenth century was also a period of unprecedented domestic
prosperity. The **national income** grew threefold from £636 million in
1855 to £1,984 million in 1910, and though some of that growth
was swallowed by the increasing numbers needing to be fed, national income per head still doubled over this period.

This was, moreover, a period of flat or falling prices. Reductions
in the import duties payable on tea and sugar brought down the cost
of those staples, while even more fundamentally the price of bread

fell substantially, especially after about 1870 when North American grain began to arrive in Britain in large quantities. In the north Midlands the 4 pound loaf cost between 5d. and 6d. in the third quarter of the century, and only 4d. to 3d. in the last quarter. In London bread prices were generally higher but showed a similar fall from the 1870s. The price of both tea and sugar fell: sugar from 4d. to 6d. a pound (1850 to 1875), down to 3d. or 2d. in the 1880s and 1890s; tea down from about 1s. a quarter to 6d. or 3d. Consumption of tea and sugar rose threefold over the second half of the century. Consumption of beer reached an all-time high in 1876 at 34 gallons per head per annum, and Samuel Smiles exhorted the nation to consider a more thrifty employment for the £60 million he calculated were being spent by the working class on alcohol and tobacco each year. Wages were essentially stable in this period, but real wages rose because of the fall in prices. It has been calculated that in Sheffield real wages rose some 30 percent between 1870 and 1900. Thus the benefits of **free trade** reached the pockets of the poorest, in the form of the massive reductions in the cost of the staples that loomed largest in their diet. Of course, not all prices fell so dramatically, but the index price of the basket of consumables tells a no less astonishing story: From its peak in 1813 at 1,881, it fell to below 1,000 in 1850 to 1852; it averaged 1,254 between 1853 and 1885, when it again dropped below the 1,000, averaging 982 between 1886 and 1913. Moreover, these low prices were achieved at a time of unprecedented economic growth. As these pages show, it is easy to achieve growth by inflating the money supply, but that raises prices. Prices can be kept low easily by restricting the money supply, but that also will inhibit growth. The remarkable feature of Britain's nineteenth-century economic performance was the combination of high growth and low prices.

Part of the explanation for such rare and favorable circumstances lay in the nature of Britain's relationship with the rest of the world. The London market, uniquely combining, as Walter Bagehot noted, economical delicacy and power, was central to Britain's international role. As wealth accumulated at home, increasing quantities were invested abroad: a total of £200 million by 1850, £1 billion by 1875, £4 billion by 1913. These investments, above all in railways across the globe, opened up new outlets for British exports and laid down the necessary transport systems required to bring cheap primary products from the rest of the world back to Britain. Often British capital was supplied as part of a package that also involved the supply of British equipment and expertise, British shipping and insurance, and British banking. Thus investments and **invisibles** paid for growing British imports of cheap food and raw materials. (Britain's visible balance of trade probably was negative throughout the century.) Rather than accumulating at home where it might stoke inflation, sterling was distributed across the world.

This, then, was the golden age of sterling, but it had a darker side. James Caird, in a series of reports for *The Times* in 1850–1851, found agricultural wages in Berkshire, Wiltshire, and Suffolk around 6s. a week, at or below the rates noted by Arthur Young eighty years earlier. Caird calculated an average wage across the south of the country as a whole at 8s. 5d. a week (Young, 1770: 7s. 6d.), and for the north, 11s. 6d. a week (1770: 6s. 9d.). In parts of Lancashire farmers had to pay as much as 15s. week for labor, which would otherwise join the migration to the mill towns in search of better pay. But in the south, where alternative, better-paid work was not so readily available, laborers were still receiving wages that left their families dependent on parish poor relief. In Wiltshire 16 percent of the population was drawing parish relief, while the figure in Oxfordshire and Dorset was 15 percent. In the northern counties, it was less than half that figure. The Royal Commission on Labour of 1893 found some improvement: 10s. a week in Dorset and Wiltshire, 18s. in Lancashire and Cumberland. In Oxfordshire in 1912 average wages ran at 10 to 12s., but these could fall to 8s. in wet weather. In 1914 Seebohm Rowntree regarded 20s. 6d. a week as the minimum wage necessary for a family of five.

Even in the towns conditions were little better, for the reality often fell some way short of the idealized picture of late nineteenth-century English industrial prosperity. In good times John Ward, a weaver in Clitheroe, was content enough. He commented cheerily, "as long as we have good health and plenty of work we will do well enough," but in doing so he put his finger on the fundamental insecurity felt by millions. The second half of the century was not, in fact, an unbroken sequence of prosperous years. Particularly from 1875 to 1895 times could be very difficult indeed. These twenty years of the high Victorian age marked what has been called "the Great Nineteenth-Century Depression."

The whole period from the Great Exhibition to the outbreak of the First World War, a period that saw huge economic progress, can actually be divided into three separate phases. The growth that was the principal characteristic of the time from 1850 to the mid-1870s was much less evident between 1875 and 1895, but picked up once more from the late 1890s until 1914. In the middle period the low and falling prices, together with the rather sluggish investment performance, which failed to respond to low interest rates, are characteristic of the down-phase of an economic cycle and in marked contrast to the boom years of the early 1870s. However, it has been questioned whether the downturn of this period really merits its title as a great depression. Most important, falling prices brought about rising real wages; a dramatic rise in living standards is hardly compatible with the idea of a depression. On the other hand, it is pointed out that real wages make little difference to a family unable to find work. *Real earnings* that reflect what people actually earned rather than what they should have earned if they were employed may tell a different story. But unfortunately the unemployment statistics, which might help resolve this problem, are also subject to disputed interpretation. What data we have come from trade union members only, and those workers most likely to suffer in a recession—the less skilled and those less well provided with trade union organization— are underrepresented in the unemployment statistics.

Thus, while some dispute the severity of the Great Depression, other historians assert that it fully deserves its title. It certainly was regarded as a depression at the time, and a Royal Commission was set up in 1886 to look into its causes. It seems clear that the pace of the economy slowed at this time, and while the living standards of those employed rose, unemployment was certainly severe in some regions and in particular sectors. Agriculture was unquestionably in difficulty. Overall, agricultural rents declined by about 30 percent between 1870 and 1900. On the Duke of Bedford's estate at Thorney rents were reduced in fifteen out of seventeen years between

1879 and 1895, by amounts ranging from 10 percent to a full half year's rent. The industrial sector also suffered. In the north Midlands iron and coal, twin pillars of the Industrial Revolution, were in difficulty. There, in Wolverhampton, Walsall, Dudley, and West Bromwich, much unemployment was masked by the widespread practice of part-time employment, which shared out the available work thinly across the workforce. Few received a viable living wage, but few were completely without some work.

In addition to the problems of adequately assessing un- and under-employment, the calculation of real wages also reopens questions about the adequacy of the price data. The items included in the price index may or may not fairly reflect spending patterns. Gambling, alcohol, and tobacco are rarely properly represented in proportion to the importance of these items in people's lives. Even more important, housing costs, which unlike most prices were steadily rising throughout this period, rarely figure in price indexes.

For all these reasons it is difficult to provide any simple measure of living standards and the purchasing power of sterling, even though there is no shortage of data. Nevertheless, it has been calculated that the minimum weekly expenditure necessary to provide a family of four with a reasonable degree of comfort, including drink, tobacco, and housing, as well as saving for sickness and old age, may have been about 25s. in 1850, 28s. in 1860, 26s. 9d. in 1870, 26s. 9d. in 1880, 23s. 9d. in 1890, and 24s. 9d. in 1900; the bare essentials of food, rent, and fuel could be had for about half these sums. Compared with these outgoings, north Midlands miners' wages varied, from about 4s. a day in the 1860s, 5s. in the early 1870s boom, 3s. at the bottom of the depression, rising to 4s. again by 1889. In contrast, engineering and laboring wages there were extremely stable across the whole period, the former taking 5s. a day and the latter half that.

Nineteenth-century sterling kept and even enhanced its value, but the surveys of Charles Booth in London in 1889 and of Seebohm Rowntree in York a decade later both concluded that as much as 30 percent of these urban populations lived in poverty. At the beginning of the twentieth century, one-fifth of the population would end its days in the workhouse, followed by consignment to a pauper's grave. One-sixth of newborn babies would not live to see their first birthday. Starvation as a direct cause of death was not unknown, and malnutrition as a contributory cause was commonplace.

Immediately before the First World War about one-third of all adult men in full-time employment in Britain earned less than 25s. a week, and so something like 2 million families, perhaps 8 million people, were maintained on that basis. A Fabian Women's Group survey of families in Lambeth living on between 18s. and 26s. a week was published in 1913, and provides much detail about housing costs as well as food budgets. A four-room house—two up, two down—in Lambeth would cost about 10s. or 11s. a week to rent. Slightly grander terraced houses with five or six rooms went for 14s. or 15s. a week. A family with an income of around 20s. a week in Lambeth normally would take a house at around 10s. but sublet one of the rooms. The best room in a Lambeth terrace house, 15 foot by 12, upstairs with two windows, could bring in 4s. a week. Nevertheless, even after subletting, a family on this sort of income would be spending about one-third of it on rent. The arithmetic was significantly different for the better off. A household receiving £500 a year might spend £85 of it on rent and rates, amounting to no more than one-sixth of income, while the more seriously rich on £2,000 per annum could rent a fine South Kensington house for £250 a year, one-eighth of annual income.

Needless to say the life choices of those at the bottom of the scale were severely limited. Those families paying less than 6s. a week rent suffered a sharply increased incidence of infant mortality—a financial as well as personal tragedy against which the poorest regularly insured themselves. Such was the humiliation felt by those reduced to a pauper funeral for their children that most Lambeth working families put aside 6d. or 1s. a week for burial insurance. A child's funeral might cost 30s. and land a grieving family in debt. Those who paid more on rent obviously had less for food, fuel, and the boot and clothing clubs to which so many subscribed another 1s. or so a week. Coal, perhaps a hundredweight a week, cost 1s. 6d. Of course it was cheaper bought by the ton or half ton, but few workers had either the cash to buy in bulk or the space to keep it. The normal diet remained dominated, as it had been for centuries, by bread, with the

4-pound loaf in London costing around 5d. or 6d. Potatoes, the other great staple, at 2 pounds for a penny, were commonly consumed at the rate of about 3 pounds a head per week. Tea, sugar, and canned milk still made up the other most essential items of the diet. Fresh milk at 2d. a pint was a luxury.

Nevertheless, such grim facts should not entirely obscure the achievements of the age. Although the poorest third of the population barely kept their heads above water, more than half of the working class did succeed in making a living. The most fortunate might work for a benevolent employer, such as Cadbury, who was actively concerned with the nutrition of its workers. The works canteen at Bournville in 1905 served 2,000 workers, providing roast meat and two vegetables for 4d.; pork pie at $1^1/_2$d.; bread and soup or egg, sausage, bacon and pudding for 1d.; and tea and cake for $^1/_2$d. Two million middle-class households earned incomes ranging from something under £100 a year up to somewhere between £300 and £1,000 at the very top of the professional middle class. In the upper classes, about 50,000 households received over £1,000 a year. For those at this end of the scale, the Lord Mayor's Banquet catered at £2 2s. per head, while the Carlton and the Café Royal reckoned to feed two in the best style for a similar sum. More modestly, though still exceeding the weekly wage of millions, Simpson's could feed three on salmon, sole, and turbot for 8s. 6d. The best taverns in London, such as the Cheshire Cheese, offered as much steak and kidney pudding as you could eat for 2s. and their best bitter for 5d. a pint. In the City, Mooney's Irish House sold Guinness at 2d. a half pint, with cheese rolls a penny. Then as now, when dining out you could spend almost any amount, but a young middle-class couple eating at home would reckon that £2 10s. would keep them and their maid for a week.

The inflation of the Napoleonic Wars was reasonably, if a little simplistically, associated with the growth of paper money, and as a consequence bankers and legislators devoted much attention in the first half of the century to the problem of controlling the supply of banknotes. The Bank Charter Act of 1844 answered this problem by limiting the fiduciary note issue (unbacked by gold) to £14 million while requiring any further notes issued by the Bank of England to be matched pound for pound by gold in the Bank's reserves. This solution had two principal weaknesses. It failed to recognize that the natural fluctuating growth of the economy created a variable demand for money, so that at times of crisis serious illiquidity problems could blow up suddenly, threatening even the soundest of City institutions. And second, the 1844 act placed too much emphasis on the note issue and its relationship to gold without sufficiently recognizing how far other financial practices, especially the use of bills and bank deposits, were changing the very nature of money.

The amount of coin in circulation almost doubled between 1844 (£36 million) and 1865 (£70 million). At the height of the boom in 1875, it reached £105 million, but further growth was sluggish during the Great Depression, and the figure was no more than £109 million in 1885. However, as the economy picked up, so did the supply of coin. On the eve of the First World War some £145 million of coin was in circulation, consisting chiefly of sovereigns. The sovereign, from 1871 with Pistrucci's George and Dragon design restored, came in the late Victorian and Edwardian era to symbolize the very essence of the gold standard. Sir William Harcourt, Prime Minister William Gladstone's chancellor, spoke for many on the importance of gold when he wrote in 1892:

London . . . is the Metropolis of the Commerce of the World to which all nations resort to settle their business. This I believe . . . to be owing to the soundness of our monetary system, London being the only place where you can always get gold. It is for that reason that all the exchange business of the world is done in London.

World gold production and the numbers of sovereigns in circulation followed a similar pattern, rising very sharply in the 1850s in the wake of the Californian and Australian finds and dipping a little in the 1870s. This slight decline in production coincided with a rise in demand for gold as more and more countries (e.g., France, Germany, Switzerland, Belgium, Holland) opted for a gold standard. The United States also increased demand for gold when it added gold to its silver standard in 1879. Thus in the 1880s there was much serious discussion about the case for a return to a bimetallic standard in

Britain to ease the shortage of gold, and there was also increasing concern for those countries, such as India, that remained on a silver standard and saw the value of their currency dwindling in terms of gold-based currencies. The debate, which occupied the minds of such serious heavyweights as A. J. Balfour, never really captured the public imagination, providing the background to Oscar Wilde's joke, "The chapter on the fall of the rupee you may omit. It is somewhat too sensational." In any event, the problem was eased by the discovery of gold in South Africa, which significantly raised production again toward the end of the century.

For Britain, the strength of its international economic position meant that it usually was able to command increased supplies of gold despite the world position. Moreover, even though sterling was the gold standard currency par excellence and the whole currency was redeemable in gold, in practice an ever greater proportion of the nation's money supply took other forms. While 25 percent of the money supply consisted of coins in 1844, that figure had fallen to 11.5 percent by 1913. Moreover, despite the early Victorian preoccupation with the note issue, the proportion of the money supply consisting of notes consistently fell from 1811 (60 percent) to 1913 (3.5 percent). Throughout the nineteenth century a steadily mounting share of the money supply consisted of money deposited in bank accounts. By 1844 that share amounted to 55 percent, rising by 1913 to 85 percent. This growing importance of bank deposits is illustrated by the observation that during the periodic financial crises of the times, hard-pressed clients often applied to the banks for loans, asserting that they would not need gold, or even banknotes, since their difficulties could be met by the right to draw checks on their bank accounts. In the same way, when the governments of the day reluctantly suspended the provisions of the Bank Charter Act, permitting the Bank to advance beyond the usual restraints, the crises often were resolved without increased note issues.

Moreover, the proportions of the money supply given here for coin, notes, and bank deposits take no account of the amount of business done by bills of exchange. We have seen in earlier chapters how such bills played an important part in inland trade. In the first half of the nineteenth century, somewhere between 40 and 70 percent of the nation's inland trade was conducted by means of bills of exchange. This form of IOU facilitated the payment of debts from one region of the country to another and also provided much-needed short-term credit. However, the role of the inland bill declined over the course of the century, exactly as that of the bank deposit, accessed by check, began to rise. While bills may have accounted for around 30 to 40 percent of business in the middle of the century, that figure had already dwindled to a mere 5 percent by 1875. The banks—above all the rising joint stock banks—were holding an ever larger part of the nation's money and arranging its business by means of checks and bank transfers.

The joint stock banks made huge strides in the second half of the century, largely supplanting the old private banks. Barclays converted to a joint stock bank in 1862, Lloyds in 1865. Toward the end of the century, the process was accentuated by a series of amalgamations; the Barclays of modern times, for example, was really born in 1896, with the amalgamation of twenty private (often Quaker) banks, even though Barclay ancestors may be traced back into the seventeenth century. The new joint stock concerns had a much larger capital at their disposal, making them less vulnerable in bad times and more influential in good. The development of their branch structure also enabled them to transfer cash from regions in surplus to those starved of funds and to settle debts with the minimum of difficulty across the country. From the days of their exclusion from the London Clearing House, the situation was completely reversed. In 1870 there were still thirteen private banks in the London Clearing House; by 1891 that figure was down to five. By 1914 thirteen out of sixteen members of the clearing house were joint stock banks.

While the joint stock banks increasingly took over many of the functions formerly performed by inland bills, the bill of exchange recovered its original essentially international character, in step with the increasingly international character of London's business. The bill of exchange, which had its medieval origins firmly rooted in international trade, had come full circle. Of course, the fully cosmopolitan character of the City was already very clear from the days of Nathan Meyer Rothschild. Many of his greatest coups were based on his trans-European connections. Equally, the rising Barings Bank was early involved in the field of international banking, raising loans for governments across the world. Joshua Bates, the linchpin at Barings in the middle years of the century, was a rather dry and driven American whose knowledge and contacts in the new world were central to an understanding of that burgeoning market. The international role of the firm was so important that Barings itself was referred to as another Great Power. But on top of all this, the increasing internationalism of British trade and finance meant that more than half the world was drawn to do business with or through Britain. As Rothschild himself had put it in the 1830s, "all transactions, in India, in China, in Germany, in Russia, and in the whole world, are all guided here and settled through this country." By 1858 this was more than ever the case, when a Select Committee was told, "The trade of the world could hardly be carried on without the intervention of English credit . . . a man in Boston cannot buy a cargo of tea in Canton without getting a credit from Messrs Matheson or Messrs Baring." In these circumstances there was naturally a huge foreign demand for credit and payment facilities in London. Great London houses such as Barings and Rothschild, from their wealth of foreign experience, were ideally placed to vet the standing of foreign merchants trading through London. By "accepting" the bills of such traders for a commission, the well-known London establishments were able to give currency to the bills of less-known merchants from distant lands.

The sheer scale of international business in London was not without its problems. Although London's role as a center for the world's trade and finance brought great wealth, links with some more financially adventurous parts of the world sometimes could be a source of difficulty. For example, the City panic of 1857 was largely American in origin. English investors provided more than half the capital needs of the U.S. railroad boom, but late in the summer of 1857 it became clear that the railroad craze had developed well beyond the needs of the time. Trollope's 1875 novel *The Way We Live Now* described one such dubious scheme for a South Central Pacific and Mexican railroad to run from Salt Lake City to Vera Cruz. For this fictional scheme, floating the company (i.e., raising cash) was more important than actually trying to lay tracks in Venezuela, but even genuine schemes could flounder if an optimistic prospectus overestimated the true level of demand for a line. As this realization dawned, railroad stocks began to fall, leading to a series of bank failures in Philadelphia and New York. As the news crossed the Atlantic, British banks and bill-brokers moved quickly to dump their U.S. holdings, and the dash for cash soon affected U.S. and non-U.S. bills alike. The bill-brokers in particular, who had been borrowing large sums very short term ("at call"), suddenly were faced with demands for the return of money lent to them, so they turned to the Bank for help. The bank rate rose to 7 and 8 percent in October and to 9 and 10 percent early in November. The U.S. minister in London, George Dallas, reported on November 6 that "All the merchants and manufacturers connected with the American trade are startled and trembling," and their problems had severe repercussions throughout the system. The Bank continued to lend and discount bills in order to help sound businesses through the crisis, and even at these high interest rates there was no shortage of those who had to borrow to try to meet their own commitments. However, the amount of accommodation that the Bank could supply was limited by the terms of the Bank Charter Act. On November 11 the City of Glasgow Bank and the brokers Sandersons (a casualty also in 1847) stopped payment, making it clear to both the Bank and the Chancellor of the Exchequer that the act would have to be suspended once again if a major City collapse was to be avoided. On November 12 the Bank, duly empowered by Downing Street, discounted a further £2 million of bills in a single day.

As in 1847, once the constraints of the act were eased, the heat quickly went out of the crisis and a high proportion of those institutions that had defaulted subsequently managed to pay in full. The leading discount house Overend, Gurney & Co. reported, "there is a much better feeling prevailing and the Bank are giving every proper facility that can be desired." A year later the bank rate was down again to 2.5 percent, but the damage to trade and industry in 1858 was very severe. In the City most observers identified the bill-brokers as the source of the problem. As Lord Overstone (Samuel Jones Loyd) summed it up:

The Bill brokers have been in the habit of holding probably from 15 to 20 Millions of Money *at call!* The whole of this sum they invest in the discount of Bills . . . and in advances upon Goods and Produce—When general pressure arises, and calls for money are made upon them by all their depositors—they have no source from which to meet these calls, except that of rediscounting at the Bank of England. Hence the enormous demands upon the Bank.

Overstone was an outspoken supporter of the rigid enforcement of the Bank Charter Act, but even those more aware of the act's shortcomings probably would not have quarreled with this analysis. The U.S. crisis caused a sudden and severe shortage of funds; the bill-brokers saw the money they had borrowed called in and therefore had recourse to the Bank. Yet the Bank's reserves, which were designed to guarantee the Bank's notes and fund the Bank's own discounting and lending activities, were not sufficient to bear the strain imposed by the bill-brokers.

Nevertheless, lessons had been learned. A system was emerging in which the Bank's lending in normal times was effectively limited by the terms of the 1844 act, but if a real crisis developed the government would reluctantly authorize the Bank to release funds beyond the limits laid down by the act. Such an eventuality usually could be prevented by early use of the Bank rate to control the normal demand for money. Since the Bank acted as long-stop for the whole banking system, other banks followed the rates it set. Generally the banks would not lend below bank rate, as they were aware that they might themselves need to borrow from the Bank at those rates. As the economy heated up and demands for loans and discounts grew, the Bank could raise the interest rate that borrowers had to pay. In normal circumstances the rising bank rate would gradually reduce the demand for loans at the same time as increasing the rewards for lending, and, in addition, higher British interest rates would draw in gold from abroad, helping to boost Bank reserves. As the economy cooled and demand for loans fell, the interest rate could be reduced. The management of the interest rate is a subtle and delicate art that even today has not yet been entirely mastered. The chief difficulty is that interest rate decisions taken by the Bank today can take months to have their full effect, involving a high degree of necessarily uncertain prophecy. In the mid-nineteenth century the Bank was coming to terms with the basic principles of interest rate management and its effects on the Bank's lending and reserves, but there was little appreciation of the full extent of the effects of interest rate changes on the economy at large. The Bank also lacked the long years of experience required for a smooth operation. Thus between 1860 and 1865 the bank rate was altered seventy times, ranging as low as 2 percent and as high as 9. The system was a long way short of perfect.

The Bank was still, of course, acting as a private institution in search of profits, at the same time it was attempting to serve as guardian of the nation's currency. Naturally the Bank was in the habit of regulating its discounting with an eye to the state of its reserves, but the 1857 crisis had shown that the Bank also had to act as reserve for the bill-brokers. As it was widely felt that responsibility for the panic lay with these brokers, the Bank announced in March 1858, as soon as things had settled down once more, that it would no longer provide discounts for the bill-brokers. Rather than relying on the Bank's reserves, in the future they would have to keep adequate reserves of their own.

This led to a brief but damaging tussle between the Bank and the most notable of the bill discounters, the firm of Overend, Gurney & Co. This firm had a long and honorable tradition in the City, going back to the early years of the century when the Quaker, Thomas Richardson, established himself as the first and greatest of bill-brokers. Richardson's links with the Quaker Gurney Bank in East Anglia led to Samuel Gurney setting up in partnership with Richardson in 1807, and Overend, Gurney was established in 1827 on the death of Richardson. Gurney made the firm the greatest discount house in the world, but his death in 1856 came at a critical time. The younger and hotter heads at Overend, Gurney resolved to give the Bank a taste of its own medicine and replied to its decision to refuse facilities to the discount houses by withdrawing £1 million on deposit with the Bank. They quickly returned the notes to the Bank, but the damage was done, and relations between the Bank and Overend, Gurney never recovered.

As early as 1861 the governor of the Bank, Bonamy Dobree, reported concerns that Overend, Gurney "does a rather reckless business and is continually incurring losses," but it was thought the firm's capital and profits were still ample. When the company went public in 1865, such was its reputation that its shares were much sought after. However, the failure of a number of finance companies involved with Overend, Gurney later brought the share price down and led to the withdrawal of much cash by depositors. In May 1866 they turned to the Bank for help, which was declined. The Bank's examination of the books revealed that the company was not solvent, and it emerged that it already was unsound when offered to the public the previous year. Nevertheless, it is possible that, but for the clash with Overend's in 1858, the Bank might have chosen to shore the firm up rather than precipitate the panic that hit Lombard Street on "Black Friday," May 11, 1866, the day after Overend, Gurney closed its doors. If Overend's, an institution ranking alongside the likes of Rothschilds, Barings, and even the Bank itself, could fail, then no one seemed safe. *The Times* reported that even the most respectable banks were besieged by depositors attempting to withdraw their cash. "Even at Lady Downshire's ball," recalled Charlotte de Rothschild, "everybody spoke of the immense City failures." Walter Bagehot warned Gladstone, then Chancellor of the Exchequer, of a "complete collapse of credit in Lombard Street," and a succession of deputations from the City pleaded with the chancellor to allow the Bank to discount and advance funds beyond the limits prescribed by the 1844 act.

For the third time since 1844 the terms of the Bank Charter Act were relaxed, though the Bank, in fact, did not need to exceed its statutory rules. It was enough to restore confidence to know that the Bank could lend to all sound institutions with security able to pay 10 percent interest for their credit. Nevertheless, there can be no doubting the severity of the crisis at its brief peak. In the calm that followed, a number of points became clearer. A simplistic interpretation of the act was now looking increasingly old-fashioned, and the possibility of a suspension of the act, *in extremis,* was more and more assumed. The primary role of the Bank, as the regulator of sterling and champion of the gold standard, was becoming clearer, and its private functions were necessarily taking a backseat. The Bank's own inclination to discount bills or make loans became a secondary consideration, as the bank rate and the reserves assumed their place as the principal monetary tools available for the defense of sterling, though this clash between the Bank's public and private roles was by no means yet fully resolved.

Of course, sterling was securely founded on the government's promise to redeem its notes in gold, and as we have seen gold coins were never more plentifully in circulation than at this time. Nevertheless, the sterling balances accumulating in British and foreign bank accounts actually far outnumbered the amount of gold in circulation, and if the public had suddenly chosen to redeem their notes and bank deposits in gold a very serious crisis would have developed. This was why the Bank had to husband its reserves and raise its bank rate at the first sign of an increased demand for gold. Anyone could, of course, choose to hold their capital in gold, but in doing so they also chose to forgo the interest they might earn. A rise in the bank rate thus increased the cost of choosing to hold gold. As the rate rose more people elected to invest their money, bringing gold into the banks.

A similar mechanism affected the choices of foreigners, but the international flow of gold also was affected by the balance of payments and the convenience of holding sterling at a time when Britain straddled the financial, manufacturing, and trading crossroads of the world. For most of this period the world at large was usually happy enough to hold sterling, but occasionally significant numbers opted instead to convert their sterling holdings to gold and take them home. This might occur, for example, as a consequence of the uncertainty created by war. The Franco-Prussian War, for example, raised the demand for gold on the continent and brought the bank rate quickly up to 6 percent in England. A drain of gold abroad also could occur if sterling became too plentiful, leading to a fall in the sterling exchange rate. If this happened, it could be worth a person's while to convert sterling bills to gold, which retained its value against foreign currencies. But these circumstances would be answered by a rise in the bank rate, for as loans and discounts became more expensive, the supply of sterling would tighten, improving the sterling exchange rate and so reducing the incentive to withdraw gold.

On the whole the system worked well for Britain, so that the Bank was able to maintain the currency with much smaller gold reserves than those held by other countries. The Bank never kept much more than £40 million in gold in its Issue Department, while the Bank of France, for example, reserved about £120 million. Moreover, although the Bank would raise interest rates to draw gold to Britain when necessary, for the most part, especially during the Great Depression, British interest rates were relatively low. These low rates allowed G. J. Goschen, the Chancellor of the Exchequer, to convert some £500 million of British government stock from the 3 percent interest it had paid to 2.5 percent in 1888. Of course, the cheapness of money in Britain at this time needs to be seen in the context of the low and falling prices of the period, but it also helps to explain the huge levels of British investment abroad, where much higher rates were paid. Yet the extent of Britain's financial links abroad also brought complications.

As already noted, the size of the Bank of England reserves was small compared with those of other countries, and extremely so given the size of sterling's international role. Moreover, the Bank also looked small compared with the increasing size and importance of the joint stock banks and of the operations being handled by merchant banks such as Barings and Rothschilds. Thus, it was to Rothschilds that Benjamin Disraeli applied for the cash to buy into the Suez Canal Company in 1875: It provided £4 million almost instantly, making £100,000 on the deal. Barings also raised large sums for foreign governments and share issues, especially in the United States and in South America. One governor of the Bank of England, William Lidderdale, sensed the difficulties the Bank might face if problems arose in a banking sector rapidly expanding beyond the Bank's influence. In 1889 he noted, "our collective liabilities are enormously increased with but a small increase in the central cash reserve of the country." The following year he recorded his concerns more fully:

I don't think anyone who has not sat for two years in the Governor's chair during the last decade can realise fully—the dependence of the English Banking System upon the Bank—the difficulty that this dependence creates in our management. Banking liabilities have enormously increased, not so Bankers' reserves, and this makes our burden much heavier than before and leads to fluctuations in rates quite out of proportion to actual movement of currency.

Lidderdale was right to worry, for trouble was brewing as he wrote. British capital was flowing into Argentina all through the 1880s, and Barings played a major part in directing that flow. The companies in receipt of these investments were not always as thoroughly investigated as they should have been, but the public's appetite for a handsome return and their faith in the recommendation of a firm like Barings usually was enough to sustain the flow of funds. However, when in 1888 Barings floated the Buenos Aires Water Supply and Drainage Company, the issue failed, leaving Barings to pick up a large number of unwanted shares. Political problems added to Barings' difficulties. Treasury official and diarist Edward Hamilton noted in July 1890 that "a revolution has broken out in the Argentine Republic, which borrowed too much—speculated & speculated . . . Barings are said to be up to the neck in Argentina securities . . ."

Well aware of the difficulties facing them, Barings borrowed heavily, and secretly, through the autumn, raising £0.5 million from Martins Bank and £0.75 million from Glyns. But such sums could provide only temporary relief from immediate embarrassments. Barings was due to pay out £1.5 million to the Russian government on November 11 alone. Barings' overall liabilities amounted to about twice the Bank of England's reserves. With Lord Revelstoke (formerly Ned Baring and head of Barings Bank) at his wit's end, and the failure of the City's leading **accepting house** looming, almost every discount house in town was threatened because so many of the bills they dealt in were guaranteed by Barings. The moment had come for Lidderdale, "a model of a calm shrewd bold Scotch man of business," to consult with the chancellor, Goschen.

In a meeting at the Bank on Monday, November 10, Goschen told Lidderdale that the government could not help, while Lidderdale replied that the Bank could do little for Barings unless the government did help the Bank. There the matter stood, but Lidderdale was in fact active behind the scenes. The Bank persuaded the Russian government not to withdraw £1.5 million from Barings at that critical time, and Natty Rothschild persuaded the Bank of France to lend £3 million in gold for the Bank's reserve. Rothschild also made it clear to the government just how serious the situation was. Lord

Salisbury, the prime minister, recalled that Rothschild "thought it [the crisis] would put an end to the commercial habit of transacting all the business of the world by bills on London." Meanwhile Lidderdale invited the much-respected bankers Bertram Currie and Benjamin Buck Greene to prepare an independent and highly confidential report on Barings' long-term solvency for the Bank. Secrecy was essential if panic was to be avoided, for as Hamilton recorded, "Though the City is very uneasy, depressed, & excited, they have not yet got word of the immensity of the storm that is brewing . . ."

The report found that Barings' long-term assets comfortably exceeded its liabilities, but payments worth up to £9 million would fall due in the next few weeks. This information took Lidderdale to Downing Street, where he told the prime minister that, without help, the Bank would have to refuse Barings' bills, which accounted for a huge proportion of the £6 million of bills estimated to be then drawn on London every day. Confronted with the prospect of a financial collapse on such a scale, Salisbury agreed that the government would bear half the cost of the Bank's continuing to take Barings' bills until Saturday afternoon. The Bank, for its part, put up £1 million and began collecting from other banks toward a Barings' guarantee fund. Glyn Mills (Currie's bank) and Rothschild both put up half a million, and the rest of the leading banks joined in. Together the five principal joint stock banks put up £3.25 million, and on Monday the *Financial Times* breathed a sigh of relief with its one-word headline "Saved." By the end of the following week there was £17 million in the kitty. "Evidence indeed," commented the Paris Rothschild, "that the English houses perfectly understood their responsibility and by preventing the catastrophe threatening the house of Baring they are shielding their self interest in as much as the house of Baring just now is the keystone of English commercial credit."

The new firm, Baring Brothers & Co. Ltd., rose from the ashes of the old and eventually the Bank's loan was fully paid off in 1895. It was to be another century before Barings once again faced a major crisis in its affairs. On the whole, given the magnitude of the disaster avoided, it was felt that the banking community had come out of the affair pretty well. The standing of the Bank and Lidderdale's personal reputation were much enhanced, for they had extracted the necessary undertakings from the government, investigated the extent of the problem, and then coordinated the united banks' rescue package. A famous *Punch* cartoon of the day represented the Bank as schoolmaster with the other banks as schoolboys being drilled in their responsibilities. But in truth the collective action of all the banks revealed a good deal of maturity and understanding that the reputation of the City as a whole depended on them all.

However, this happy cooperative spirit born of crisis evaporated as the dangers receded, and despite a good deal of agreement about the diagnosis of the fundamental problem, sharp differences soon arose about the appropriate treatment. At the heart of the matter was the fact that the nation's reserve held by the Bank had not grown in step with the size of the nation's business. Moreover, a very large proportion of the whole world's business was also then being transacted in sterling through bills on London. Cornelius Rozenraad, the London-based foreign banker, observed in 1907 that "bills on England are negotiable everywhere, and transactions between two countries having no direct or no sufficient exchange relations are settled by bills or cheques on London." The Bank's reserve, never much more than £40 million at best, was recognized as an increasingly inadequate foundation for so much business. The Baring collapse had shown clearly that this reserve was dwarfed by the size of London's national and international commitments.

In the same way, the Bank's principal weapon for the defense of the currency, the bank rate, was seen to be dangerously ineffective at times, when the volume of lending offered by the London money market as a whole was so much greater than that offered by the Bank. Goschen warned bankers in the clearest possible terms in 1891 that "it is a false system and a dangerous system to rely significantly upon the aid the Bank of England can give in a crisis." To encourage other banks to keep more adequate reserves themselves, Goschen proposed to require them to publish regular accounts detailing their reserve position. He also floated the idea of a new fiduciary £1 note to replace the sovereigns in circulation, so that this gold could be added to the banking reserves.

Neither proposal found favor with the banks. The size of the reserves kept by the joint stock banks and the Bank of England had a
critical bearing on the competition between them. The banks were
not content to increase their reserves and deposits kept with the
Bank, if the latter used those increased reserves to finance its own
lending, in direct competition with the joint stock banks. For neither
the first nor the last time, the two roles of the Bank, as a private
profit-making concern and as a national central bank, were seen to
be in conflict. Nor were the joint stock bankers sympathetic to the
notion of replacing the gold sovereign with a pound note. The sovereign circulated more plentifully in the currency of these years leading
up to the First World War than any gold coin had ever done before
in Britain. Its ready availability made the gold standard a reality for
all but the poorest members of society, and that availability contributed significantly to the confidence placed in sterling banknotes.
And in addition to the confidence engendered by the metal, and the
pleasure instilled by the beauty of the coin, sovereigns were popular
because people simply had gotten used to them. As Bertram Currie
put it, anonymously, in a letter to *The Times*, "there are few things
upon which mankind are so much the slaves of habit, or so suspicious of change as in regard to the money which they are accustomed to handle in their daily transactions." It is a sentiment as true
today as it was in 1891.

The same conservative instinct in monetary matters put paid to a
renewed burst of bimetallic campaigning later in the decade. In an attempt to economize on gold, it was noticed that the provisions of the
1844 act allowed the Bank to keep up to one-fifth of its reserve in silver. However, the suggestion that the Bank actually should do such a
thing was met with howls of protest. Natty Rothschild felt it necessary to warn A. J. Balfour, who was now in government (1897),
"that an intense feeling has been raised in this city against any concessions being made here in London to the bimetallist party. The
idea that the Bank of England might keep a portion of its reserve in
silver has raised quite a storm of indignation." Part of the problem
that the bimetallists wished to address was that western dependence
on gold had raised the price of gold in silver terms so far as to cause
serious difficulties in India, which operated a silver standard for the

rupee. In short, a silver rupee was losing value because of the high demand for gold. Since financial opinion blocked an extension of the use of silver in the West, a solution to Indian problems was sought by extending the use of gold in the East. Although India was not brought on to the gold standard, the sovereign was introduced there as legal tender in 1898.

Such an extension of gold, and the final collapse of the last of the bimetallic schemes, was accomplished only in the context of sharply increased gold production (above all from the mines of South Africa) and against the background of a significant economic revival that began in the last years of the century. While this growth helped to cut the ground from beneath the feet of the bimetallists' lobby, it did nothing to resolve the problem of the size of the Bank's reserve in relation to the volume of business sterling was required to service and in comparison with the activities of the other banks. Thus while Bank of England deposits had stood still (£38 million in 1879, £43 million in 1899), deposits at the National Provincial Bank alone had outgrown that figure. The London and County Bank also had deposits in excess of the Bank's at the turn of the century, and two or three other joint stock banks were also reaching similar levels. Although the problem of the competitive relationship between the Bank and the banking community at large remained unsolved, there was a broad measure of agreement that the national gold reserve was not adequate and that the joint stock and private banks were handling so much business that they would have to build up reserves of their own rather than depend on the Bank alone to bail them out of difficulties.

Given this general simmering level of concern about the gold reserve and the almost universal conviction that gold was a fundamental element in the global trade and financial system of the age over which Britain presided, it is difficult to avoid the conclusion that gold mines were an important factor in Britain's quarrel with the Boers in South Africa. The question may be put more generally in terms of the whole of the British Empire and the extent to which territorial acquisition was driven by economic motives. The issue is hotly debated, and an alternative school of thought argues that the empire was acquired in a "fit of absence of mind." In some cases economic motives look clearer than others. For example, it seems difficult to separate the annexation of Egypt from the government investment in the Suez Canal, and the much longer history of the British involvement in India clearly grew out of trading origins. Edward Hamilton recorded general opinion on the annexation of Burma in 1885–1886: "The fact is (as I heard someone appositely remark in the railway carriage this afternoon) jingoism is popular so long as it brings profit; and traders confidently expect to make a profit out of the new Burmah." In December 1902 England and Germany together blockaded Venezuela to prevent the repudiation of its debts, extending the concept of national interest to include the protection of private citizens' investments. But there are equally clear examples of a refusal to get involved in support of the investments of British citizens in far-flung corners of the world (such as Argentina) if there were no other British strategic concerns. In each case British decisions emerged from a potent cocktail of political and economic considerations, which contained elements of European rivalry and nationalist pride as well as a rather vague, and not always well-founded, expectation of profit.

As far as sterling itself is concerned, the international role of the British currency was already well established long before the great surge of imperial ambition associated with the later years of Victoria. For most of the twentieth century sterling was much affected by imperial links. After all, at the simplest level, after 1914 sovereigns were struck more often in the empire than in London.

Whatever the underlying causes of the Boer War (1899–1902), there can be no doubt of public support at its outset. This was nowhere more evident than in the City, where news of the war was greeted with enthusiastic displays of patriotism. The reality of the conflict, which proved much tougher than anticipated, did not seriously weaken national feeling, but it did confront the City with war's financial cost. The *Financial Times* headline for October 14, 1899, "Another Dismal Day: Prices Flat on War News and Dear Money," says it all. Bad news depressed the stock market and raised the cost of borrowing. That month, even before the outbreak of hostilities, the Bank rate was raised from $3\frac{1}{2}$ to $4\frac{1}{2}$ percent. As the war dragged on, the government repeatedly turned to the City for funds, beginning with the "Khaki" loan of £30 million early in 1900. Two issues of Exchequer bonds followed, before another major loan of £60 million was raised in Consols in the spring of 1901, with a further £32 million borrowed early in 1902.

However, despite such government borrowing and Stock Exchange nervousness about news from the front, the economy as a whole continued the recovery already evident from the late 1890s. Although British domestic growth averaged little more than 1 percent per annum from 1899 to 1913, the growth of world trade has been calculated at just over 3 percent per annum between 1893 and 1904, rising to over 4 percent per annum from 1905 to 1913, and the profits of the City's merchant banks grew in step with this. The deposits of the leading joint stock banks nearly doubled in the last decade before the First World War. Nor was the Stock Exchange entirely under a Boer cloud. In the early summer of 1901 traders caught enough of America's enthusiasm for railroad shares for London stockbrokers to sell some 150,000 more shares in Northern Pacific Railroad than actually existed.

The industrial production of the United States (and Germany) had rivaled Britain's increasingly seriously from the 1880s. By 1910 Britain had an annual balance-of-payments deficit with the United States of about £50 million a year. But America's growing financial importance, marked by New York participation in four large loans raised for Japan in 1904 and 1905, also posed a challenge to London. The first three loans were split equally between Wall Street and the City, with German involvement added for the last loan. America's financial coming of age also began to disturb Britain's control of the bullion market. The early years of the century saw the development of a special kind of bill of exchange, known as a finance bill, as opposed to a commercial bill. All bills involved credit, but whereas the commercial bill was closely linked with a particular consignment of merchandise, finance bills lost the link with trade. Ever since the Middle Ages, the bill of exchange sometimes was used for credit as distinct from trade, but the use of the finance bill in the first decade of the twentieth century put things on an altogether different scale. By 1913 nearly two out of three bills were finance bills rather than commercial bills. In the autumn of 1906

Americans were borrowing hundreds of millions in sterling in finance bills, which they converted to gold and shipped to the United States. There every sovereign could form the basis of a rapid expansion of bank loans. The Bank of England discriminated against finance bills, but its main line of defense when faced with a foreign drain of gold was the tried and tested expedient: a rise in the Bank rate in October from 4 percent to 6 percent. In addition, the Bank of France sent £2.5 million to London, hoping to prevent the Bank from pushing its rate right up to 7 percent.

These measures did the trick, but such high rates of interest, made necessary to protect sterling and the Bank of England gold reserves, inevitably restricted trade and industry at home. The Bank brought its rate down again as soon as possible, and it was back at 4 percent for most of the following summer, but the autumn of 1907 saw a renewed drain across the Atlantic, this time driven by rumblings on the U.S. stock exchange. As U.S. shares fell in London and New York, the safety of gold looked increasingly attractive. The failure of the Knickerbocker Trust Co. in the United States triggered a major panic. Natty Rothschild reckoned 100,000 shares were sold in a morning in London, and the gold drain to the United States intensified, with New York offering 78s. an ounce compared with the standard English buying price, set by the 1844 act, of 77s 9d. The act also required the Bank to pay sterling notes in sovereigns, which amounted to selling gold at the rate of 77s. 10½d. an ounce. On Tuesday, October 29, 1907, £1.6 million in gold was withdrawn from the Bank in a single day, almost all of it for America.

With New York again outbidding London for gold, the only defense was to raise the price of sterling by raising the bank rate again. It went to 5.5 percent on Thursday and to 6 percent on the following Monday. The Bank asked Rothschild to approach the Bank of France, and £3 million in gold was made available by Tuesday. Still the hemorrhage continued, until, with the Bank's reserve below £18 million, the bank rate was raised on Thursday, November 7, to 7 percent, its highest rate since 1873.

This was the sternest test of the system since the Barings crisis, but it worked. Seven percent, they used to say in the City, would bring gold from the moon, but it certainly turned the flow, drawing £7 million in gold from Germany and more from America and Australia. Yet so high a bank rate was not without cost. W. R. Laesione, a financial journalist and a member of the Stock Exchange, had described even 6 percent as "a war measure in time of peace," and prophesied serious discomfort among commercial borrowers. The very high bank rate raised the serious question of how far the interests of trade and industry were compatible with those of the financial sector. From a banking point of view, it appeared that the use of the bank rate enabled the Bank to regulate the supply of sterling to keep it always in a steady relationship with gold, permitting a genuinely free and open market for gold to operate and guaranteeing the metallic basis of the sterling currency without requiring every pound of bank money to be actually physically represented by gold. However, away from the City, in the real world where goods were made and traded, sharp fluctuations in the cost of borrowing were seriously damaging. Moreover, it was also argued that the whole organization of company funding had more regard to the generation of profits in the City than to the provision of regular funding for sound business. As *The Times* complained in 1909:

in Great Britain money for industrial purposes has to be raised through the independent financier, who looks upon the "industrial" as a means of making promotion money or profit on the Stock Exchange, rather than a steady income, and to him a successful flotation is of more importance than a sound venture.

Whether an industrial concern sought to borrow money at interest or by launching shares on the stock market, it was likely to find the City practice and institutional structures more attuned to the needs of bankers and brokers than to the requirements of the manufacturer. It was a complaint still being made over a century later by writers such as Will Hutton lamenting the lack of an industrial investment bank, or by the Trades Union Congress (TUC) and Confederation of British Industry (CBI) bemoaning the effects of high interest rates and a strong pound in 1998.

In the 1900s a similar clash of interests lay behind the emerging controversy over free trade and tariff reform. Nineteenth-century orthodoxy held that Britain's best interests as a trading nation were well served by the free trade regime, which brought cheap food and raw materials tariff-free into the country and put sterling into the hands of other nations, enabling them to buy British goods and services. The absence of import duties helped make London, Liverpool, and Glasgow preeminent international trading centers and made the sterling bill on London current throughout the world. In the unlikely event that the international trader should find no need for a means of payment in London, he could always be sure of being able to convert his sterling credit into gold. Free trade and the gold standard went hand in hand. However, while the City delighted in the simplicity of mechanisms that brought gold in and out of the country as required with a touch on the bank rate, manufacturers began to complain that other nations protected their industries with tariff barriers, making British goods expensive, while British markets had no protection from competing foreign imports. Those same manufacturers also asked why they should be the ones required to pay high interest charges for money they borrowed, because foreign banks and stock markets chose to take their gold from London, the only free bullion market in the world.

The whole question of the gold reserve also brought the relationship between the Bank and the rest of the banking community to the fore again. The Bank recognized that its national and international responsibilities left it little room to compete with the clearing banks for ordinary banking business, while the clearers also realized that cooperation with the Bank on the question of the gold reserves was essential. The clearing banks did increase their gold reserves, which just about doubled from around £25 million to about £50 million between 1900 and 1913, although their total liabilities (current and deposit accounts) also at least doubled. The Bank's gold reserve, of around £40 million, was also made more effective by various expedients designed to influence the supply of money without going as far as changing the Bank's rate. For example, the Bank might on occasion itself borrow from the joint stock banks, to mop up a surplus of funds. If the clearing banks were able to buy gold on occasion, it would save the Bank having to do so. Equally, if the banks sold gold for export, it would spread the load formerly borne only by the Bank. In 1911 the Clearing Bankers' Committee began to hold quarterly meetings at the Bank of England, symbolizing a new mood of cooperation. In the absence of agreement on more formal schemes for reform, such as the old proposals for the more frequent publication of accounts or the issue of pound notes to replace sovereigns in circulation, the coordination of Bank and clearing bank actions went some way to improve control of total gold reserves.

The government was as keen as anyone to find ways to regulate the money supply without recourse to the bank rate, since the government was an increasingly heavy borrower. Although the heavy borrowing of the Boer War was temporary, spending on the navy rose in response to demands for more Dreadnought battleships. As the government sought to borrow more, the price of Consols fell. Thus the Treasury sold £100 worth of stock for, say, £91, but paid interest on the full £100 worth. The reforming Liberal government, brought to power by a landslide victory in the 1906 general election, had to choose between expensive borrowing and unpopular taxation in order to fund its program. It is a choice that confronts government to this day. A third option, to inflate the currency to finance government expenditure, allowing prices to rise and the exchange value of sterling to fall, was to be discovered under the pressure of two world wars and indulged in a postwar world hungry for social improvement, but such an approach was no more possible for a gold standard Britain than it is for 1990s governments committed to low inflation.

In 1909 the government chose taxation to fund the social expenditure proposed in Prime Minister Lloyd George's "People's Budget." By modern standards the level of social provision and of taxation were extremely meager, but opposition in the City was intense. In financial circles it was widely asserted that death duties, income and super tax would lead to a flight of capital, discouraging investment and ultimately reducing the employment and wages of those the budget was intended to serve. In fact, British investors already had shown a marked preference for foreign investments decades earlier, but the terms in which the debate was now couched would set the tone for the whole of the rest of the century. Reduced to its simplest terms, it involves a balance between the value of men and the value of money. The City explained that this unparalleled assault on property would damage the credit of the nation, but against this view Frank, Earl Russell spoke for "those people who are to be seen homeless every night on the Embankment, . . . who are unemployed up and down the country, . . . who are starving, . . . who are being sweated and unable to compete on fair terms for a livelihood in the labour market of the world." Russell told the House of Lords that "some of us felt that a slight disturbance in the temples of high finance is worth while if something is done to alleviate the lot of those unfortunate people, and to bring stability and enjoyment of life to a larger portion of the population of this country."

Their lordships voted with the City, but subsequent general elections confirmed the will of the people, and the House of Lords eventually bowed to democracy. The fears of the monied classes were exaggerated, and action for the plight of the poor was long overdue. Nevertheless, as the twentieth century unwound, the time would come when arguments from the City about the value of money would have to be listened to more carefully.

7

From Sarajevo to Bretton Woods:
1914 to 1944

... because our rulers are as incompetent as they are mad and wicked, one particular era of a particular kind of civilisation is very nearly over.
—J. M. Keynes, in private correspondence, December 1917

In roughly thirty short years from 1914 to 1945 Britain fought two bitter and costly world wars. The price of victory, both in human and in financial terms, was enormous. The country was brought from a position of unassailable financial strength to the brink of ruin. Sterling, for so long as good as gold and as solid as the Bank of England, was suddenly shown to be vulnerable. After 1918 millions discovered that the country that needed them in war had no use for them in peacetime. Yet by the time the nation emerged from these three troubled decades, a consensus was growing which suggested that sterling's separation from gold could turn out to be a liberation and that the accidental lessons of war finance could be applied in future to improve the material lot of ordinary people.

The century ending in 1914 was a period of very dramatic economic progress especially in Europe. The Edwardian Indian summer, postscript to a Victorian age of prodigious achievement in arts and science, in industry and trade, appears in retrospect as the highwater mark of British international supremacy. Of course there were clouds on the horizon before the thunderclap over Sarajevo: Industrial unrest, suffragettes, and Ulster had all begun to ruffle the Edwardian brow; other industrial nations also had enjoyed growth, and Germany and the United States were already serious rivals. But part of the secret of nineteenth-century success had been the establishment of an international system of free trade with a minimum of tariff barriers for the mutual benefit of trading partners. This shared prosperity had proven to be in the interests of all, and if manufacturing nations had benefited rather more from their inventiveness than the producers of raw materials, from a European point of view that seemed fair enough. This very satisfactory state of affairs prevailing in nineteenth-century Britain seemed very close to the natural order of things, and that which was natural was closely identified with that which was good.

British exports, which had grown fourfold in the first half of the century, grew eight times by value between 1850 and 1913. As well as exporting its own manufactures, in the half century before the First World War Britain also invested hugely abroad. The London capital market alone raised about half the world's total of exported capital, and the City was additionally the theater for the negotiation of a huge proportion of the world's commodity trading, insurance, and shipping. This dominant position in trade and finance made London, and sterling, of paramount international importance. Many of the world's transactions, whether directly involving Britain or not, actually were settled by the transfer of sterling balances from one London-held account to another. As a Royal Commission was told in 1887, "A New York merchant wishing to buy goods in the East is obliged to supply himself with a credit upon England," for "Bills upon London are always in the market; everybody has debts to pay in London, therefore everybody wants bills on London." And confidence in the whole procedure was guaranteed by the knowledge that such sterling balances were, if necessary, fully redeemable in gold bars or sovereigns. As the commission heard, "Great Britain is the only country where there is a real gold standard, the only place where, if a man has a bill for £100, he knows what he has got, and he knows that in all cases he can obtain for his bill for £100 a certain quantity of gold at a certain weight and fineness." When particular international transactions did call for an actual physical transfer, such payment was likely made in sterling. Thus the French indemnity paid to Berlin after the Franco-Prussian War in 1871 was made at least partly in sterling, and 1,000 sovereigns from this payment, still in their original linen bags, spent by Germany in Copenhagen, actually returned to the Bank of England in 1915.

Thus from 1821 until 1914, the gold standard came to represent an important part of the confidence and security of nineteenth-century Britain. The strength of sterling on the gold standard was founded on Britain's massively impressive industrial and trading performance but also contributed to it. Other nations imitated Britain's currency, producing gold currencies of their own and contributing to a sort of de facto currency union that benefited international trade. Of course, as we have already seen, this currency system was not immune to periodic crises. But by 1914 the successful negotiation of a series of financial panics of varying seriousness over almost a century had built up a reservoir of experience and confidence which suggested that although things might get difficult from time to time, and individual banking houses might, if badly managed, go under, the system as a whole was sound. This was the world that had to come to terms with the Austrian ultimatum to Serbia on July 24, 1914.

Paradoxically, the very dominance of Britain's position in the world of international finance was the root cause of the 1914 crisis triggered by the war. Bills of exchange drawn on London financed most of the world's trade, and we have already seen how such bills were accepted and discounted in the City. About £350 million of such bills were under discount in London in the summer of 1914, mostly on foreign accounts. The Bank of England played long-stop for the whole system, so houses that were fundamentally solvent but experiencing some unexpectedly large calls on their liquidity normally could rely on it to help them out in the interests of maintaining the whole interdependent structure. Ultimately, of course, even the vaults of the Bank of England were a finite resource, and the whole system depended on regular remittances of goods, gold, or other securities from the drawers of such bills to their acceptors to enable them to meet maturing bills. Under threat of a major European war, with continental ports and financial markets closed, this flow of resources dried up, leaving the entire interlocking system of London brokers, banks, discounting and accepting houses starved of cash. Saturday, July 25, 1914, saw the worst Stock Exchange falls since 1870, and the discount market seized up. Gaspard Farrer, a leading merchant banker with H. S. Lefevre & Co. and Barings, commented that bill-brokers were unable to find takers for even the best-accepted bills at the most attractive rates. The following week the joint stock banks added to the pressures on the Stock Exchange and the money market by calling in the debts owed to them and withdrawing the gold in their accounts at the Bank of England. Walter Cunliffe, governor of the Bank of England, assured Sir John Bradbury, permanent secretary at the Treasury, that the Bank was still in control on Wednesday, July 29. But ever since the Barings crisis of 1890 there had been some tension between the clearing banks and the Bank of England. The Bank had inceased the size of its reserves to strengthen its position in the event of such crises, but, as managers of a profit-seeking institution in its own right, the directors were loath to leave what in normal times seemed excessively large reserves idle. Equally, the clearing banks were reluctant to enlarge their balances at the Bank, which they increasingly regarded as a competitor. In consequence, the Bank of England's reserves were perhaps not as large as they might have been if it had been less ambivalently established as a central bank. Fortunately, whatever the element of bluff, Cunliffe, who was later described as "a curious character, [who] looked like a farmer, was definitely a bully, and [who] had withal a certain cunning," was the right sort of man to tough it out. Nevertheless, things got a lot worse in the following days.

On July 30 the City figure Smith St. Aubyn reported in his diary, "A very bad day. People are getting really alarmed and are flocking to the Bank of England to change notes for gold. Discount houses have practically ceased business." On that same day the bank rate was increased from 3 to 4 percent, after the Bank had paid out £14 million to the discount market in three days. In the nineteenth century, the Bank had established its willingness, at a price, to bail out the discount houses from time to time. Raising that price—the bank rate—usually had been enough to limit the calls made upon the Bank of England. But the next day, Friday, July 31, the bank rate had to be doubled and the Stock Exchange closed. The clearing banks were paying out sovereigns only with the very greatest reluctance, and long queues were forming at the Bank of England. On Saturday the bank rate hit 10 percent, and on Sunday, August 2, vividly illustrating the frenzied urgency of the situation, John Maynard Keynes dashed from Cambridge to the Treasury in a motorbike sidecar for consultations.

As we shall see, Keynes was to play a major role in the history of sterling, but in 1914 he was no more than a highly able university economist who had worked briefly in the India Office on monetary questions before winning a fellowship at King's College, Cambridge. He was a witness to the emergency measures required that August, which Lloyd George later recalled grandiloquently under the title "How we saved the City." In fact, the measures taken were fairly standard short-term crisis management procedures. As in 1847, 1857, and 1866, the Bank of England requested and received the permission of the Chancellor of the Exchequer to issue more notes than its gold reserve normally would have justified under the 1844 Bank Charter Act. The joint stock bankers also pressed for the suspension of gold payments, but the Bank and the Treasury, which were inclined to blame the joint stock banks for the whole crisis, believed this would be unnecessary. They argued that the issue of more Bank of England notes together with the new Treasury currency notes for £1 and 10s., hurriedly being printed to ease the demand for sovereigns and half sovereigns, should be enough to ease the liquidity crisis without the formal suspension of gold payments. Significantly, the new currency notes, called Bradburys as they bore his signature, did not repeat the traditional Bank of England promise to pay the value of the note in gold, and sovereigns did in fact disappear from circulation in the early years of the war. All this occurred gradually and informally, however, rather than as a result of a dramatic and formal announcement suspending gold. It simply became unpatriotic to demand payment in gold.

The bills of exchange problem was eased by the Postponement of Payments Act. The Bank holiday, which had mercifully fallen on Monday, August 3, and provided much-needed respite, was extended until August 7, to allow time for the printing of the new Treasury notes. The panic was sufficiently defused so that on the reopening of the banks it was possible to cut the bank rate from 10 percent to 6, and again on the next day to take it down to 5 percent. Finally, on August 13 the government agreed to make good any losses incurred by the Bank of England in discounting bills at the bank rate if the bill eventually remained unpaid because of the inability of the drawer to remit the necessary funds in wartime. Although the Stock Exchange did not formally reopen until January

1915, it is fair to say that the financial crisis of 1914 caused by the outbreak of war had been weathered. Paying for the war itself, however, was quite another problem.

In the First World War almost 2.5 million British troops were killed or wounded. Nearly one-tenth of all British men of fighting age perished. What is more, they died in conditions of muddy misery and futile slaughter that largely obscured the heroism of their sacrifice. This was a war that made human life shamefully cheap, but iron and steel and high explosives still proved very expensive. In addition, quite apart from funding the direct costs of the war, the government soon found that, as a consequence of the disruption of international trade, it had to introduce controls and assume powers of requisitioning to ensure that the general population as well as the armed forces could be fed and clothed. Government purchasing soon accounted for 85 percent of imported food, and the controls on imported materials, industrial production, and transport were all-embracing. Before the war government spending had accounted for only 8 percent of national income, but that figure rose to about 50 percent as the government assumed ever greater responsibilities and the entire nation's resources were mobilized for the war.

Curiously, a government that did not hesitate to ask its people to make the supreme sacrifice balked at asking them to pay taxes that even remotely reflected the true financial costs. The balanced budget of 1913–1914 was replaced by a large deficit in 1914–1915, when a very modest rise in income tax fell far short of expenditure, which had more than doubled. In 1915–1916 government income was significantly increased but met only just over a quarter of its soaring expenditure. In the next three years only about one-third of government expenditure was met out of revenue. By 1918–1919 revenue had more than quadrupled since 1913–1914, but expenditure was up twelvefold. The gap between income and spending could be met only by borrowing; thus almost £5.5 billion was added to the national debt over this period. This sum was raised through a mixture of short-, medium-, and long-term loans. The biggest single item was the 1917 5 percent **War Loan** of which £2,067 million were issued, and to which most holders of the earlier 1914 and 1915 War Loan stocks converted. Exchequer and National War **Bonds** and

War Savings Certificates raised most of the rest, but more than £1.4 billion of Treasury bills and Ways and Means Advances were also important.

Huge government borrowing and the emergency measures of August 1914 put apparently unlimited sums of money into the system. It has been estimated that the combined sum of notes and coin in circulation in 1914 amounted to less than £200 million but that by the middle of 1919 it stood at more than £580 million. Yet this inflated note issue was dwarfed by the increase in bank deposits. Total purchasing power in the summer of 1919 stood at £3.15 billion, almost double its level at the end of 1913. Before the war, banknotes payable in gold had limited the growth of the supply of money, and demands for more resources were met only at higher rates of interest. The rising bank rate gradually extinguished the domestic demand for more cash while simultaneously attracting more funds from abroad, to reestablish equilibrium. During the war, however, the Bank of England lent to the government, which spent the money that soon found its way into bank accounts of the government's contractors and other creditors. These swollen accounts encouraged the banks to lend to their customers or to the government by buying Treasury bills or other government securities. The original injection of cash thus not only increased the supply of money but financed further advances several times the size of the original loan. Even the Currency Notes Redemption Account of the Bank of England, set up to back the new currency notes, suffered the same fate, being lent to the government and then plowed back into the banking system where it financed new loans. There was now in practice an unlimited supply of legal tender notes.

We have already seen that in earlier centuries a rise in the money supply was, other things being equal, likely to lead to a rise in prices. This observation, though sometimes disputed, had become increasingly commonplace since the sixteenth century. In the late nineteenth and early twentieth centuries, however, two economists, Irving Fisher in the United States and Alfred Marshall in Cambridge, had begun to refine this general idea into a more precise statement that became known as the quantity theory of money. Fisher's version stated that the money supply (M) times the velocity of circulation

(V) equals the general price level (P) times the number of money transactions (T). Thus, MV = PT. In other words, the price level would depend on the amount of money available, with an allowance for how often that money could be spent (V) and how much business there was in the economy for the money to do (T). If V and T were unchanged, a rise in M would cause a rise in P (**inflation**). Equally a fall in M would lead to a fall in P (**deflation**). Marshall refined this idea by concentrating on cash balances (k), the amount of money people need to keep ready available to spend. This waiting money was the opposite (or inverse) of velocity V, so k = 1/V, and M = kPT. In due course, John Maynard Keynes was to explore the idea of these cash balances more fully, drawing an important distinction between savings and investment. It also proved useful to replace the transactions concept T with a measure of the size of the economy, Y, which corresponds with gross domestic product (GDP). All these ideas form the common heritage of Keynesian and monetarist economics, which together have dominated economic thought throughout the twentieth century. At its simplest, it means that the total amount of money in the economy and how often it changes hands have a direct effect on how much things cost.

The First World War provided a particularly vivid example of a link between money supply and the level of prices: Between 1914 and 1918 both soared. Thus, in the course of the war, bank deposits roughly doubled. A rise in prices was already apparent before the end of 1914, and by the Armistice wholesale and retail prices stood 120 to 130 percent above their prewar levels. In addition, wages during the war had risen faster than prices. Of course, as we have already observed, the measurement of prices and wages is not straightforward, and different indexes calculated on different assumptions, and based on other samples, can produce varied figures. Moreover, the basic "other things being equal" proviso of the quantity theory rarely can have held less true than in an economy undergoing the stresses and strains, the controls and the exigencies, of war. Nevertheless, like the Napoleonic Wars a century earlier, the First World War illustrates particularly clearly the effects of a relaxation of credit, a booming money supply, and a large government deficit.

In ordinary circumstances this combination of factors might be expected to produce a fall in the value of money both at home in the form of rising prices and abroad in the form of a falling exchange rate. At home the value of the pound did indeed fall: By the spring of 1919, the cost of living was double that of 1914, which is another way of saying the pound lost half its purchasing power. The value of the pound abroad can be illustrated by a look at the sterling–dollar exchange rate. The normal prewar gold standard pound stood at $4.86, and there were clear signs of it slipping early in the war. Apart from inflation at home, Britain also had balance-of-payments problems, as its exports were disrupted by the war, while it continued to import military equipment and raw materials for war production. By the spring of 1915 sterling had fallen to $4.79, and in August of that year it hit $4.56. It was at this time that the Chancellor of the Exchequer, Reginald McKenna, told the Cabinet that Britain could not expect both to support its allies financially and to sustain an army of seventy divisions. However, despite the huge financial burdens that Britain attempted to shoulder at this time, it did more or less succeed in managing its exchange rate with the dollar. In 1916 the Treasury contrived to peg the rate at $4.76^{7}/$_{16}$, and though there were many close calls, once the decision had been taken—Cunliffe at the Bank of England had been opposed to the policy—it proved possible to defend this rate.

The problem of defending sterling was all the more difficult since Britain not only had regular foreseeable obligations to meet debts in America and repay loans, but the pound was also vulnerable to irregular runs reflecting the latest gossip about the state of the government and the progress of the war. If the outlook for Britain darkened, holders of sterling were likely to sell pounds for dollars, and if significantly more people were looking to sell pounds than to buy them, the price—that is, the exchange rate—would fall. The Treasury then would buy pounds to shore up the price, but to be able to do so it first had to gather together as much gold or foreign currency as it could, whether by selling British-held securities in America; using gold held in Ottawa; issuing bonds in the United States; or borrowing from U.S. banks, especially J. P. Morgan. Any and all of these expedients were used to raise dollars for Britain that could then be sold for pounds in order to protect the dollar–pound exchange rate. In October 1916 Keynes, who was one of the Treasury officials supporting the pound on a daily basis, reckoned the Treasury was having to find $2 million a day to support the pound. At the end of that year it was costing $5 million a day.

One way or another the pound hung on. New loans brought temporary relief, or a turn of the war in Britain's favor reduced the severity of the runs against sterling for a time, but ultimately only the entry of the Americans into the war eased the financial situation. Even then, the Americans were astonished at the amount of help Britain sought. The United Kingdom was asking for a $1.5 billion loan, and the United States was advancing $300 million. In July 1917 Keynes told the U.S. Secretary of the Treasury:

In short our resources available for payments in America are exhausted. Unless the US Government can meet in full our expenses in America, including exchange, the whole financial fabric of the alliance will collapse. This conclusion will be a matter not of months but of days.

Ultimately it was America that allowed Britain to sustain the exchange rate. Although the circumstances in which this assistance became necessary were hardly normal, this American aid marked a watershed in the relations between the two countries. In a nutshell, in the summer of 1917 the United States succeeded Britain as the world's dominant financial power. It would take the rest of the century for the British to come to terms with that.

In the short term, however, all this seemed like a temporary expedient to see Britain through a particular difficulty, and as the prospect of an end to the war came into view, plans were laid to restore the old familiar prewar financial landscape as soon as possible. The Cunliffe Committee on Currency and Foreign Exchange was established in 1918. As might be expected from a committee chaired by a former governor of the Bank of England, it recognized the evils of almost unlimited wartime monetary expansion and was concerned about the loss of gold overseas. Every ounce spent abroad supporting the exchange rate was one ounce less at home available to guarantee the convertibility of the note issues. The levels of expenditure made necessary by the war, together with the financial expedients to which the government had had recourse, while understandable in the circumstances, should not, the committee felt, be allowed to continue longer than was strictly necessary. Thus the government's borrowing should be reined in and its debts paid off. The note issue should be cut back from year to year, and the parallel issues of the Bank of England and the Treasury should be amalgamated. The overall size of the fiduciary issue should be limited and a gold reserve of £150 million reestablished. All these sound and sober measures would permit a return to the gold standard, the cornerstone of Britain's prewar system. It practically went without saying that the gold foundation of sterling should be at the 1914 rate, with the Bank selling gold at £3 17s. 10^1/$_2$d. per troy ounce (916 parts in a 1,000 pure) and a parity against the dollar of $4.86.

Of course, it was recognized that this could not be achieved overnight, not least because of the considerable support required to hold the pound at its wartime peg of $4.76. But it was assumed that after the war, with government spending, credit, and the note issue cut back, normality might be expected to return. In March 1919, as a first step, official support for the pound was suspended, though in the following month the export of gold without official Bank of England permission had to be prohibited to put some sort of a brake on the loss of gold. Even so, by February 1920 the unsupported pound had sunk to $3.20, so an act was brought in that year formally controlling the export of precious metals. It was obvious that things were very definitely not yet back to normal, but the time limit on this act—it was due to expire at the end of 1925—would in due course assume an importance not then appreciated.

Although the return to gold was identified as one of the targets of government policy even before the end of the war, the immediate postwar mood was not compatible with the sort of stern and sober economic management necessary to reestablish the government finances. The order of the day, especially at election time, was for a land fit for heroes rather than for an austerity package that would confront the public with the economic cost of the war. The victorious allies were worried that the end of wartime spending, combined with massive demobilization, could lead to severe unemployment. With revolution taking hold in Europe, it was no time to tell a battle-hardened workforce that their services were no longer required for peacetime employment. Accordingly, there was no immediate attempt to balance the budget or restrain the burgeoning money supply. The fiduciary note issue peaked in 1919 at £320,600,000. The national debt, a mere £650 million in 1914, stood at £7.435 billion by the spring of 1919. Moreover, the removal of wartime price controls further stoked inflation, and companies eagerly took on staff and invested in new plant to take advantage of the rising prices, in turn pumping up the postwar boom. As a consequence, far from a recession, 1919 saw a wave of optimism, with prices, wages, and employment all rising at unprecedented levels. In the last eight months of 1919, wages and the cost of living both rose 11 percent, and the length of the average working week fell without any reduction in wages. Austen Chamberlain's budget of April 1919 did aim to cut the government's 1919–1920 deficit substantially, but spending proved much more difficult to restrain than expected and the eventual shortfall of £473 million was almost double the original estimate. It was difficult to argue with the feeling that those who had survived the war deserved to enjoy the peace.

That peace of 1919 was, of course, formally enshrined in the Treaty of Versailles. Apart from redrawing the map of central Europe and reallocating a number of erstwhile German colonies to Britain, France, and Belgium, the peace treaty had an important influence on the history of sterling. The settlement of interallied war debts was intricately bound up with the related question of the reparations payments that Germany was to pay to the victors. Britain owed huge sums to the United States but was in turn owed millions by its allies, especially France. France, however, where much of the actual fighting had taken place, was recognized as the most deserving recipient of the reparation payments to be made by Germany. Unfortunately, the sums demanded from Germany were far beyond what it was capable of paying, and any measures subsequently taken to extract payments forcibly, such as the French occupation of the Ruhr, reduced still further the German capacity to pay. In consequence, most of the 1920s were devoted to a series of international, and largely fruitless, negotiations designed to try to unlock the related problems of German and interallied war debts. Most dangerously, the mistakes of Versailles contributed to the sense of German grievance that prepared the way for Adolf Hitler. Additionally, the obstacles placed in the way of a just and rapid settlement of war debts seriously complicated the reconstruction of the international financial system and prolonged the difficulties Britain was to have in trying to stabilize the relationship between the pound and the dollar.

The future of sterling was further affected by the Treaty of Versailles in a small but not insignificant way. Maynard Keynes had attended the negotiations in Paris as a British Treasury official, and his work had convinced him of the inadvisability of attempting to exact payments from Germany that took no account of that country's ability to pay. In June 1919 he finally left the Treasury, and over the next few months he prepared a devastating indictment of the unjust and shortsighted treaty, which he published that autumn as *The Economic Consequences of the Peace*. The book, which contained a number of wickedly telling verbal sketches of the principal protagonists as well as a rigorous and authoritative economic analysis, was a huge and instantaneous success. Its importance for the history of sterling lies in the fame—even notoriety—that it conferred on its author.

John Maynard Keynes (1883–1946) was to become unquestionably the most important individual affecting the history of sterling in the twentieth century. Even after his death, his influence, as an inspiration or bête-noire, has continued to dominate. Though working for the government in both world wars, he otherwise held no major posts beyond a few minor City directorships and his fellowship at King's College, Cambridge. His enormous influence was exercised through his writing and through the advice—both solicited and unsolicited—that he offered to friend and foe by letter, in government committee, or in the press. In person, as Lytton Strachey observed, he could argue with "great incisiveness and vigour . . . His rapidity and dexterity in answering . . . and making his meaning clear were extraordinary." His writing, on the most complex economics, was a model of lucid clarity, readily intelligible to the layman. Even his scholarly magnum opus, *The General Theory of Employment, Interest and Money* (1936), reads beautifully, with the technical apparatus largely relegated to the end of the book. On less technical questions he possessed startling clarity of vision, great descriptive powers, and a ready wit, which on occasion could develop into devastating and withering scorn. He was, in short, a most formidable opponent who had mastered the emerging theoretical basis of his subject when many of those charged with the actual conduct of economic affairs had not. Moreover, he was an accomplished publicist who understood the growing importance of popular opinion and was not afraid to appeal directly to it, over the heads of government.

Keynes's biographers are divided about the extent to which his readiness to go public reduced his private influence at the Bank, the Treasury, or 11 Downing Street, but those who ignored his views must have realized that his powers of invective and analysis, and his ready channels of communication through the press to the general public, were bound to make him a powerful adversary. To the bankers of Europe and America, Keynes may have seemed a brilliant academic, but one wonders if many of them can have thought him sound. Though the homosexual encounters of his youth were no doubt unknown to them, his association with the pacifists and bohemians of Bloomsbury can hardly have lent weight to his theories. Furthermore, as the economic situations with which they were required to deal grew more precarious, orthodox Bank and Treasury men were understandably less and less ready to experiment with new theories that often ran counter to established practice. As Cunliffe put it in 1916, "Mr Keynes ... in commercial circles ... [is] not considered to have any knowledge or experience in practical Exchange or business problems ..." Cunliffe certainly thought he had extracted a government assurance that "Mr Keynes should not meddle again in City matters." Most infuriatingly of all, Keynes had the annoying habit of usually being right, combined with a readiness to change his mind as circumstances changed, which was a liberty more institutional figures rarely enjoyed.

And the circumstances of 1920 did indeed change markedly, the boom of 1919 giving way to a fierce recession. Alarmed by the very high prices and labor shortages of the boom, the bank rate was raised in the autumn of 1919 to 6 percent and in April 1920 to 7 percent, where it stayed for almost a year. This was a rate not to be reached again until 1957. It was certainly too high, too late, and kept for too long, but to some extent it was forced on the government by the pound's very low exchange rate and by the difficulty of finding takers for Treasury bills at lower rates. Interestingly in light of his posthumous reputation, Keynes too had been appalled by the inflation of 1919–1920, which he feared would "strike at the whole basis of contract, of security, and of the capitalist system generally." Inflation redistributed income in a way that many people found thoroughly alarming. This sort of concern about the social effects of inflation was part of the background to the call for measures to claw back excess war profits and to Baldwin's memorable remark (reported by Keynes) that many of his new Conservative colleagues elected in 1918 were "a lot of hard-faced men who look as if they have done very well out of the war." Accordingly, Keynes too called for a "swift and severe dose of dear money" to combat inflation.

The rise in interest rates to reduce the money supply—making borrowing less attractive by making it dearer—would certainly put a brake on the boom. But with hindsight it seems clear that the boom was running out of steam even before the introduction of the 7 percent rate. The Stock Exchange had peaked in March of that year and was 25 percent down by August. The chancellor, Austen Chamberlain, became dimly aware that the measures he had introduced to cut government spending and restrain the boom were coming into effect only in time to deepen the recession. Unemployment, still only a modest 4 percent in October 1920, was over 15 percent the following spring, when the Bank rate was belatedly cut. Unemployment continued to rise to the end of 1921, despite a further rate cut in November. By the middle of 1922 the Bank rate was down to 3 percent. Prices, and even wages—traditionally slower to move—were dropping like stones, down below the 1919 levels and well on the way to the 1914 figures. A very similar picture in France, a boom and slump of extremely severe proportions from 1919 to 1921, suggests that national governments were wrestling with international conditions. However, in these circumstances, increased taxation and government spending cuts bringing the budget into a surplus of almost £240 million in 1920–1921, compares with the £1.690 billion deficit of 1918–1919, came as a body blow to the British economy. Unemployment among trade union members rose from 1.4 percent to 16.7 percent within a year and for the rest of the decade never fell below 9 percent.

For many, confronted with the extreme fluctuations of the years 1919 to 1921, the rock-solid certainties of the prewar gold standard looked ever more attractive. There was widespread agreement: A return to gold was enshrined in the program of reconstruction outlined by the Cunliffe committee and endorsed by subsequent governments, whether National, Conservative, or Labour. For the most part, it was not so much a question of whether the pound should return to the gold standard but *when*. And the question of the appropriate valuation or parity for the pound on gold was even less discussed: For most people the only possible rate was that of 1914, which is to say £1 to $4.86. It is not entirely facetious to suggest that Britain's return to the gold standard in 1925 was much more thoroughly discussed after the event than before it.

Cunliffe and Montagu Norman, his successor as governor of the Bank of England, saw gold as the only possible guarantee for sterling. This was a reasonable point of view for the time, but the assumption that gold, sterling, and the dollar should all return to 1914 values was rather less reasonable. Keynes, Cunliffe's old adversary, saw that the prewar pound–dollar parity would overvalue sterling by about 10 percent. Moreover, if the pound was to be worth as much in 1925 as in 1914, domestic prices and wages would have to fall too. Keynes realized that such a process was likely to be economically, socially, and politically damaging. Winston Churchill, Chancellor of the Exchequer in 1925, was well aware of these arguments and genuinely concerned about them, but ultimately, with the technical experts so divided, the decision was largely forced on him by the weight of political and financial expectation that had built up. So on April 28, 1925, as part of his budget speech, Churchill brought Britain back onto the gold standard. It was a decision he quickly regretted and, years later, still regarded as the biggest mistake of his life.

Under the gold standard of 1925, however, notes were not to be payable in gold coin but in large gold bars at £3 17s. 10½d. an ounce, so there was no reprieve for the prewar sovereign. This world-famous coin had disappeared from circulation in 1915. Throughout the war its use was discouraged, and asking for it was widely regarded as unpatriotic. Moreover, the gold backing reintroduced in

1925 was not a reality for the man in the street unless he wanted to spend over £1,500 on a 400-ounce bar. This limitation of the actual role of gold in ordinary people's lives, which was an idea going back to Ricardo over a century earlier, was actually quite a large national psychological stepping-stone. It came very shortly after the reduction in the silver content of the coinage in 1920, when the ancient sterling silver standard was replaced by coins of only 50 percent silver. This change was made necessary because wartime inflation had made the silver in an old halfcrown (2s. 6d. = 12$\frac{1}{2}$p.) worth 3s. 4d. Of course, the direct link between the face value of the silver coinage and its intrinsic content had been broken in 1816, but the abolition of the sterling standard did mark a break with the past as did the disappearance of the sovereign. With or without the gold standard, the money in use in Britain now consisted of paper, bronze, or debased silver. Whatever the illusions of precious metal, and as we have seen it was never an immutable standard, its passing meant that the value of people's money no longer lay at all in their own hands; it was now at the mercy of more, or less, competent and more, or less, well-intentioned governments and international financiers.

From 1928, when the Treasury and Bank of England note issues were finally amalgamated, new, and actually very beautiful, £1 and 10s. notes were produced. A limited fiduciary issue of £260 million was authorized, though the small print of the act actually provided a good deal more flexibility than under the old Bank Charter Act of 1844. It speaks volumes for the reputation of the Bank of England, now rehousing itself in a massively towering fortress of modern design on its old Threadneedle Street site, that paper bearing its promise to pay so easily replaced precious metal for daily use.

The establishment of this modified gold standard went off calmly. The dollar credits negotiated by Montagu Norman in readiness for some expected exchange turbulence were not required, since the markets generally had anticipated and welcomed the move. There was a widespread belief that it would bring the stability which international trade required and that longer-term benefits would accrue. International confidence in the wisdom of the return to gold can be gauged by the scramble to follow suit by France in 1926, Italy in 1927, Norway in 1928, and Portugal in 1929. Almost all the countries on gold before 1914 were back on it before 1930. Annual growth in Britain's GDP from 1925 to 1926 was a respectable 2 percent. And once the step had been taken, even the opponents of the move did not call for its reversal. So irrevocable did it all seem that when the National government of 1931 did eventually devalue and abandon gold, its Labour Cabinet predecessors complained that no one had told them you could do that.

In 1925 Keynes too thought the matter settled, but he rapidly and eloquently stated his objections to the return to the gold standard in a series of articles published in the Beaverbrook paper the *Evening Standard*. Dawson, the editor of *The Times,* had found them "extraordinarily clever and very amusing" but too embarrassing to print; in establishment circles, "clever" is never a recommendation. The *Standard* articles were then quickly republished by Keynes's Bloomsbury friends the Woolfs in a Hogarth Press pamphlet entitled *The Economic Consequences of Mr Churchill.* Keynes warned prophetically that the gold standard would not be painless, for "Deflation does not reduce wages automatically. It reduces them by causing unemployment," at a time, moreover, when a million men were already without work. More specifically, Keynes wrote that "Like other victims of economic transition in past times, the miners are to be offered the choice between starvation and submission." In fact, the miners chose both: The general strike broke out on May 3, 1926; the miners stayed out until November 12 and then went back to longer working hours and a pay cut.

Churchill took a fairly glum view, writing in 1927:

We have assumed since the war, largely under the guidance of the Bank of England, a policy of deflation, debt repayment, high taxation, large sinking funds and Gold Standard. This has raised our credit, restored our exchange and lowered the cost of living. On the other hand it has produced bad trade, hard times, an immense increase in unemployment involving costly and unwise remedial measures, attempts to reduce wages in conformity with the cost of living and so increase the competitive power, fierce labour disputes arising therefrom, with expense to the State and community measured by hundreds of millions . . .

Keynes's forecast of the uncompetitiveness of British industry at the $4.86 exchange rate was also borne out by events. From 1925 to

1930 Britain's current account surplus was no longer sufficient to fund its traditional levels of investment overseas, which now pushed the country into an overall deficit. Moreover, the outer **sterling area** countries, many of whose staples (wool, wheat, sugar) were anyway faced with oversupply and dwindling demand, found the high value of the pound an additional obstacle to their exports. The trading deficits of these independent sterling area countries thus added to United Kingdom sterling problems.

This deteriorating trading position soon affected the exchanges. In 1926 the pound had remained strong, partly because of a high bank rate and partly because French bankers had preferred sterling to a franc in the hands of socialists. However, from 1927 onward the pound required increasing support, not least as the New York Stock Exchange boom sucked in funds from Europe that had to be converted to dollars. To protect the pound, the bank rate had reached 6.5 percent by September 1929. Such high interest rates, with unemployment already over a million, were seriously damaging to the economy as a whole. Nor did the Treasury much like them, as it struggled with the cost of government debt. Debt service charges, which had run at 11 percent of government spending in 1913 and 24 percent in 1920, hit 40 percent in 1930. The Wall Street crash of October 1929 stemmed the flow of **hot money** into New York. As soon as investors were no longer selling pounds to buy dollars to invest in Wall Street, the Bank of England no longer had to support the sterling exchange rate. Indeed, far from having to sell gold to buy sterling, the Bank was able to replenish its gold reserves and to cut the bank rate, which by May 1930 was down to 3 percent. However, unemployment jumped to over 2 million that summer, as the effects of the stock market collapse reverberated around the world. This was the situation faced by the Labour government elected in 1929 to do something for the unemployed.

In the best Whitehall and Westminster tradition, this appalling situation, which Ramsay MacDonald described vividly but without exaggeration as an "economic blizzard," was referred to a committee. The Macmillan Committee was set up in November 1929, and most of the leading British economic and financial experts of the day either sat on it or gave evidence to it. Perhaps significantly, Montagu

Norman gave a curiously lackluster performance. Though he was to remain as governor at the Bank of England until 1944, in 1931, because of ill health and the stress of the situation, he was near the end of his tether. The relief that the Wall Street crash had brought the pound late in 1929 proved to be short-lived. A large part of the problem was that though the crash reduced the demand for dollars to play the markets, it turned out to be so severe that it triggered a major crisis in world trade, which hit sterling particularly hard. The decline in shipping and financial services, together with low interest rates that reduced Britain's income from its overseas investments, dramatically reduced the contribution of invisibles to the balance of payments. The eventual current account deficit in the balance of payments for 1931 was to be a record £114 million. Already by the second half of 1930 the pound again needed to be supported in Paris and New York. Though the possibility of devaluation was studiously avoided, in the winter of 1930–1931 Philip Snowden, as chancellor, was warning the Cabinet that the gold and foreign currency reserves were under mounting pressure, and there were early signs of speculation against the pound. Unemployment reached 22 percent of the insured labor force.

Everything came to head in July 1931, when two major European banks in Germany and Austria collapsed. Sterling assets abroad were frozen in a major European liquidity crisis. At the same time, the Macmillan Committee report appeared, arguing that a devaluation of sterling would damage confidence and that, in any case, even a 10 percent devaluation would hardly do enough to boost exports or dent unemployment. In addition, the report revealed the extent of Britain's short-term indebtedness, which hit the pound further. In the last half of July the Bank of England spent heavily buying pounds to support the exchange rate and raised the bank rate a full point, to $3\frac{1}{2}$ percent on July 23 and to $4\frac{1}{2}$ percent one week later. European bankers were particularly worried about budget deficits, which had begun the German inflation and also caused serious exchange depreciation of the franc. Americans, on the other hand, wanted the Bank of England to spend its gold more freely to support the pound, though this would require a larger fiduciary banknote issue, since once gold was spent buying pounds it would not be available in the reserve to back the note issue. But any such increase in the unsupported portion of the note issue immediately rang European alarm bells. From the middle of July the Bank of England spent £200 million of its own and borrowed reserves in two months trying to defend the pound.

The political crisis over the budget deficit (£23 million for 1930–1931) was brought to a head by the report of the May Committee, which estimated the likely deficit for April 1932 at £120 million, later revised to £170 million. To meet this deficit the report called for tax increases of some £24 million and cuts in spending of £97 million. Of the spending cuts, £67 million was to fall on unemployment benefits, where spending was to be reduced by 20 percent. Even before the proposed cuts the weekly benefit for a family of four was already aimed at the very barest subsistence level of about 30s. Of course, so clear a statement of the budget problem only damaged the pound further, especially since it was widely recognized that such cuts as might prove acceptable, with reluctance, to a Labour cabinet would be most unlikely to be enough to satisfy the financial markets. Ernest Harvey, deputizing for Norman, frankly told Snowden, the Labour chancellor, on August 6 that "the sign which foreigners [in Paris and New York] expect from this country is the readjustment of the budgetary position." Norman believed he had only to frighten MacDonald and Snowden enough to make the cuts for gold to be saved, but on August 23 the Labour government resigned. The Cabinet was unable to reach agreement and knew that the Labour party in the House of Commons would not vote for cuts, while the Liberals and Conservatives would not allow tax increases. Ramsay MacDonald formed a National government, an act of treachery still remembered with a kind of macabre fascination by Labour historians, and his new Cabinet announced proposed cuts to Parliament on September 10. Keynes described the proposals as "the most wrong and foolish things which Parliament has deliberately perpetrated in my lifetime." For a moment the exchanges appeared to steady a little, although they still required support, but exaggerated reports of a naval "mutiny" at Invergordon over pay cuts triggeed a renewed hemorrhage from the reserves and a fall on the Stock Exchange. On September 18 and 19 almost £30 million was spent supporting the traditional exchange rate of $4.86, and the next day Britain came off the gold standard, never to return. Sterling fell immediately to $3.94, and lost another 50 cents in the following months. Montagu Norman, who was returning from Canada at the time of the devaluation on an Atlantic steamer, received the news from his deputy, Harvey, in an obliquely worded radiogram: "Sorry we have to go off without you and cannot wait to see you before doing so." Appropriately enough, Norman failed to understand it.

The great majority of the population no doubt failed to understand it either. Snowden performed the usual acrobatics required of every devaluing chancellor, explaining how the devaluation, which had been an unthinkable catastrophe a few days before, was now all for the best in the circumstances and would not make any difference to the money in the shops and pubs of Britain.

For most ordinary purposes, the money did continue to function very much as before. Domestic prices, the measure of the value of the pound at home, did not rise after the 1931 devaluation, but what could a pound buy in the 1920s and 1930s? For Virginia Woolf, *A Room of One's Own* (1929) and £500 a year provided the independence and security that any woman would require, if she were to be able to write. But in 1934 the average gross earnings of a miner in Britain lucky enough to be in work was £115 11s. 6d. Of course, the middle-class intelligentsia of Bloomsbury were accustomed to living rather well. The lady author Woolf described used one of her new 1928 10s. notes to pay 5s. 9d. for lunch in a small restaurant near the British Museum.

Curiously, that very sum, 5s. 9d., was identified by dietitians at the time as the minimum sum required for adult subsistence for one week. It was a matter of some debate, as George Orwell describes in *The Road to Wigan Pier* (1937), for such calculations informed decisions about the level of the dole. An unemployed adult man received 17s. per week when first out of work, 15s. when his insurance stamps were exhausted, then 12s. 6d. on the PAC (Public Assistance Committee). A typical family of four would get about 33s., of which a quarter went on rent. An old-age pensioner received 10s. a week. If there were 2 million people drawing dole, that suggests at least 6 million were living on it. Moreover, full-time wages were often little better: In the cotton mills in Preston, for example, a survey revealed only 640 people earning over 30s. a week while 3,113 earned less. In consequence, Orwell suggested, somewhere between 10 and 20 million British people were underfed.

As an indication of retail food prices in the 1930s, you could buy three wholemeal loaves for 1s., a pound of cheese for 7d. An unemployed man's family typically spent 1s. a week on tea, which Orwell called the Englishman's opium, and 1s. 9d. on about eight pounds of sugar; dentists in working-class areas found it unusual for people over thirty to have any of their own teeth left. An occasional bag of chips and access to a radio were "luxuries" to which even the poorest aspired, and for which, if necessary, they would sacrifice "essentials."

As we have already seen in earlier centuries, small details of this sort not only bring a touch of reality to impersonal price index numbers, they also serve to remind us of the essential difficulty of any price index: that is, that the basket of goods devised to represent the cost of living is often very far away from many people's actual purchases, and the calculation of a single cost-of-living index cannot hope to give a true reflection of the impact of changing prices and wages on the lives of either Virginia Woolf or an unemployed miner. Nevertheless, it is still worth looking at the price index between the wars. Prices for 1914 more than doubled by 1918; prices thereafter peaked in 1920, fell sharply in 1921 and 1922, picked up a little until 1925, and then fell steadily to 1932. The average price level throughout the 1930s was very close to that of 1914 and very significantly below the prices of the 1920s. To that extent, the juxtaposition of Woolf's middle-class 1920s prices with Orwell's working-class world of the 1930s is a little unfair, but it makes the important point that any price index looks very different from the top or the bottom of the social scale. Yet whatever the inadequacies of the huge generalizations of which any price index is composed, and however different indexes may vary from one another, the movement of prices summarized in this way still provides our only measure of the fluctuating value of money.

These low prices, combined with the stubbornly high unemployment figures, express the statistical essence of the Great Depression of the 1930s. Official unemployment peaked in August 1932 at 23 percent of the insured workforce and stood at over 20 percent for two full years. Including uninsured groups (agricultural workers, domestic servants, the self-employed), the total number unemployed has been estimated at its peak at 3,750,000. The real meaning of these figures in terms of human misery is difficult to grasp. Yet the reality of that depression was more vividly expressed by the Jarrow march, or by the visit of Edward VIII to South Wales with his acknowledgment that "something must be done," or by Keynes's observation that every five shillings saved put another man out of work for a day. For the long term, mass unemployment, the dole, and its attendant means test scarred the British social and political landscape for the next fifty years.

Yet despite, or perhaps because of, the clarity of this lasting impression, other views have emerged, pointing out that in America, or in Germany where 4 million had been out of work, things had been worse. Indexes of industrial manufacturing levels (1913 = 100) show that while production in the United States fell from 113 to 58 between 1929 and 1932, and the fall in Germany over the same period was from 108 to 65, in Britain it fell only from 110 to 90. And there were also some British signs of 1930s recovery, or rather renewal, since most of the new growth came in developing sectors—housing, motor vehicles, and electrical goods—which made good at least some of the ground lost by the old giants—coal, iron and steel, shipbuilding. Fords built a plant at Dagenham for 15,000 new workers. Hoover built a factory on the western road into London, the architecture of which still expresses all that was most optimistic in the age. Could it be that however grim and bitter the memories of the 1930s may be, the involuntary devaluation of 1931 and the fall from grace represented by going off gold actually made for a significant improvement in Britain's economic performance between 1931 and 1939?

Improvement there certainly was: Britain's GDP grew steadily through the 1930s, with manufacturing production rising 50 percent from 1932 to 1937. This period has been described as "a sustained cyclical upswing marked by a growth of manufacturing production unparalleled in Britain's twentieth century experience." The balance of payments, which had contributed so significantly to the 1931 sterling crisis, did improve dramatically thereafter. Deficits on the current account were reduced by 50 percent from 1931 to 1932 and by 75 percent the following year; in 1935 a surplus was achieved. Of course, import tariffs played a part in this, but, thanks to the weaker pound, Britain's exports were cheaper abroad, allowing the decline in United Kingdom exports to be checked, if not reversed. Devaluation also made imports dearer, reducing the import totals in the balance of payments and stimulating domestic industry to supply the home market more energetically. It has been calculated that every 1 percent rise in the price of imports led to a 2.2 percent rise in the demand for British goods. Yet the advantages of devaluation did not last forever. Initially, in the autumn of 1931, the pound fell by more than a dollar from its traditional $4.86, but many other countries, including most of the empire, devalued with sterling, so the *effective* exchange rate, allowing for what countries Britain actually was trading with and in what proportions, was down only 13 percent. Even that did not last, for America too came off gold in 1933, the dollar stabilizing in early 1934 at $35 an ounce, only 59 percent of its earlier value. Thereafter, the pound and the dollar were more or less back where they started; only continental Europe remained for the time on gold, with France, for example, not devaluing until September 1936.

Even more important than tariffs or the reduced international value of sterling was the liberating effect on government policy of no longer having to try to defend the pound at an unrealistic valuation. In fact, the Exchange Equalization Account, set up to prevent destabilizing fluctuations, was more often active in the market selling sterling, to keep its price down, rather than buying it. That meant that from early in 1932 interest rates too could come down, in stages, eventually reaching 2 percent. The stimulating effects of cheap money for the domestic economy were soon evident. As interest rates fell, shares rose, doubling in value between 1932 and 1936. The housing market responded too from 1932 to 1939, with a notable boom in buildings of instantly recognizable style, still visible in towns and villages all over the country. In the 1930s a new three-bedroom house in London's suburbs could be had for about £750 and much more cheaply outside the capital. At the height of the boom, about 360,000 new homes were being built nationally. However undeservedly, even the Treasury began to benefit from low interest rates, which lowered the cost of government debt. It was possible to convert the old 5 percent War Loan to 3.5 percent. Devaluations and tariffs soon lose their power, most notably when rival economies follow suit, but the freedom to set interest rates with an eye to the needs of the domestic economy, rather than according to the dictates of the foreign exchanges, did confer more lasting benefit. Nevertheless, the improvement of the mid-1930s had a distinctly southeastern feel to it, for the old industries of Wales and the north, where the depression always had been worst, enjoyed very little relief. Of course, any national movement of economic indicators will necessarily contain countermovements within it, but despite a marked upturn, unemployment remained stubbornly over 1 million. Indeed the sharp recession of 1938, when industrial activity in Britain fell more than 10 percent, emphasized the fragility of the mid-1930s recovery. For the poor souls on the dole and their hungry dependents, no really fundamental and lasting improvement occurred before the huge economic stimulus provided by the Second World War.

Despite the value of Keynesian insights, it was really only the coming of war which ended the depression. Rearmament and recruitment into the armed forces were to replace the dole and the means test. By the middle of 1940 unemployment was down to 600,000 and was still falling. Soon it was labor rather than work that became scarce, and, as in the first war, the labor shortage brought millions of women into the labor force for the first time. By the end of 1943 over one-fifth of the United Kingdom workforce was enlisted in the armed forces and a further third was directly involved in war production. The hunger marchers who had begged for work now had plenty, but such a major shift in manpower resources was not without its problems. This time, however, the lessons of 1914 to 1921 provided a stark warning about the consequences of a wartime boom, and the chief concerns from an early stage were inflation (i.e., the strength of the pound at home) and the exchange rate (the measure of the pound abroad).

On the home front, the authorities were very quick to recognize the importance of the cost of living and were ready to subsidize the cost of key items in the index. As we have seen, the precise composition of the index—that is, the statistical weighting given to the different items of typical expenditure—could make a significant difference. However, the index in use in 1940 was the same as that used in the First World War, which in turn was based on a consumption survey of 1904. It was still assumed, reasonably enough, that some 60 percent of working-class income was spent on food, but some items, such as electricity, were completely omitted. To keep the cost-of-living index down, subsidies were targeted at the most heavily weighted items, while luxuries, especially if they were lightly weighted, such as tobacco and alcohol, were more heavily taxed. This policy was extremely successful: Although the wholesale price index (1939 = 100) rose to 140 by 1940 and to 174 by 1945, the cost-of-living index rose only to 121 by 1940 and only to 132 by the end of the war. In 1940, £72 million was spent subsidizing food, rising to £250 million in 1945; the full cost of wartime food subsidies exceeded £1 billion.

Yet it would be a mistake to think that the British wartime consumer was cosseted. In the Second World War government was much quicker to confront the people with taxation reflecting the financial cost of the war. Less than a month after the German invasion of Poland, Sir John Simon, Chancellor of the Exchequer, raised income tax from 5s. 6d. to 7s. in the pound (35 percent) and increased the surtax on the rich. Nevertheless, Keynes called the sums raised chicken-feed in relation to what was required, and already before the end of 1939 he urged a more radical approach in his *How to Pay for the War*. Keynes was asking what level of spending the whole nation, rather than the government, could afford. The following April British expenditure was running at £40 million a week, but *The Economist* carried an article that month showing it was still well below the level of war spending in Germany. Simon raised income tax again to 7s. 6d. and introduced the purchase tax. In July 1940 the bill reached £57 million a week; by August 1940 Britain was buying 3,000 aircraft a month from the United States. Careful calculations of the kind of war the taxpayer could bear, and of how long sterling reserves might hold out, were cast aside as it became clear that husbanding resources for a three-year phony war of modest proportions looked likely to result in defeat in a matter of months. The disastrous course of the war in 1940 was driving the government to accept Keynesian solutions to problems that were rapidly getting out of hand.

Keynes arrived as an advisor at the Treasury in June 1940, soon after Dunkirk, and his influence was quickly writ large in Sir Kingsley Wood's April 1941 budget. The essence of the Keynesian approach was to move toward a system of national accounting. Keynes was attempting to mobilize the resources of the whole country rather than trying to balance the income and expenditure of government alone. The national accounts showed that the greater levels of expenditure required were affordable, if a larger portion of national wealth was entrusted to government, either through tax payments or through saving. Unfunded government expenditure, paid for only by printing money, caused inflation, and the extent to which expenditure exceeded the sum of tax and personal savings lent to government constituted the "inflationary gap." An increase in tax and personal savings that could bridge the gap would prevent inflation. Accordingly, in the 1941 budget income tax was raised to 10s. in the pound, but the cost of living was stabilized.

About half of all government spending still had to be covered by borrowing from the nation's savings, and in this the wartime regime was extraordinarily successful. The National Savings Movement mobilized small savings through National Savings Certificates, Defence Bonds, and the Post Office Savings Bank, while the clearing banks funneled idle bank balances into the war effort through Ways and Means Advances, Treasury bills, and the slightly longer-term Treasury Deposit Receipts paying fractionally more interest. On the whole, however, money remained cheap and the war was essentially funded at 3 percent. Over the period 1939 to 1945 some £14,800 million was raised through government borrowing; in all only £770 million of increased government spending was left to be printed in increased fiduciary banknote issues.

In this way the war was funded without serious inflation: The internal domestic value of the pound sterling only fell by some 30 percent between 1939 and 1945. Different arrangements were needed to safeguard the international position of sterling. The pound was set at $4.03 for the duration of the war, but the resources available to keep it there were tiny compared with the demands that were to be made upon it. An Exchange Equalization Account had been established in 1932 and in September 1939 held £525 million in foreign assets. In addition there was about another £250 million in foreign securities held by British individuals. The plan, as before, was to convert these assets to dollars, which then could be spent buying pounds to shore up the price of sterling on the exchanges. The earliest estimates suggested the government might hope to manage like this for about three years, but the critical military situation in 1940 brought things to a head much sooner.

Quite apart from the course of the war, the underlying balance-of-payments situation was much less healthy in 1939 than it had been in 1914. That situation deteriorated further as resources—materials and (wo)manpower—were diverted from exports to the manufacture of munitions and domestic needs. In 1939, 9.5 percent of the workforce had been producing exports; by 1945, that figure was down to 2 percent. Over the war as a whole Britain incurred debts of £16.9 billion, which were met by exported goods and services worth £6.9 billion, sales of capital worth £1.2 billion, grants chiefly from America and Canada worth £5.4 billion, and running up debts to other patient and understanding countries, especially India and Egypt, to the tune of £3.5 billion. These debts usually were referred to as **sterling balances**, being money owed by Britain that was not paid over, but frozen in sterling accounts for settlement at some stage after the war. India and the Middle East, with a standard of living well below that of even wartime Britain, agreed to provide goods and services in exchange for indefinitely postponed payment. The Canadian contribution, in gifts, aid, goods, and services, was even more heroic and, as a proportion of its available resources, rivaled the generosity of the United States. The American contribution, despite various gifts and accommodations early in the war, was dominated from December 1940 (a full year before the United States entered the war as a belligerent) by the Lend-Lease scheme.

Lend-Lease is a very misleading name, for there was no question of any payment or of the return of the materials lent. Goods and services needed by Britain, and available in the United States, were supplied free. The United States sent $27 billion to Britain in this way, receiving $6 billion back from the United Kingdom in reverse Lend-Lease goods and services. It was an arrangement that was hugely beneficial to Britain, without which the war could not have been fought. Although it took a couple of years for the supplies really to come on stream, merely the existence of the deal on paper provided a massive financial guarantee for Britain's rather precarious wartime finances; it solved the dollar exchange problem and so took the pressure off sterling. The importance of Lend-Lease was to be vividly illustrated by the near-devastating effect of its precipitate withdrawal in August 1945.

The deal, however, was not totally without strings. When the Lend-Lease agreement was finally drawn up, Article VII included a reference to "the elimination of all forms of discriminatory treatment in international commerce and the reduction of tariffs and other trade barriers." President Franklin Roosevelt privately assured Prime Minister Churchill that this meant an agreement to work toward a bold new international economic order, not a simple ditching of Imperial Preference, the system of tariffs that safeguarded Britain's trading relationships with the empire. On the basis of this assurance, and because in reality it never really had much choice, Britain signed the agreement. This undertaking was to be the origin of a series of long and difficult meetings trying to hammer out the sort of arrangements that should govern postwar international finance. The negotiations, which reached their climax at Bretton Woods, New Hampshire, in the late summer of 1944, were a mixture of genuine idealism and tough, old-fashioned Anglo-American horse-trading. Unfortunately for Britain, America held all the horses.

Keynes led the British team of negotiators, while the American side was dominated by Harry Dexter White and his assistant, Edward Morris Bernstein. On one fundamental point there was no disagreement. As Keynes put it, "In 1918 most people's only idea was to get back to pre-1914. No one today feels like that about 1939." There was nothing in the 1930s to be nostalgic about. Nevertheless, despite a good deal of agreement and growing personal respect and understanding, the American and British diagnoses of the causes of the ills of the interwar period diverged. While America concentrated on removing obstacles to trade, especially tariffs and currency restrictions, Britain (and many of the other nations that attended the final Bretton Woods stages of the talks) were more worried about an international shortage of dollars. Nevertheless a final act eventually was hammered out that all parties felt able to recommend back home. It proposed the establishment of an International Monetary Fund (IMF), to promote international trade and stable exchange rates and to establish a reserve fund of international liquidity over and above individual countries' gold and foreign currency reserves. Subscribing countries would contribute in proportion to their wealth. These subscriptions, or quotas as they were called, were payable in a mixture of gold and the subscriber's own currency, but countries experiencing a temporary imbalance resulting in a shortage of any particular currency could buy the scarce currency from the fund with its own currency at fixed parity rates. In practice, the shortage currency was almost always going to be dollars, but there were limits; persistent borrowers paid a rising charge and in any case could draw only up to the limit of their quota. On the other hand, protective barriers were permitted against any country running a persistent surplus. Otherwise, members should not devalue, or erect tariff barriers or currency restrictions, unless a persistent imbalance had been established. The General Agreement on Tariffs and Trade (GATT, 1947) would work toward the reduction of such barriers. In addition, Bretton Woods proposed a Bank for Reconstruction and Development to manage longer-term loans of up to $10 billion.

These proposals eventually received domestic approval, but acceptance either by Parliament or by Congress was no foregone conclusion. In Britain Keynes found the proposals opposed on the left by those who feared the fixed exchange rate and free trade obligations might force deflation and unemployment on the government, and on the right by Bank of England conservatives who did not "allow for the fact that vast debts and exiguous reserves are not, by themselves, the best qualifications for renewing old-time international banking." In recommending acceptance, he reiterated his own radical financial credentials:

I have spent my strength to persuade my countrymen and the world at large to change their traditional doctrines and, by taking thought, to remove the curse of unemployment. Was it not I, when many of today's iconoclasts were still worshipping the Calf, who wrote that "Gold is a barbarous relic"?

The IMF scheme sought to provide the stability of the gold standard without its rigidity. Bretton Woods, with its fixed exchange rates underpinned by international agreement and umpired by the IMF, established the broad outlines of a scheme that would last until the 1970s. However, the special circumstances of Britain's position in the immediate aftermath of a second massively debilitating war were always recognized. Some sort of transitional arrangements were required. However, instead of a gentle transition, the precipitate termination of Lend-Lease within less than a month of the end of the war triggered a major crisis. With Churchill and Roosevelt gone, conservative Democrats were disinclined to continue to subsidize a rival empire now in the hands of socialists; in any case, now that the war was over, it could be argued that Lend-Lease was no longer legal. A more charitable interpretation was that the U.S. government had no idea of the true state of Britain in 1945 and that when it became clear to them that the sudden end of Lend-Lease was likely to trigger the economic collapse of their partner in victory, they stood ready to do the decent thing.

Once again, an increasingly frail and exhausted Keynes was sent across the Atlantic to negotiate a loan that could save an increasingly enfeebled national economy from complete collapse. A victim of a severe and dangerous heart condition sought a transfusion of funds for a chronically weakened and rapidly aging great power. In the end, a loan was forthcoming. It was "cut somewhat too fine" for Keynes's liking and allowed no margin for unforeseen circumstances. It amounted to $3.75 billion plus $650 million for Lend-Lease items now needing settlement. Canada added a further $1.25 billion. The loans were charged interest at 2 percent, a generous rate (though Keynes had hoped for a gift), interest and capital repayments becoming payable only in 1951. Most ominously, the package was conditional on Britain agreeing to honor Bretton Woods commitments to make the "sterling balances" fully convertible by July 1947.

Keynes had been hoping for a rather more open-handed American response, but he understood that the U.S. government had to take account of a series of requests from other countries as well as Britain. Moreover, American public opinion was not sympathetic: A Gallup poll in October 1945 suggested that 60 percent of U.S. citizens opposed a loan to Britain, with only 27 percent in favor. Realistically, though, America had little choice but to make some loan, rather than see Britain bankrupt and international trade still further disrupted. Equally, Britain had no choice but to accept the terms. Keynes ridiculed the alternative, a sterling area siege economy, summarizing it as a plan

to build up a separate economic bloc which excludes Canada and consists of countries to which we already owe more than we can pay, on the basis of their agreeing to lend us money they have not got and only buy from us and one another goods we are unable to supply.

Nevertheless, getting the loan killed Keynes early in 1946, and accepting the terms very nearly destroyed the British economy in 1947.

8

Sterling Since the War

Clearly money has something to do with life.
—Philip Larkin, *Money,* 1973

Britain emerged from the end of the Second World War triumphant and broke. In financing the war it had spent one-third of its gold reserves and sold one-third of its overseas assets. Other overseas assets had been destroyed. At home three-quarters of a million houses needed to be replaced or repaired. Taxation had risen dramatically, but debts of £3.5 billion still had accumulated. In addition to the costs of the war just concluded, Britain still had to carry the financial obligations associated with its continuing international role as a victorious and imperial great power. The decision to grant independence to India was certainly not seen at the time as the beginnings of the end of the empire, and British armed forces still were required to carry out a host of tasks all across the globe from occupied Germany to the Middle and Far East. In the aftermath of a heroic victory, no one imagined that Britain's days as a great power were over. And finally, on top of the expense of the war and of a continuing imperial role, all British political parties had come to recognize an obligation to the British people. Providing proper living standards, which it was increasingly felt the people had earned, would cost money too.

Faced with substantial debts and extensive commitments at home and abroad, the British government immediately made arrangements to borrow. Keynes set off to America with high hopes of negotiating an interest-free loan or gift of $5 billion. Hugh Dalton, the Labour Chancellor of the Exchequer of the time, later recalled the disappointing reality:

As the talks went on, we retreated, slowly and with bad grace and with increasing irritation, from a free gift to an interest free loan, and from this again to a loan bearing interest, and from a larger to a smaller total of aid; and from the prospect of loose strings, some of which would be only general declarations of intention, to the most unwilling acceptance of strings so tight that they might strangle our trade, and indeed, our whole economic life.

In the end the loan was much smaller than Keynes had expected, but the most important string, to which Dalton referred, was the British commitment to restore the **convertibility** of sterling. During the war the government had suspended the free exchange of pounds for dollars on the open market. Import and exchange controls enabled the government to limit the sale of pounds for the purchase of dollar goods. The terms of the Lend-Lease and Bretton Woods agreements both looked forward to the time when such impediments to free international trade and exchange would be removed, and the American negotiators consistently demanded British agreement to such a commitment as the price of U.S. aid.

Keynes thus may have felt that the commitment to convertibility was nothing new. He probably agreed with it in principle as part of the Bretton Woods scheme. However, he allowed what was little more than a pious long-term hope to develop into a firm commitment to restore convertibility for current transactions from July 1947. Neither he nor the Americans expected this commitment to apply to Britain's wartime debts to countries like India and Egypt, which were known as the sterling balances.

In the winter of 1945–1946 there was much disappointment about the size of the American loan and some concern about the convertibility clause. Aneurin Bevan and Emanuel Shinwell on the left argued for rejection of the loan in Cabinet, and in the Commons the Conservative Robert Boothby called for rejection, putting his faith in the empire and the sterling area. Some officials believed it might have been better to look for a smaller, commercial loan without strings rather than accept the American conditions. The Bank of England was worried about the impact of convertibility at $4.03 to the pound. Nevertheless, the opponents of the loan were not really able to provide a convincing answer to the question "What is your alternative?" Moreover, most of the Cabinet had a pretty clear idea of what the alternative was. It was described by Dalton who prophesied "greater hardships and privations than even during the war," including "practically no smokes, since eighty per cent of our tobacco cost dollars."

In the end the loan and its terms were accepted because they bought a little time. The choice between an immediate crisis and one in eighteen months time was a simple one. There would be time to make arrangements to cope with the problem, and something might turn up. Unfortunately, what turned up was the worst winter of the century in 1947, a foreseeable fuel crisis that put 2 million temporarily out of work and hit British exports, and a growing awareness that it might not be possible to separate current sterling transactions from long-standing sterling balances. During the war Britain had paid for a huge supply of goods and services by crediting what were essentially frozen sterling accounts. Over £1 billion was owed in India alone; £356 million was owed in Egypt. The total bill in 1945 was estimated at £2.39 billion. When convertibility was written into the U.S. loan agreement in 1945, it was not envisaged that it would apply to these sterling balances. However, it was to prove extremely difficult to separate them from current expenditure, which would be convertible. As the negotiations for Indian independence proceeded, it became clear that it would not be possible to write off these debts or to exclude them from convertibility. India remained much poorer than Britain. For years India had faithfully repaid money borrowed from England. Now that the roles were reversed, Britain could not simply refuse to pay. Although Britain did manage to negotiate a great deal of patience from the holders of the sterling balances, these debts were coming home to roost and would greatly exacerbate the problem of convertibility.

However, in 1946, with the American loan under his belt and British industry picking up rapidly, Dalton was able to finance the founding of the welfare state. Under the National Insurance Act of 1946, a single pensioner would receive 25s. a week and a couple 42s.

Lloyd George's maximum means-tested pension had been 5s. (raised to 10s. in 1918). Since prices in 1946 were only about 2.3 times higher than before the First World War, the new pension, which was not means-tested, was very significantly more generous. Moreover, food was still heavily subsidized.

The year 1946 also saw the nationalization of the Bank of England. Although in one respect this may be regarded as a predictable and ideological objective for a new socialist government, in fact both the politicians and the Bank treated the affair less controversially. Two world wars had comprehensively completed the Bank's journey from an independent, private, profit-seeking financial institution into a national central bank. Early steps on this journey had been taken in the nineteenth century, and it was then already becoming incumbent on the Bank to put the stability of sterling, and of the whole banking system, before private profit, but it was above all the wars that confirmed the unquestioned priority of the national interest for the management of the Bank. Thus formal nationalization merely confirmed a development that was already taking place. The Bank served the Treasury and chancellor, advising as an experienced manager of the markets, but ultimately following instructions to put government policy impartially into practical effect.

All in all, Dalton regarded 1946 as an *annus mirabilis,* and even as late as April 1947 he confidently told the Commons "that the new Britain . . . has taken the cost of social security in its stride; the measures have been passed, the money has been found, and the benefits are being enjoyed by those entitled to them." Chancellors always do their best to generate confidence, but behind the scenes things were very different. Dalton later recalled, "Very often during these months [leading up to July 1947], I lay awake at night doing mental arithmetic. We had so many dollars; last month we spent so many; if we spend the same next month, we shall only have so much left. But we mustn't let our dollar reserves fall below so much, or we shall be sunk." The actual figures that kept him awake were these: In 1946 the gold and dollar deficit had been running at about $50 million a month. By February 1947 the figure was up above $200 million. These figures could only get worse after convertibility was resumed on July 15, 1947. Civil servants prepared dire assessments of the prospects for the economy without dollars. It was calculated that the food ration would have to be cut to 1,700 calories a day, over 1,000 calories below the wartime ration, and less than that necessary for the subsistence of laboring adult males. Under stress, poor Dalton lost sleep, was plagued by boils, and kept himself going on Benzedrine.

Britain could and probably should have approached the U.S. Congress for agreement to defer convertibility, but both the Bank and the Treasury feared that such an approach could increase concerns about the pound and trigger the very panic they were trying to avoid. Sterling duly became convertible on July 15, exposing it to the forces of a relatively uncontrolled free market. In the context of an international dollar shortage (born of the U.S. balance-of-payments surplus, for only America was in a position to supply the goods the rest of the world so badly needed), the opportunity to buy dollars at four to the pound was too good to miss. That month the drain on Britain's gold and dollar reserves rose to over $500 million as the government struggled to defend the official exchange rate. In August the drain amounted to more than $600 million. Dalton likened the experience to watching a child bleed to death. Although the government organized a massive export drive and simultaneously cut back sharply on imports, a large part of the dash for dollars arose from capital movements as well as from the current balance of payments. Given the relative strengths of the U.S. and British economies, it is hardly surprising that so many people chose to hold dollars rather than pounds. When, on August 20, 1947, convertibility was again suspended, all but $400 million of the American loan had been expended and sterling's frailty had been exposed.

Dalton, a broken man, introduced an emergency budget in November, increasing taxes and freezing food subsidies. He subsequently resigned in the wake of a fuss about unguarded remarks he had made to a journalist while on the way to deliver his budget speech. Of course, it was really convertibility that destroyed him. With hindsight it has been argued that the U.S. loan should never have been accepted on those terms, but refusal of the loan was not a viable political option in 1945. Perhaps more should have been done early in 1947 to renegotiate the convertibility commitment or to prepare a more rapid response to the bleeding.

Dalton was replaced as chancellor by Sir Stafford Cripps, a rather lean and hungry figure whose appearance and demanding personal standards fit well with the time of austerity with which his name is associated. Those who worked closest with him were deeply impressed by his kindness and the sincerity of his Christian principles, but his public image was rather more forbidding. In fact, he inherited a situation that contained a number of redeeming features. The very severity of the convertibility crisis obliged Cabinet members in future to pay more attention to their new chancellor than they had to their old one. Moreover, Dalton's final budget of November 1947, which had aimed at a surplus of some £350 million, in fact yielded nearly double that. Thus a 1946–1947 deficit of £569 million turned into a 1947–1948 surplus of £635 million. Finally, Cripps enjoyed the enormous benefit of Marshall Aid.

The U.S. Secretary of State, General George Marshall, first hinted at the scheme of aid that would bear his name in June 1947. Ernest Bevin, the foreign secretary, deserves credit for the speed with which he took the hint and organized a European response, but it was not until June 1948 that the Cabinet finally signed up to the Marshall Aid agreement. Although it thus came far too late to relieve the convertibility crisis, Marshall Aid was to play an enormous part in European reconstruction. As America came to regard the Soviet Union as a threat, and the Cold War began, Congress became aware once more of the case for a more generous attitude to Europe. It takes nothing away from American generosity to realize how closely it was linked to the American national interest. The United States was much more interested in helping allies who were useful in the present rather than bailing out old friends for the sake of auld lang syne. America was equally clear-sighted about Britain's role, encouraging Britain to take a leading part in the moves toward European integration that the U.S. government was encouraging. Britain, for its part, demonstrated from the very beginning a grudging lack of vision that has characterized its attitude to Europe for half a century and repeatedly left it struggling to catch up with developments that it could have led. In the context of the time, and given the distribution of British trade, it was understandable that Britain should have put its faith in the commonwealth and the sterling area, rather than in Europe, but the same attitudes persist, with less justification, to this day.

The shortage of dollars in the postwar world was a fundamental problem that affected America, Europe, and the sterling area. Any assessment of the relative strengths of the British and American economies indicated a marked shift in favor of the United States, but the official sterling–dollar exchange rate was frozen at the level set on the outbreak of war. In the meantime, while European production had been destroyed or depleted by the war, U.S. production had been massively and successfully stimulated. Foreign exchange and import controls prevented this imbalance from working itself out in the market, but sterling area profits could not pay for dollar imports. In these circumstances the case for a small but early devaluation of sterling was urged in some quarters (notably by Otto Clarke, an official in the Treasury), but a number of other arguments seemed to run the other way. Keynes believed the dollar was overvalued and that the cost of British labor was already competitive. Exports would recover anyway as resources were no longer devoted to the war effort, and most imports still were largely government-funded and under government control. A devaluation that would raise the price of imports also would raise government spending. It also would seem like a betrayal of British allies who were waiting patiently for repayment of the sterling balances owed to them for wartime goods and services. British debts that had been incurred with the pound worth $4 should also be settled at that rate. With hindsight the long-term situation would have justified devaluation, but at the time there were good reasons for the attempt to hold the pound steady.

In fact, Britain did succeed in raising its exports sharply while restricting the growth of imports. Exports grew strongly in 1946 and 1948, and disappointed only in 1947 as a consequence of the power crisis and early in 1949 as a result of the recession in the United States. However, the reemergence of a balance-of-payments deficit early in 1949 reopened the question of devaluation. Sterling area customers were finding American goods cheaper than British, whenever they could find the dollars to buy them. It was also becoming clear that capital flows accounted for much of the preference for dollars. Even if Britain could achieve a balance-of-payments surplus in current spending, U.S. long-term prospects looked better than British, and low interest rates—an absolutely fundamental element in Labour party thinking—did nothing to attract money to Britain. Moreover, American policy began to favor a British devaluation as an essential first step toward reestablishing a free and open foreign exchange market. American pressure for a British devaluation intensified in the spring and early summer.

In May Cripps tried to dampen rumors of a possible devaluation with an explicit denial. As a general rule it is usually true that once a chancellor has to deny the possibility of a devaluation, it is already too late to stop it. On July 7 he told the Commons, "the Government have not the slightest intention of devaluing the pound." This was still true of the Cabinet. Some feared the effect of a devaluation and its impact on the cost of living as an election approached. Cripps was working with the commonwealth to cut the dollar spending of the sterling area and with his colleagues to cut government spending. Some spending ministers felt that without cuts in government spending devaluation would not work, but that with such cuts devaluation would not be necessary. The Bank of England opposed devaluation because it feared this might give the government an excuse not to cut spending sufficiently. Nevertheless, despite the heavyweight opinion ranged against devaluation, the drain on the reserves mounted, from £82 million in the first quarter of the year to £157 million in the second. With the total reserve down to £400 million, Labour ministers recalled the traumas of 1931 and 1947.

In the middle of July Cripps repaired to a Swiss sanatorium, suffering from a gastric ailment no doubt exacerbated by overwork and stress, which made eating and sleeping difficult. Within two days of his departure, the junior ministers entrusted with the care of the economy in his absence—Hugh Gaitskell, Douglas Jay, and Harold

Wilson—had agreed to press for a devaluation, and in August Clement Attlee wrote to Cripps informing him that the Cabinet now favored devaluation, principally as the best means to slow the drain on the reserves. It was felt that the expectation of devaluation was already delaying the purchase of sterling goods and encouraging the sale of sterling. The choice of the new rate remained open, and the timing of the announcement was delayed by Cripps's schedule. On his return from Switzerland he was due to visit Washington with Ernest Bevin.

Thus in September 1949 Bevin, who suffered from a heart condition, and Cripps, with his gastric complaint, warned the Americans of the impending announcement and discussed the appropriate exchange rate for sterling. Bread, so often in this history the most fundamental measure of the value of sterling, loomed large in the discussions. Sir Edwin (later Lord) Plowden recalled, "Ernie said what would $2.80 do to the price of the [28-ounce] loaf? I said it would raise it from 4¹/₂d. to 5¹/₂d." And so the pound was devalued 30 percent from $4.03 to $2.80. But it was a condition of Bevin's agreement that the dearer bread should also be whiter. He hated the austerity loaf, with its higher bran content, while Cripps preferred the extra roughage and thought it scandalous to charge the public more for a loaf that was not as good for them. There can be little doubt that Bevin's view was more in touch with public opinion.

The devaluation was announced on Sunday, September 18, 1949. The sterling area and many European currencies followed suit. The failure to notify continental governments prior to the devaluation was another affront to Europe. Although the devaluation against the dollar was 30 percent, most of Britain's other trading partners also devalued to some extent, so the trade-weighted devaluation of the pound only amounted to 9 percent. That so many countries followed the British example tends to support the judgment that a fundamental readjustment of the international value of the dollar was overdue. The success of the new rate, which lasted for the next eighteen years, supports that assessment. The flow of the gold and dollar reserves was successfully reversed, and Britain and the sterling area moved into a balance-of-payments surplus against the dollar. Inflation remained modest. By most measures the devaluation thus appears as the appropriate response to the postwar dollar situation, and if it had been introduced earlier in a deliberate and considered way, instead of reluctantly in the face of a dollar crisis, it might have been regarded as less of a defeat.

The outbreak of the Korean war in June 1950 still makes it difficult, even today, to evaluate the 1949 devaluation. It may, however, have contributed to the electoral fortunes of the Conservative party, which was brought to power in 1951, and remained in government till 1964. The business of postwar reconstruction brought generally prosperous times in the 1950s. Sterling's convertibility was restored gradually, and the fixed exchange rate system worked well. But major problems were looming. The United Kingdom's share of world trade fell from 29 percent in 1948 to 16 percent in 1960. Moreover, successive chancellors were finding it increasingly difficult to balance the budget. Full employment and lingering British imperial dreams were proving too costly. Those dreams turned quickly to nightmare in 1956, when the Suez Canal fiasco put sterling under additional heavy pressure. The markets judged that Britain could not afford to spend 9 percent of its GDP on military expenditure, especially in a cause that America did not endorse. At its worst during the post-Suez crisis some £26 million was lost from the reserves in a single day. It was only after Britain's ignominious withdrawal from Egypt that the United States allowed Britain to draw from the International Monetary Fund the funds necessary to protect the sterling exchange rate.

The lesson of the second half of the century, which United Kingdom governments were slow to learn, was that the willingness of the IMF or other central banks to lend to Britain was strongly influenced by the financial policies of the British government. Lenders would support the pound only if they saw the government taking action to improve the financial outlook. The commitment to full employment, a welfare state, and great power aspirations made any such improvement very difficult to achieve.

This was the background to a famous interview between Harold Wilson and the governor of the Bank of England, Lord Cromer, in November 1964. Cromer's sympathies undoubtedly lay with the Conservatives, while "capital" always has been suspect in left-wing circles ever since Marx. When Cromer more or less told Wilson that his policies would require the approval of international financiers as well as that of a democratically elected House of Commons, Wilson responded with two threats: to call another general election to reinforce the democratic mandate and to float sterling. Floating—that is, abandoning the government support for sterling at its official exchange rate and allowing it to find its own level—would have precipitated an international crisis striking at the system of fixed exchange rates of currencies around the world. Nevertheless, it had been much discussed in government circles since the 1950s. Although Cromer knew a new election would cut little ice in Switzerland or America, central bankers faced with the choice of supporting sterling or coping with the collapse of the Bretton Woods fixed rate system were likely to prefer the former. Accordingly Cromer did approach other central banks to win short-term loans amounting to $3 billion. However, such support would not continue indefinitely, and the help of the international banks and the behavior of speculators betting against the pound remained crucially influenced by their interpretation of government policies.

Fixed exchange rates cannot be held in place solely by government declarations. As well as specifying the intended value of the pound, the government had to be ready to defend it. It could do this in three main ways. If the government held, or could borrow, sufficient reserves of gold or foreign exchange, it could buy pounds to keep up the price of sterling. But the government also could adjust the Bank rate to support sterling. By raising interest rates at home, it could encourage an influx of foreign capital looking for higher returns and also reduce spending in Britain by making money dearer there. The problem with this approach was its effect in terms of rising unemployment. The third possibility was a tightening of fiscal policy—that is, government taxing more and spending less, which is seldom democratically popular.

The failure to implement any of these three policy options with sufficient conviction led so inexorably to the 1967 devaluation, which reduced the pound from $2.80 to $2.40. The devaluation, together with cuts in government spending and increased taxes, brought the British economy back on course by 1970, but three big issues lay ahead. War in the Middle East had demonstrated the importance of oil for the economies of the West. Second, by 1970, 38 percent of British exports were being sold in Europe compared with 28 percent in 1960. The corollary was that British exports to the sterling area were down to 23 percent in 1970 compared with 35 percent in 1960. These were the irreducible facts that brought Britain into the European Economic Community (EEC). And the third big issue, though in 1970 perhaps no bigger than a cloud on the far horizon, was inflation. In the 1970 election campaign the Conservatives argued that on present trends, the pound of 1964 would be worth only 10s. by 1974, and a party political broadcast on television showing a pound note being steadily snipped away was judged a particularly telling visual moment in the campaign. Edward Heath's very first election press conference warned of the imminent arrival of the 3s. loaf (15p.). The *Daily Express* picked on this issue for the best scare headline of the campaign on June 2, shortly before polling.

Despite changes to our daily bread over the centuries, changes in the price of the loaf probably give us as close an understanding of the value of money in the past as we are likely to get. Throughout this history we have seen that government was particularly sensitive to the price of bread and its association with the value of money. From the medieval assize of bread, to the Free Trade and Tariff debates of the nineteenth century, to Bevin's concerns at the time of the 1949 devaluation, and to Heath's choice of the topic as a crucial election issue in 1970, the link between bread and money is clear. Indeed, as slang, "bread" often means money. Yet it is interesting to note that after 1970, bread rather falls out of the picture. Its importance in an increasingly affluent diet has declined, to the dismay of the nation's nutritional experts. In the same way, food in general now accounts for a dwindling proportion of disposable incomes in the developed world. As more and more of our spending becomes discretionary, fashion and choice have begun to influence the purchasing habits of a growing proportion of the population. To the extent that price is becoming a less dominant factor affecting purchasing behavior, economics becomes an increasingly complex matter.

The Conservative government, elected rather to everyone's surprise in the summer of 1970, correctly identified inflation and unemployment as the two principal economic problems requiring attention, but its failure to decide which of the two evils should be addressed more urgently revealed a fatal ambiguity at the heart of policy. At this time inflation and unemployment were both rising, and Cabinet indecision about how much of the one they could tolerate in order to cure the other left the government ill-prepared to cope with some extremely testing international economic and financial developments.

Most notably, in August 1971 President Richard Nixon suspended the convertibility of the dollar for gold, allowed exchange rates to float, and introduced a 10 percent surcharge on imports to the United States. This was a response to mounting American balance-of-payments problems resulting from heavy spending in Vietnam and the rising price of primary produce required to feed the booming industries of the developed world. Various arrangements were made to try to provide for partially refixed rates that were allowed to fluctuate more than the old fixed rates, but only within prescribed margins. The Smithsonian agreement of December 1971 allowed for fluctuations up to 4.5 percent from the central rate, while the German **snake** established by the EEC in April 1972 permitted only 2.25 percent variation. Sterling joined the snake but was quickly driven out as the markets judged that British economic policies were incompatible with the discipline required by the snake. However, all these attempts to introduce some stability to the system of free-floating currencies could not conceal the fact that the Bretton Woods scheme of fixed exchange rates, which had operated since the war and coincided with a period of very considerable world economic expansion, was now no more. It was the end of an era of government control and international cooperation.

Floating did have advantages that had long commended it to some in Britain. With sterling no longer committed to a fixed exchange rate, British gold and foreign currency reserves would not need to be spent buying up unwanted pounds on the world markets. If there were more sellers than buyers for sterling, then the rate would be allowed to sink. No longer would the state of the reserves constrain government freedom. However, variable exchange rates made it more difficult for companies and governments alike to plan, and in practice it would be necessary to set some limits to the extent to which they were prepared to see their currencies rise or fall. This was a whole new world with new freedoms and new pitfalls.

It was also a world in which the long postwar boom of recovery and reconstruction was approaching its peak. Primary producers were beginning to charge more for the raw materials needed by the industrial world. Even before the oil shock of 1973, this trend was already apparent, and rising international prices were contributing to domestic inflation. The float, which effectively devalued sterling by about 9 percent in 1972, also raised the price of imports. When the Organization of Petroleum Exporting Countries (OPEC) raised the price of oil fourfold, imported inflation became even more severe.

By chance, just at the time that inflation was taking hold, Britain finally chose to abandon its old money. Shillings and old pence (d.) were replaced with a new decimal currency with 100 new pennies (p.) making a pound. The pound itself was unchanged, but the decimalization of 1971 was firmly associated in many people's minds with rising prices. The real causes were mistaken government policies and from 1974 the full effects of the OPEC oil price rise. In August 1975 the annual rate of inflation peaked at 26.9 percent. The 3 s. loaf prophesied by Heath in 1970 became a reality, though because of decimalization it was now 15p. (One old shilling was equal to 5 new pence.) As prices rose, workers naturally demanded higher wages, adding another twist to the inflationary spiral. In the twelve months from July 1974 to 1975 hourly wages rose 33 percent, while retail prices rose 26 percent.

However, both major political parties and the IMF were more worried about the oil shock causing a worldwide recession than about inflation, and the British government failure to hit the brakes in 1974 and 1975 was accepted as internationally helpful. In the background, though, other economic theories were taking hold. As inflation soared, economists once more began to associate the falling value of money with its rising supply. Money supply (M) was measured once again with increasing interest. Alternative definitions proliferated, giving rise to Mo and M1 to M5. More and more attention was also paid to government borrowing defined by the Public Sector Borrowing Requirement (**PSBR**).

As we have seen, the idea of an association between the supply of money and its value was an old one. But in the 1970s the newly liberated international financial markets became increasingly influenced by M and PSBR figures. Huge sums of money moved around the world, in and out of the main international trading currencies, in response to the announcement of new forecasts. Unfortunately, these forecasts of M and PSBR were often extremely inaccurate. As a result, when the financial markets woke up to the fact that the performance of the British economy in the early 1970s necessitated a reduction in the value of sterling, the necessary adjustment was in fact an overreaction based on inaccurate forecasting. The fall in the value of sterling in 1976—down to around $1.60—was in fact greater than the formal devaluations of 1949 and 1967 and was greater than the situation required. Bolstered by IMF loans and stern (if belated) government action, sterling bounced back above $2.00 in 1977. Nevertheless, confidence in sterling at home and abroad had been severely damaged. Internationally the old certainties of the Bretton Woods era had been replaced by floating currencies of fundamentally unstable value, making it difficult for government and business alike to plan.

Although the worst inflation of the mid-1970s had been brought under some sort of control before the end of the decade, the problem of rising prices remained at the heart of British politics. Rising prices legitimized a demand for higher wages, and each group of workers measured its prosperity against the pay rises won by other groups. Pay differentials established over generations were eroded in months, and society constantly had to renegotiate the "going rate for the job." Pay and prices did not move equally and in step in response to the falling value of the currency. Instead stresses and strains developed within society as inflation eroded the position of some while elevating that of others. Thus the problem of the value of sterling assumed mounting importance among the concerns of government, and few governments in British history were ever more exercised by monetary questions than that brought to power by the general election of 1979.

Margaret Thatcher's government was firmly committed to a monetarist response to inflation. It believed that rigorous control of the money supply alone would be enough to curb inflation, which could reasonably be defined as too much money chasing too few goods. This was the quantity theory of money ($MV = PT$, see pp. 204–205) elevated to a philosophy of government. In some ways it is surprising that the Conservative party, traditionally the most pragmatic of institutions, should have committed itself so wholeheartedly to dogma, but the theory had a number of features that appealed to the Tory instinct to limit government's role, power, and spending. There was to be much less government intervention, since the necessary national economic management could be achieved through money supply targets alone. Specifically, prices and incomes policy would be cast aside and the value of money safeguarded instead by limiting its supply.

The theoretical probability of a relationship between money supply and the price level (an assumption that runs through this book) was, however, rather more difficult to apply in government. In the first place, unknown time lags between possible cause and possible effect made the theory an uncertain guide to policy. Moreover, M was essentially an international phenomenon. Fully convertible sterling, freed of exchange controls in October 1979 and aided by modern technology, was even more volatile than seventeenth-century Spanish-American silver had been. Above all, it was necessary, but extremely difficult, to define the money supply. Were prices influenced by "broad money" or by "narrow money"? When it became clear that it was broad money that mattered, it proved impossible to forecast and extremely difficult for government to influence—not least since government had foresworn the "corset" that had limited bank lending. In consequence the government would eventually take refuge in the much less significant Mo, which it could estimate and control with a reasonable degree of accuracy, although its relationship to the price level was little more than notional. Within a very few years the monetary targets were downgraded in the government armory, and much greater reliance was placed instead on the PSBR and the minimum lending rate (**MLR**), which dictated the price of credit.

Whereas in the Middle Ages and early modern period the supply of credit had been closely tied to the supply of coin, and the rights of the early banks to create credit had equally been limited by their cash reserves, in a world of deregulated financial services and "market forces," credit was now controlled only by its price. Thus attention shifted from money supply figures to the interest rate, which proved to be a more than adequate brake on the economy. MLR rose to 17 percent in November 1979, falling only to 16 percent in July 1980, and unemployment soared toward 3 million, for not only did the high price of money squeeze the domestic economy, it also sucked in funds from abroad, raising the sterling exchange rate to $2.40 in September 1980 and pricing British exports out of the market. The overvaluation of the pound, which now was also boosted by the arrival of North Sea oil, directly contributed to the loss of 1.5 million jobs in British manufacturing industry in the early 1980s. Parts of Britain's leaner, fitter industry began to look distinctly anorexic.

All this was judged to be a price worth paying, for although inflation had been successfully reduced to single figures by less draconian measures in the late 1970s, the disease was shown to be still virulent as prices rose at a rate of 21.9 percent per annum in May 1980. Much of this inflation was, in fact, directly attributable to the effects of Geoffrey Howe's first budget, which raised the value-added tax (VAT) from 8 percent to 15 percent (flying in the face of an election promise not to do so). This change alone added 3.6 percent to the retail price index (RPI). A further boost to inflation came from the electorally expedient undertaking to honor the recommendations of the Clegg Commission on public service pay.

Inflation and unemployment were rising and the government's targets for money supply and the PSBR were constantly overshot. Doubts were growing in the Cabinet, but the prime minister contemptuously dismissed such fears and encouraged Howe to persevere. In the 1981 budget he raised taxes by some £4 billion at a time of already severe recession. It was a kick in the teeth for Keynesian economics, which would have looked rather to stimulate demand to get the economy going once more, and some 364 economists of varied persuasions, appalled by what the chancellor had done, wrote to *The Times* prophesying deepening depression, the erosion of the industrial base, and an endangered social and political fabric. Sure enough, unemployment hit 3 million, and output tumbled in a manner reminiscent of the 1930s, with the added dimension of rioting in Liverpool, Manchester, Bristol, and Brixton.

Eventually, however, the reduction in public borrowing permitted a reduction in interest rates. In due course this brought the pound down on the foreign exchanges, from a high of $2.45 in October 1980 to $1.54 in April 1983. Thus lower interest rates released the stranglehold on the economy and simultaneously restored the competitiveness of what remained of British industry. And to put the icing on the cake, inflation was falling—squeezed out of the domestic economy by the recession and helped by a global fall in world commodity prices.

When Nigel Lawson succeeded Howe as chancellor after the 1983 general election, he showed himself increasingly concerned about the valuation of sterling and its impact on exports. Sterling's exchange rate was watched with ever greater attention in the Lawson Treasury.

Lawson took an opportunity early in his chancellorship to declare "It is the conquest of inflation and not the pursuit of growth and employment, which is or should be the objective of macroeconomic policy." But in fact it was the growth record of his time in office that reads best. Four percent growth in 1983 was followed by 3 percent over 1984–1985, reflecting the impact of the miners' strike, before returning to 4 percent again in 1986. With inflation then at 2.5 percent, North Sea oil output peaking, and exports generally strong, all the indicators for 1986 looked good. It seemed as if the difficult anti-inflationary decisions of the early Thatcher years were now bearing fruit, and the fundamental changes that had been made in the economy, based on the deregulation of financial services, trade union reform, and the extension of a share- and property-owning democracy would permit wider prosperity without inflation. Income tax was cut by 1p. in the pound in 1986, and further, larger cuts followed in 1987 and 1988, bringing the basic rate down to 25 percent. GDP grew at a rate of 4.5 percent per annum in 1987 and 1988. In May 1988 interest rates were cut to 7.5 percent, the lowest level of the Thatcher years, and 1 million unemployed found work the same year.

The harsh reality of the situation was actually rather different. Despite the Lawson boom, unemployment remained over 2 million at the end of 1988. In any case, the growth of the early Lawson years was a natural cyclical reaction, after the very difficult period from 1980 to 1982, and the booming economy of 1988 was not merely enjoying the fruits of Tory reform but rather contained within it the seeds of a subsequent sharp downturn, for as demand was allowed to exceed capacity, the economy was overheating. Nothing fundamental really had changed, and the eternal verities of boom and bust, stop and go, still held sway. The unsustainable Lawson boom joined those of the 1960s and 1970s in the list of false and costly dawns. Inflation rose to 8 percent in 1989 and double figures in 1990, while interest rates soared to 15 percent in October 1989 and unemployment remained high.

In the 1980s the economy had become carried away by its own exuberance. But there was an emerging technical problem. Lawson found he could rely little on the accuracy of the money supply figures and came instead to place increasing reliance on the exchange rate. Sterling–dollar rates were still liable to wild fluctuation, but he found the sterling–Deutschemark (DM) rate a useful guide. However, Lawson never managed to convince Thatcher of the need to stabilize the relationship between sterling and the DM. For him, a stable pound would be a bulwark against inflation; for her, it was never a priority that justified less than optimal domestic interest rates. Lawson was prepared to try to manipulate the exchange rate; Thatcher preferred to leave it for the markets to settle. The differences between them came to a head over the question of Britain's membership of the Exchange Rate Mechanism (**ERM**) of the European Monetary System (**EMS**). The ERM fixed the ratios among a group of leading European currencies. In effect, it was a group of weaker currencies nailing their colors to the DM mast. Lawson wanted in, but Thatcher would have none of it. She first rejected the idea in November 1985, but the chancellor and prime minister remained in harness together, despite mounting difficulties, until Thatcher publicly appointed her own economic advisor, Alan Walters, to buttress her instinctive rejection of Lawson's policy. The chancellor's long-anticipated resignation finally came on October 16, 1989. The resignation of Geoffrey Howe (then deputy prime minister) and of Thatcher herself were soon to follow. Sterling and the ERM had graduated from being a technical economic issue and had come to symbolize fundamental notions of British identity and Britain's appropriate relationship with the rest of Europe.

The European question did not disappear with Nigel Lawson. The new chancellor, John Major, also favored British membership of the ERM, on the grounds that it would help convince the markets of the seriousness of the government's commitment to the fight against inflation. If the markets were so convinced, it should be possible to lower British interest rates without triggering a flight from sterling. Reluctantly, on June 13, 1990, Thatcher told Major that she would no longer oppose joining the ERM. She probably was more influenced by the need to reduce conflict within the government and the Conservative party than by the economic arguments. Certainly the eventual announcement of Britain's membership of the ERM was highly colored by political considerations. It was timed for the eve of the Tory party conference in October 1990 and combined with a 1 percent cut in interest rates (against the advice of the Bank of England and of most Treasury officials). Perhaps more important, the choice of the rate at which sterling was to join the ERM, equal to DM2.95, was very much toward the top end of the possible range. It may have gone down well with the party conference that week, but many observers, including the Bundesbank, prophesied that DM2.95 could prove difficult to defend in the longer term. Indeed, it quickly slipped below this target parity, but the government was obliged by the rules of the ERM to pursue policies that would keep the pound within 6 percent of par.

Thus Britain was committed to a strong pound at a time when the marked fall in consumer demand in the years 1989 to 1991—a hangover from the champagne days of the Lawson boom—was causing a fall of almost 2 percent in GDP in 1991. Of course, the strong pound also restricted the growth of British exports. Moreover, the collapse of the old Communist regimes in eastern Europe and especially the reunification of Germany brought about much higher interest rates on the continent. The all-important German interest rate rose from around 3.8 percent in 1988 to over 8 percent in 1989 and nearly 10 percent in the third quarter of 1992. The British government was obliged to keep its interest rate above that of Germany to attract investors, even though the condition of the domestic economy would have called for lower rates otherwise.

By September 1992 the whole ERM was under very severe strain. The Italian lira devalued and left the mechanism on September 13, after the Bundesbank had spent DM24 billion unsuccessfully trying to support it. In the same way the markets bet heavily that sterling too would have to abandon its intended parity, obliging the Treasury and the Bundesbank to buy pounds in an attempt to keep up the price. On Black Wednesday, September 16, 1992, an exhausted chancellor, Norman Lamont, admitted that the game was up. Sterling's membership of the ERM was suspended, and although the lira rejoined, there was never any question of Britain doing so. Much of the Conservative party developed a marked antipathy to Europe, blaming the Bundesbank for failing to continue to support sterling, as it in fact supported the franc when it too came under pressure. It is true that German support for sterling might have been stronger if Germans had been defending a sterling–DM parity they believed in.

The aftermath of Black Wednesday was rather curious. Lamont, relieved of the task of defending an indefensible exchange rate, was devaluation happy, and the whole British economy began to bounce back. With the new low value of sterling, British exports seemed good value abroad, and the economy picked up on the back of genuine export-led growth. Interest rates, no longer kept high to support sterling, were allowed to fall. By the spring of 1993 they were down to 6 percent. Unemployment, though still high, began again to fall. The Stock Exchange rose steadily. Exports in 1994 were up 20 percent (by volume) over those of 1993. Nevertheless, despite all the good news, the government's financial credibility was irretrievably damaged. Lamont was sacked as a scapegoat in 1993. The bluff good humor of his successor, Kenneth Clarke, together with the favorable turn of the economy went some way to restore confidence, but much of the country, including many Conservatives, were left with the feeling that the reelection of the Major government in April 1992 had been an unfortunate democratic accident. If it had been a mistake, the electorate made amends in 1997, when they emphatically evicted the government, despite generally favorable economic conditions.

The new Labour chancellor, Gordon Brown, moved quickly to assure the markets that sterling was safe in his hands by entrusting the control of interest rates to a newly independent Bank of England and its Monetary Policy Committee (MPC). The MPC began a series of interest rate increases that brought the rate to 7.5 percent in 1998, keeping inflation on target and significantly strengthening sterling, which even reached DM3. Inevitably, the stronger pound made British exports harder to sell abroad again, and led to demands from manufacturers especially that rates must come down again if a recession was to be avoided in 1999. The old puzzle of how to achieve economic growth with prosperity and jobs without also causing inflation remains. This time, however, some new factors are coming into play. Most important, the global economic climate has turned distinctly wintry. International price trends seem to be turning firmly down, as the Japanese economy remains in the doldrums, the Asian tiger economies have run into major banking and currency crises, and the collapse of the ruble raises fears of a huge international credit squeeze. Fears of a major international recession are real, but of course similar fears after the OPEC shock and the stock market crash of 1987 proved unfounded in the past. Nevertheless, it does seem clear that at the moment deflation is becoming a greater danger to the world economy than inflation. In two months in the autumn of 1998 this insight led fifty-four separate central banks to cut their interest rates. The new European Central Bank talked tough but cut rates like everyone else.

The turbulence in the world currency and stock markets in 1998 makes the European Single Currency—the euro—at once more dangerous and more desirable. The particularly chaotic state of the financial markets and institutions in a large part of the world does make the euro's start date of January 1999 seem unpropitious. On the other hand, if the euro succeeds, a strong and powerful currency supported by the collective resources of Europe's united central banks stands a better chance of weathering the storms ahead than isolated national currencies. Moreover, if the world should decide in the years to come that the deregulation of global finance has created too much instability and that certain controls are called for, a reduction in the number of different major currencies in play would simplify the business of reimposing some control.

However, this begs the question of whether the euro will work and the related question of whether Britain should give up sterling in favor of a common European currency. The two questions are obviously related, since it seems clear that if the euro is successful, Britain will certainly join it. Whatever patriots may say about sovereignty (and there can be no doubt that currency and sovereignty are closely linked), if the public is offered the choice of a prosperous common European future or a noble but impoverished independence, the person on the Clapham omnibus will choose the former. Indeed, the recent history of sterling shows that the idea of independent control of the currency is largely illusionary. The American role in the devaluation of 1949 and the German influence on sterling in or out of the ERM show clearly that already the chancellor is barely master in his own house. Even if a British government were able to achieve a degree of real freedom from Washington and Berlin, it would remain a slave to the markets in London, New York, Frankfurt, Tokyo, and Hong Kong.

Furthermore, sterling's record for the best part of a century can scarcely justify blind and unthinking loyalty. It may be that it is time to trade in our old currency, rather as one might reluctantly say farewell to a pair of much-loved but increasingly ill-fitting old slippers. A sentimental appeal to almost a thousand years of tradition would miss the point that sterling has lasted so long only because it has adapted successfully over the years to change.

Nevertheless, if the worst fears of the euro-skeptics should turn out to be justified, if the single European interest rate should give rise to civil unrest in those member countries not well served, then British caution suddenly would appear so much more valid than visionary continental dreams.

This, in a nutshell, is the choice that will sooner or later be put before the British electorate in a referendum. In a sense it is a little like a brain surgeon asking a patient if the surgeon should operate. It is a highly technical question that most are ill-equipped to answer. In another more important sense, however, the referendum places responsibility where it truly belongs, because each citizen will have to live with the consequences of the collective decision Britain makes. The country will be significantly richer or poorer according to whether the right decision is made.

Inevitably contemplation of the history of Britain's currency over nine centuries does prompt certain observations. In the first place, despite the very physical character of medieval money, it is clear that money always has been essentially a social convention. Governments, with either more or less popular involvement, have settled the value of money and agreed what the nature of that money should be, and the people, encouraged by government's willingness to accept such money in tax, generally have been prepared to accept it too. This is not to deny that people always have been instinctively conservative about their money. People are understandably reluctant to tamper with something so fundamental to all our lives. Nevertheless, the nature of British money has changed markedly over time. It has moved from silver to gold. The actual precious-metal content has varied. Paper and base metal have supplanted gold and silver. Plastic and electronic impulses have assumed a dominant role. But whatever the physical composition of money, its basic, essential, and enduring characteristic is its acceptibility as a social idea. That is why even ancient monies are relevant to our understanding today.

But if the idea of money is enduring, its value has been anything but. The apparently inexorable rise of prices over at least eight centuries, demonstrated in the appendix, records an almost relentless fall in the value of sterling. Reducing the behavior of prices to a single index, however convenient, is nevertheless potentially misleading, since it conceals the truth that all prices do not move in unison. Some prices fall, even within a general price rise, and the rates of change vary. Moreover, the effects of price changes affect different people in various ways, creating winners and losers with little regard to any concept of economic or social justice. Changing prices usually have been socially corrosive in some degree, setting one group against another.

Nevertheless, the history of prices suggests that despite the undesirable effects of inflation, generally it has been combined with economic growth, while zero inflation or deflation has led to stagnation or recession. This is, of course, a sweeping generalization requiring much refinement. Inflation much over about 8 percent per annum, if sustained for any length of time, soon can erode confidence in the value of money, undermining trade and opening the way to stagflation. Yet despite this, few people would now regard zero inflation as a desirable or sustainable goal, especially in an international context.

The international character of Britain's money is another feature that marks its entire history. In the Middle Ages the absence of precious-metal mines in Britain capable of meeting the nation's monetary needs forged a close link between Britain's trade and its currency. That link has grown even more clear in the twentieth century with the abandonment of precious-metal money. Sterling always has been an international currency. Whatever its future, it will have to be hammered out in an international environment. Global developments will continue to play a crucial role, and policy-makers in Britain will not be able to turn their back on them. It may well be that even before we can resolve the problem of sterling in Europe, the most pressing difficulties will concern financial and cultural relationships between the developed and the developing world.

Appendix
THE PRICE INDEX

Repeated references have been made in the text to the price index prepared by Henry Phelps Brown and Sheila Hopkins, originally published in *Economica* in 1956. This index covered the period from 1264 to 1954. For this index the average price of a fixed group of commonly purchased essential goods in the period 1451 to 1475 is represented by the figure 100, and the annual price of those (or similar) goods for other years is calculated relative to that 1451 to 1475 base period. Thus an index number of 50 would indicate that prices were half the level of 1451 to 1475; an index of 200 would mean that prices were double those of the base period.

For certain specialist purposes various other indexes have been prepared for shorter periods, but the sheer range of the Phelps Brown–Hopkins index makes it the obvious choice on this occasion. Following the practice used by Douglas Jay in his book *Sterling. Its Use and Misuse: A Plea for Moderation* (1985), I have spliced the modern retail price index (RPI) on to the Phelps Brown–Hopkins Index. In purist terms, such a procedure is indefensible. Most obviously the earlier index was based substantially on wholesale prices, while the RPI is of course a *retail* price index. More fundamentally, the problems of comparing index prices for a representative group of common purchases over centuries are severe. Typical purchases in the Middle Ages differ from those of the eighteenth century, and by the late twentieth century the proportion of average purchasing power devoted to food has dwindled to a fraction of what it had been earlier. Moreover, different kinds of prices behave in different ways; property prices, for example, often diverge from food prices. Equally, earnings sometimes behave differently from prices: Since the early 1960s, while prices have risen something like tenfold, average household weekly earnings are now about twenty times greater. Social changes, such as the rise of the two-income household, can have a profound influence on the value of money. In short, strictly speaking, it simply is not possible to compare the purchasing power of sterling over the seven and a half centuries for which we have data. Nevertheless, so long as the very approximate and rough and ready nature of these calculations is understood, the case for providing some indication of how the value of our money has changed seems unanswerable.

Various points emerge from the figures set out. Periods of fairly flat prices have alternated with long periods of sustained inflation. There is good evidence to show that by the 1260s, when the Phelps Brown–Hopkins Index begins, prices already had been rising fairly steadily for almost a century. Thus the thirteenth century stands out as a period of marked price rise comparable with the period 1540 to 1650. However, the inflation of the second half of the twentieth century has been by far the most severe, although it has coincided with the period of the greatest general prosperity and economic growth. If, as is sometimes suggested, Britain and the world economy are about to embark on a period of lower prices, there must be some danger that it will be accompanied by greatly reduced levels of growth or even recession. It may be, therefore, that the twenty-first century will find more interest in comparisons with the periods of flat prices characteristic of the fifteenth century, the early eighteenth century, and the late nineteenth century.

Decade	Price Index	Decade	Price Index
1260s	79.8	1350s	128.5
1270s	101.2	1360s	141.5
1280s	92.8	1370s	130.8
1290s	101.5	1380s	107.8
1300s	99.3	1390s	108.6
1310s	141.5	1400s	110.4
1320s	123.2	1410s	113.2
1330s	106.7	1420s	103.7
1340s	95.6	1430s	115.1
1440s	100.7	1720s	608.0

1450s	99.2	1730s	553.0
1460s	104.1	1740s	598.8
1470s	94.3	1750s	628.2
1480s	116.0	1760s	703.6
1490s	101.3	1770s	805.3
1500s	104.3	1780s	824.4
1510s	111.2	1790s	997.7
1520s	148.0	1800s	1474.0
1530s	155.1	1810s	1601.0
1540s	192.1	1820s	1221.4
1550s	289.2	1830s	1145.8
1560s	278.8	1840s	1136.0
1570s	314.7	1850s	1153.7
1580s	357.0	1860s	1266.5
1590s	472.0	1870s	1330.0
1600s	474.9	1880s	1059.0
1610s	528.4	1890s	964.7
1620s	515.8	1900s	1006.9
1630s	615.8	1910s	1483.0
1640s	617.4	1920s	1755.4
1650s	636.1	1930s	1180.8
1660s	646.4	1940s	2300.1
1670s	614.6	1950s	4309.6
1680s	576.8	1960s	5910.5
1690s	646.8	1970s	13070.6
1700s	590.7	1980s	36101.0
1710s	663.1	1990s	58130.1

It should be stressed that these are ten-year average figures. The price index for individual years, to which reference sometimes is made in the text, is of course available in the original work by Phelps Brown and Hopkins and in the published RPI.

Glossary

I have tried to write this book for the general reader, assuming no prior knowledge or familiarity with specialist terms. However, it has not always been possible to explain all the unusual words at the point where they occur in the text. Instead, terms that may be unfamiliar to some readers are printed in bold, when first or significantly mentioned, and briefly discussed in this glossary. The explanatory notes that follow do not attempt to be thoroughgoing definitions, but merely flesh out a little of the fuller meaning of each term as it has been used in this book. For a more comprehensive treatment, the reader may care to consult one of the many excellent dictionaries of economics that are available.

Accepting houses Financial institutions that, for a fee, guarantee that the bills of exchange which they accept will be paid when they fall due. Thus, if there are insufficient funds in the account against which the bill is drawn to allow it to be paid, the accepting house will honor the bill.

Angels English gold coins introduced by Edward IV in 1470. They had an image of St. Michael the Archangel slaying a dragon on one side and a stylized ship on the other. They were worth 6s. 8d., which is half a mark. The angel denomination continued to be struck into the seventeenth century, though by then their monetary role had declined and they were mostly sought after as a charm to ward off disease.

Assay Determination of the purity of a precious-metal alloy. In historical times this was usually done by cupellation, which involved heating the alloy to a very high temperature, at which impurities are removed. By weighing the sample before and after cupellation, the assay can establish the original degree of impurity.

Balance of payments   The balance of the nation's account with the rest of the world. This is composed of a current account and a capital account. The current account reflects the current trade balance—the value of imports subtracted from the value of exports. This can be broken down further to distinguish between visible trade, consisting chiefly of raw materials and manufactures, and invisibles, consisting chiefly of services such as shipping and insurance. The capital account reflects the flow of investment money in or out of a country. Large flows on the capital account can run counter to the current trading position.

Bank rate   The rate at which the Bank of England discounted or re-discounted bills. When money was scarce, the Bank would be prepared to lend to basically solvent institutions against good bills at this interest rate. The announcement of the bank rate would influence other lenders and discount houses, which would be unlikely to lend much below the bank rate, in case they themselves found they had to borrow from the Bank. From 1971 to 1981 the bank rate was replaced by the minimum lending rate (**MLR**), the interest rate charged by the bank to discount houses. From 1981 this was called base rate. Bank rate, MLR, and base rate all indirectly governed the interest rates charged by other lenders.

Base rate   See **bank rate**.

Bills of exchange   Originally devised to enable merchants to conduct trade abroad in foreign coin without having to export bullion or specie. A banker in one country would arrange payment by a colleague in another. As well as facilitating the exchange of one currency for another, the time necessarily allowed for the transaction (say two or three months) would introduce an element of short-term credit, for which a charge would be made. In due course bills, which were essentially promises to pay in a specified place and currency some time in the future, began to change hands like money before they became due for payment. Those who accepted such bills instead of money would usually discount them by a percentage (see **discounting**), reflecting the delay before they became due for payment and the risk that eventually they might not be paid at all. The system proved so invaluable to international merchants and bankers that bill of exchange soon began to be used in the same way to facilitate trade and payments within Britain. Obviously inland bills involved no exchange element, but the credit and remittance features alone were sufficient to make the use of such bills an indispensable part of British domestic trade and banking. Bills thus came to augment the supply of ordinary notes and coins serving as money rather as a modern check would do, but with the additional possibility that they might circulate as discounted, negotiable instruments during their lifetime before maturity. (See **negotiable bills**.) The government also issued Treasury or Exchequer bills in the same way as short-term promises to pay.

Bimetallic flows A bimetallic monetary system sets an official value on coins of both gold and silver. The respective values set on the two metals establish an official silver–gold ratio, which might fluctuate from as little as about 9 units of silver to 1 of gold, up to as much as 15 or very occasionally more. If Britain placed a higher value on gold than, for example, France, French merchants would choose to pay their debts in England in gold. Conversely, English merchants would be likely to send silver to France. Thus the combination of disparate metal prices together with the normal settlement of trading debts could draw one metal into the country while sending the other abroad. This process is known as bimetallic flow. When such factors were at work, mint output would be characterized by a plentiful supply of one metal combined with a severe shortage of the other. For example, the latter half of the reign of James I was marked by heavy gold output and a dearth of silver. For most of the eighteenth century, Britain so undervalued silver that little was struck, and in the nineteenth century Britain adopted a gold standard in which silver and copper coins made up the small change but the value of the pound was defined only in terms of gold.

Bonds IOUs, similar to bills, but with a longer period of at least a year or more before maturity. Like bills, bonds can be discounted, that is, cashed by a third party before their due date for a value below their face value. They can also be traded on the Stock Exchange, where their value might rise or fall. As interest rates rise, the market price of bonds falls. Government bonds are known as gilt-edged investments (gilts) because of the reliability with which they are paid. Consols are a special form of undated government bond that pays interest reliably but is only repaid in full when/if government chooses.

CBI The Confederation of British Industry. An organization of British companies, mostly involved in manufacturing, that acts as a pressure group and mouthpiece expressing the bosses' viewpoint.

Circulating capital The cash resources of a company necessary to acquire stock and finance business. Where an eighteenth-century author might speak of circulating capital, a modern writer might speak of cash flow.

Clearing banks The main public banks participating in a clearing system that settles the checks drawn by the customers of each bank with every other bank. Since many payments are paid into each bank as well as out of it, only the end credit or debit balance at the end of each day's trading requires a transfer.

Consols Consolidated funds. See **bonds**.

Convertibility Refers to the possibility of changing one form of currency for another. Thus paper money might be convertible into gold, or not; sterling might be convertible into dollars, or not.

Corset A 1970s scheme for **special deposit**s made by the banks in order to limit their lending. The system was abandoned by Geoffrey Howe in the early 1980s because it was thought to merely divert lending from the banks to other financial institutions. The abolition of the scheme, however, did contribute to an explosion of credit.

Debasement A reduction in the purity of metal in a precious-metal coinage. By extension, the term is often used to describe any reduction in the intrinsic pure metal content of a currency, whether that reduction is achieved by lowering the purity of the metal, by reducing the weight of the coin while leaving the alloy unchanged, or by leaving the coinage physically unaltered while increasing its face value. Sometimes a combination of these three methods might be used, but in any case a debasement may be said to have occurred whenever and however the precious-metal content of a given face value of a currency is reduced. The economic effects of debasement were very similar to those of **devaluation**, tending to raise the price of imports while making exports seem better value abroad. Debasements usually increased the money supply and raised prices. In small doses the process usually boosted economic activity, but repeated debasements could destroy confidence in the currency and disrupt trade.

Deflation A reduction in the price level often resulting in reduced trade. Falling prices often can be associated with a reduction in demand, sometimes attributable to a shortage of money.

Depreciation See **devaluation.**

Devaluation A reduction in the value of one currency in terms of other currencies. In an era of floating exchange rates, this can take place gradually over time reflecting market demand for the currency in question, when it is often called depreciation. With fixed exchange rates, devaluation occurs as a deliberate (though usually reluctant) act of government. Its economic effects are similar to those of **debasement**: Exports become cheaper in foreign currencies while imports get dearer in the devalued currency. This process tends to improve the balance of payments, until inflation erodes the competitiveness of domestic industry.

Discounting A process that allows the holder of a bill or bond to sell it for less than its nominal or face value before it is due for payment. The buyer is, in effect, lending cash to the seller on the security of the bill, and the discounted value of the bill reflects interest payable on the loan.

Double patards A silver coin denomination struck in the Burgundian Netherlands in the second half of the fifteenth century. Their intrinsic value was almost exactly equal to that of an English groat of the same period, and a monetary agreement concluded between England and Burgundy provided for the circulation of both coins in both countries.

EMS The European Monetary System, which was established to coordinate the monetary policy and exchange rates of member countries, leading toward European Monetary Union (EMU).

ERM The Exchange Rate Mechanism of the European Monetary System. It attempted to limit the degree of fluctuation between the currencies of member states, as a desirable end in its own right and as a prelude to greater monetary union. Britain's unhappy membership of ERM lasted only from 1990 to 1992.

Fiduciary notes That part of the currency which is not backed by gold reserves.

Free trade   Trade unencumbered by import and export tariffs, subsidies or quotas. Strong countries, such as Britain in the later nineteenth century and America in the twentieth, favor free trade, while weaker trading countries often seek some degree of protection.

Funds   "The Funds" referred to interest-bearing government stock, which paid a regular annuity though the principal could be redeemed only at the government's wish. See also **bonds**.

Gazumping   A seller refusing to go through with the agreed sale of a house because he or she has accepted a better offer subsequent to the original deal. It is usually a symptom of sharply rising house prices.

GDP   Gross domestic product, which is a measure of the total of all finished goods or services produced within a country over a year. It can be calculated by measuring national output, income, or expenditure, and can be expressed in either current or constant prices. The calculation of GDP per capita allows the activity of small and large countries to be compared.

Hard currencies   Also known as strong currencies. Those whose price in terms of other currencies is stable or rising. They are readily convertible on the exchange markets. Such currencies also hold their values well in terms of goods, leading to lower inflation than in countries with weaker or softer currencies. Among precious-metal currencies, hard coinages have a higher and more stable intrinsic content than weak coinages. Hard currencies often are associated with countries enjoying a strong **balance of payments**. However, if a country's currency is too hard, given its underlying economic strength and competitiveness, it can give rise to unemployment. In such circumstances, controlled **devaluation** or **debasement** can stimulate growth by improving competitiveness. The benefits of this sort of adjustment, however, tend to be short-lived.

Hot money   Cash that is likely to move quickly from one country to another in search of the best investment opportunities. International investors shun currencies that are expected to fall in value against goods or other currencies but can be induced to invest in currencies with bad inflation or balance-of-payments records by the offer of high interest rates. Speculative runs into or out of a currency can develop their own momentum, raising or depressing the price beyond that suggested by rational explanations. As the amount of international capital looking for a home grew to levels far exceeding the sums involved in international trade, and as exchange controls were swept away, hot money came to contribute very significantly to the increasing currency instability of the late twentieth century.

Inflation A persistent rise in the general level of prices.

Inland bills See **bills of exchange.**

Intrinsic worth The value of the precious metal contained in a coinage. Currencies also have a nominal or face value, usually set by the issuing government about 5 percent above the intrinsic value. The difference between the intrinsic and face value of a coinage reflects the premium enjoyed by coin, authenticated and guaranteed by government, over bullion.

Invisibles Services available in international trade, as opposed to visibles, which are typically raw materials and manufactures. Invisible traded services include shipping, airlines, tourism, banking and financial, medical or educational services.

Joint stock companies or banks Those in which investors hold shares and receive distributed profits in proportion to their shareholding while leaving the management of the company to elected directors. This arrangement allows for the accumulation of more resources than normally can be provided by individuals or smaller partnerships.

Legal tender Refers to money that must be accepted in settlement of payments or debts. Thus although a creditor might prefer payment in gold, he would be obliged to accept it in notes if they had been declared legal tender.

Livres tournois French pounds, on which the French accounting system was based until the Revolution. As in England, there were 240 pence (*deniers*) to the French pound (*livre*), or 20 shillings (*sols*), each of 12 pence. However, the silver content of the French *denier* fell much earlier and farther than that of the English penny, making it a much weaker currency than sterling.

Macroeconomics This term is concerned with the economy as a whole rather than with the performance of individual businesses. It looks, for example, at total output, consumption, imports, exports, and money supply for the entire national economy as well as at the overall price level. Per capita figures are also macroeconomic because they are derived from aggregate data.

Mercantilism   The theory that national prosperity depends on a large and increasing national supply of bullion, which had to be acquired by mining or through a favorable trade balance. Mercantilist legislation attempted to promote exports, restrain imports, and augment the bullion stock. The theory failed to recognize that wealth consists in the goods and services which money can command rather than in money itself. However, mercantilism, or bullionism as it is sometimes known, did contain a kernel of truth, recognizing that both domestic and international trade depended on an adequate money supply. In an age when money was overwhelmingly coin, prosperity did depend on an adequate supply of bullion. This was still true, even in an age of paper money, so long as notes were backed by gold.

MLR   See **bank rate**.

Monetarism   A theory that holds that the quantity of money determines the level of prices and the tempo of the whole economy. As an economic theory, it enshrines the truism that if money supply grows faster than the economy as a whole, prices will rise. As a practical government policy, however, monetarism never solved the problem that it was impossible to measure the money supply or the size of the whole economy accurately. Nor was it possible to predict the exact relationship between money supply and the price level, even if it had been possible to establish them. More controversially, monetarists generally have argued that the economy tends toward a natural rate of unemployment and output and that therefore demand management policies will be ineffective in the long run.

National income   Sometimes represented by the symbol Y, corresponds (loosely) with gross national or domestic product. See **GDP**.

Negative equity   Describes the position of a house owner whose mortgage debt exceeds the value of the house. This phenomenon tends to occur when house prices suddenly fall back after a period of sustained price increases.

Negotiable bills   Those that circulate like money at a discounted value negotiated between seller and taker. See **bills of exchange** and **discounting**.

OECD The Organization for Economic Cooperation and Development promotes the growth and financial stability of its members, which include most of western Europe, plus Turkey, together with North America, Australasia, and Japan. Mexico and the Czech Republic also have joined recently.

Price index See the appendix.

Promissory notes Promises to pay issued by goldsmiths or bankers. Since such banknotes were convertible to gold, they were thought as good as gold and were in some respects more convenient. Even to this day modern banknotes still list a now-meaningless "promise to pay."

PSBR The Public Sector Borrowing Requirement is the amount the government has to borrow to bridge the gap between its annual income and its expenditure.

Quantity theory A theory of money which asserts that there is a connection between the supply of money (M) and the general level of prices (P), though the velocity of circulation (V) and the level of transactions (T) in the economy will also play a part. The theory is neatly expressed in the equation $MV = PT$, though more sophisticated versions of the equation have been developed. Historically and in the long term, there is much evidence to support the theory, though prices can go on rising beyond the levels indicated by money supply if there is an expectation of a continuing price rise; likewise, if money supply falls, a general reluctance to lower prices and wages can reduce levels of business rather than lowering prices. The application of the theory to modern national economic management has not been a conspicuous success, not least because of the difficulty of defining money supply and collecting accurate monetary data.

Quarter A measure of grain equal to eight bushels. The bushel in use until the nineteenth century was equivalent to 35.2 liters. In 1824 a slightly larger "imperial" bushel was introduced. A bushel of wheat normally weighed 55 to 60 pounds.

Real terms These calculate values after making allowances for changes in the price level over time. For example, real wages would recalculate actual nominal wages in terms of the changing purchasing power of money at different dates.

Real wages See **real terms**.

Seignorage   The profit derived by the crown from a tax on minting, paid by the mint's customers. Seignorage was charged in addition to the mintage charge, which was paid to the mint staff for the actual cost of coining. (Modern economists sometimes use this term to include both revenue from issuing money and the "inflation tax" derived from the reduced purchasing power of the money already in circulation. This sense of seignorage is not used in this book.)

Snake   A system linking the exchange rates of a group of European currencies in a fixed relationship to one another.

Soft currency   See **hard currencies.**

Special deposit   Deposits made by the banks at the Bank of England, over and beyond normal bank reserves. They were called for as a means of limiting bank lending, when it was thought desirable to restrict credit without raising interest rates.

Specie   Coin, usually of precious metal, as opposed to other forms of money.

Sterling area   A group of mainly Commonwealth countries that linked their currencies to sterling and held their reserves in sterling lodged in London.

Sterling balances   Balances earned by various countries, such as India and Egypt, especially for goods and services provided during the Second World War. They were frozen in London and became a particular problem when Britain attempted to reestablish free convertibility of sterling.

Strong currency   See **hard currencies.**

Tallies   Used in the Middle Ages to record debts. A tally was a long, thin piece of wood on which notches of different sizes were cut to record the sum of money owing. The tally was then split lengthways to form two complementary records of the debt, one for the debtor and the other for the creditor. When the creditor presented his part of the tally for payment, it could be checked against the other part to see that they "tallied." The system often was used privately but was a particularly important part of the medieval Exchequer's mode of operation, and continued into the eighteenth century when it was increasingly replaced by the Exchequer bill. In the nineteenth century a bonfire of old Exchequer tallies caused the fire that destroyed the old House of Commons.

Testons or testoons The new shilling coins introduced by Henry VII, and struck more plentifully by Henry VIII and Edward VI especially during the debasement. In the course of the second half of the sixteenth century, the term testo(o)n was replaced by shilling.

Threshold payments Wage increases triggered as the price index crossed certain prearranged thresholds.

Tontine A loan scheme in which subscribers received an annuity for their lifetime.

Tower pound Weight used exclusively for coining purposes at the mint in the Tower of London. It was equal to 5,400 troy grains.

Treasury bills See **bills of exchange**.

Troy weight Based on the troy grain, the troy pound weight, which replaced the Tower pound in the mints from 1526, weighed 5,760 troy grains.

TUC The Trades Union Congress is an organization representing and promoting the trade union movement.

Usury Money-lending at excessive interest.

Velocity Velocity of circulation (V) expresses not the rapidity or frequency of money payments, but rather the ratio between the size of the money supply (M) and the size of the economy (represented by T or y in the quantity theory) ($V = y/M$).

War Loan Government borrowing from the public to finance the war.

Weak currency See **hard currencies**.

Wirtschaftswunder An economic miracle. The German term refers particularly to the recovery of the West German economy after the Second World War.

Further Reading

This is a short book about a big subject. Much detail has been omitted. For further information, and for an appreciation of the sources on which this book is based, the reader is referred to the following works and to the references (bibliographies and footnotes) in them. This list could be much longer, but it is already long enough for it to be worth picking some out for special mention. Without Sir Albert Feavearyear's book, it is improbable that the idea for this book would ever have occurred to me. The work is still a classic, and there is a strong case for a new edition to bring the story up to date. For coinage across the whole period, Christopher Challis's *New History of the Royal Mint* provides an authoritative summary. For the Middle Ages Peter Spufford's *Money and Its Use in Medieval Europe,* though of European scope, sets the scene in which the English currency operated. The books by Dyer and Nightingale, though presenting very different points of view, can very profitably be read together for an agricultural and a mercantile picture. The issues in the early modern period have been well summarized by Outhwaite and Ramsey, while Challis and Gould dominate discussion of the debasement. Supple and Kepler are important for the seventeenth century. Tawney is still a classic. David Mitchell is important for early banks, and Horsefield and Cameron provide the framework for any quantitative understanding of the emergence of paper money and its use alongside coin. For the eighteenth century Bowen and Hoppit lead the field, though Carswell's telling of the South Sea Bubble story should not be missed. In the nineteenth century I have relied heavily on the very readable work by Kynaston for the City of

London. Pressnell is still the last word on the provincial banks. In the twentieth century Moggridge's *Maynard Keynes* has dominated me as much as his subject has dominated sterling, and Cairncross provides the rare combination of scholarly detachment with active personal experience of the events described. Among the political memoirs Healey's and Lawson's stand out, while Dell's view of the last fifty years is compelling and extends far beyond his own personal involvement.

I have gone to some lengths to avoid referring to particular authors by name in the text, because this book is intended as an introduction for the general reader who should be spared too much academic debate. As a consequence some issues are inevitably skated over, and many scholars may feel I have done scant justice to their work. To them I apologize. If they are kind enough to write to me, I will be able to take better account of their thoughts in my future work.

Alcock, N. W. (1981). *Warwickshire Grazier and London Skinner 1532–55: The Account Book of Peter Temple and Thomas Heritage.* London.

Alford, B. W. E. (1972). *Depression and Recovery? British Economic Growth 1918–1939.* London.

Alston, L. M. (ed.) (1906). *Sir Thomas Smith's De Republica Anglorum 1550.* Cambridge.

Ashton, T. S. (1953). "Bills of Exchange and Private Banks in Lancashire, 1790–1830," in T. S. Ashton and R. S. Sayers (eds.), *Papers in English Monetary History.* Oxford.

Bagehot, Walter (1873). *Lombard Street.* London.

Barnsby, George (1971). "The Standard of Living in the Black Country during the Nineteenth Century," *Economic History Review,* 2nd ser., 24.

Beckett, Francis (1997). *Clem Attlee.* London.

Beckett, J. V. (1986). *The Aristocracy in England 1660–1914.* Oxford.

Besly, E. (1990). *Coins and Medals of the English Civil War.* London.

Bindoff, S. T. (1973). *The Fame of Sir Thomas Gresham.* London.

Black, John (1997). *Oxford Dictionary of Economics.* Oxford.

Bowen, H. V. (1995). "The Bank of England during the Long Eighteenth Century, 1680–1820," in Richard Roberts and David Kynaston (eds.), *The Bank of England.* Oxford.

Brenner, Y. S. (1961). "Inflation of Prices in Early Sixteenth Century England," *Economic History Review,* 2nd ser., 14.

Briggs, Asa (1962). *The Age of Improvement 1783–1867.* London.

Burnett, John (1979). *Plenty and Want.* London.

Butler, David (1971). *The British General Election of 1970.* London.

Cairncross, Sir Alec (1992). *The British Economy since 1945: Economic Policy and Performance 1945–1990.* Oxford.

Cairncross, Alec, and Eichengreen, Barry (1983). *Sterling in Decline: The Devaluations of 1931, 1949 and 1967.* Oxford.

Cameron, Rondo (1967). "England, 1750–1844," in his *Banking in the Early Stages of Industrialisation.* New York.

Cannadine, David (1990). *The Decline and Fall of the British Aristocracy.* New Haven.

Carswell, J. (1993). *The South Sea Bubble.* Stroud.

Challis, C. E. (1978). *The Tudor Coinage.* Manchester.

—— (1989). *Currency and the Economy in Tudor and Early Stuart England.* London.

—— (ed.) (1992). *A New History of the Royal Mint.* Cambridge.

Chartres, J. A. (1977). *Internal Trade in England 1500–1700.* London.

Clarkson, L. A. (1971). *The Pre-industrial Economy in England 1500–1750.* London.

Clay, C. G. A. (1984). *Economic Expansion and Social Change: England 1500–1700.* Cambridge.

Cornwall, J. C. K. (1988). *Wealth and Society in Early Sixteenth Century England.* London.

Day, J. (1978). "The Great Bullion Famine of the Fifteenth Century," *Past and Present,* 79.

Defoe, Daniel [1726] (1987). *The Complete English Tradesman.* Gloucester.

Dell, Edmund (1997). *The Chancellors: A History of the Chancellors of the Exchequer 1945–1990.* London.

Dyer, Christopher (1994). *Standards of Living in the Later Middle Ages: Social Change in England c. 1200–1520.* Cambridge.

Feavearyear, Sir Albert (1932). *The Pound Sterling* (revised by E. Victor Morgan, 1963). Oxford.

Foreman-Peck, J. (ed.) (1991). *New Perspectives on the Late Victorian Economy.* Cambridge.

Fussell, G. E. (ed.) (1936). *Robert Loder's Farm Accounts, 1610–1620.* London.

Gould, J. D. (1970). *The Great Debasement.* Oxford.

Grierson, Philip (1961). "Sterling," in R. H. M. Dolley (ed.), *Anglo-Saxon Coins: Historical Essays Presented to Sir Frank Stenton*. London.

—— (1988). "An Early Reference to Sterlings," *British Numismatic Journal, 58*.

Healey, Denis (1989). *The Time of My Life*. London.

Hennessy, Peter (1992). *Never Again: Britain 1945–1951*. London.

Holderness, B. A. (1976). *Pre-Industrial England: Economy and Society 1500–1750*. London.

Hoppit, Julian (1986). "Financial Crises in Eighteenth-Century England," *Economic History Review, 39*.

—— (1996). "Political Arithmetic in Eighteenth-Century England," *Economic History Review, 49*.

Horsefield, J. K. (1960). *British Monetary Experiments 1650–1710*. London.

Hutton, Will (1995). *The State We're In*. London.

Jay, Douglas (1985). *Sterling. Its Use and Misuse: A Plea for Moderation*. London.

Johnson, Christopher (1996). *In with the Euro, Out with the Pound: The Single Currency for Britain*. London.

Kepler, J.S. (1959). *The Exchange of Christendom. The International Entrepôt at Dover 1622–51*. Leicester.

Kerridge, Eric (1988). *Trade and Banking in Early Modern England*. Manchester.

Kynaston, David (1994). *The City of London* (2 vols.). London.

Latham, R. C. (ed.) (1970). *The Diary of Samuel Pepys*.

Lawson, Nigel (1993). *The View from No 11: Memoirs of a Tory Radical*. London.

Lennard, Reginald (1959). *Rural England 1086–1135*. Oxford.

McCulloch, J.R. [1856] (1954). *Early English Tracts on Commerce*. Cambridge.

Macfarlane, A. (ed.) (1976). *The Diary of Ralph Josselin*. London.

Marshall, J. D. (ed.) (1967). *Autobiography of William Stout of Lancaster 1665–1752*. Manchester.

Mathias, Peter (1969). *The First Industrial Nation*. London.

Mayhew, N. J. (1995). "Modelling Medieval Monetisation," in Richard H. Britnell and Bruce M. S. Campbell (eds.), *A Commercialising Economy: England 1086 to c. 1300*. Manchester.

—— (1995). "Population, Money Supply, and the Velocity of Circulation in England, 1300–1700." *Economic History Review, 48*.

Melton, F. T. (1986). *Sir Robert Clayton and the Origins of English Deposit Banking 1658–1685.* Cambridge.

Mitchell, B. R., and Deane, Phyllis (1962). *Abstract of British Historical Statistics.* Cambridge.

Mitchell, David (1995). "Innovation and the Transfer of Skill in the Goldsmiths' Trade in Restoration London," in D. Mitchell (ed.), *Goldsmiths, Silversmiths and Bankers: Innovation and Transfer of Skill, 1550 to 1750.* London.

Moggridge, D. E. (1995). *Maynard Keynes: An Economist's Biography.* London.

Mui, Hoh-Cheung, and Mui, Lorna H. (1989). *Shops and Shopkeeping in Eighteenth-Century England.* Kingston, Ontario.

Nichols, J. G. (ed.) (1848). *The Diary of Henry Machyn, Citizen and Merchant Tailor of London 1550–1563.* London.

Nightingale, Pamela (1995). *A Medieval Merchant Community: The Grocers' Company and the Politics and Trade of London 1000–1485.* New Haven.

Orwell, George (1937). *The Road to Wigan Pier.* London.

Outhwaite, R. B. (1970). *Inflation in Tudor and Early Stuart England.* London.

——— (1971). "Royal Borrowing in the Reign of Elizabeth I," *English Historical Review,* 86.

Pember-Reeves, Maud [1913] (1979). *Round About a Pound a Week.* London.

Petersen, Christian (1995). *Bread and the British Economy c. 1770–1870.* Aldershot.

Phelps Brown, E. H., and Hopkins, Sheila (1956). "Seven Centuries of the Price of Consumables, Compared with Builders' Wage-Rates," *Economica,* 23.

Pimlott, B. (1985). *Hugh Dalton.* London.

Pollard, S. (1969). *The Development of the British Economy 1914–1967.* London.

Postan, M. M. (1944). "The Rise of the Money Economy," *Economic History Review,* 14.

Pressnell, L. S. (1956). *Country Banking in the Industrial Revolution.* Oxford.

Quinn, Stephen (1996). "Gold, Silver, and the Glorious Revolution: Arbitrage between Bills of Exchange and Bullion," *Economic History Review,* 49.

Ramsey, Peter H. (ed.) (1971). *The Price Revolution in Sixteenth-Century England*. London.

Redwood, John (1997). *Our Currency, Our Country: The Dangers of European Monetary Union*. London.

Roberts, Richard, and Kynaston, David (eds.) (1995). *The Bank of England: Money, Power and Influence 1694–1994*. Oxford.

Rogers, J. E. Thorold (1866–1902). *A History of Agriculture and Prices in England, 1259–1793*, 7 vols. Oxford.

Roover, R. de (ed.) (1949). *Gresham on Foreign Exchange*. Cambridge, Mass.

Smith, Adam (n.d.). *An Inquiry into the Nature and Causes of the Wealth of Nations*. London.

Spufford, Peter (1988). *Money and Its Use in Medieval Europe*.

Styles, John (1980). "Our Traitorous Money Makers," in John Brewer and John Styles (eds.), *An Ungovernable People*. London.

Supple, B. (1959). *Commercial Crisis and Change in England 1600–1642*. Cambridge.

Tawney, R. H. [1926] (1990). *Religion and the Rise of Capitalism*. London.

Tawney, R. H., and Power, Eileen (eds.) (1953). *Tudor Economic Documents*. London.

Taylor, Arthur J. (1975). *The Standard of Living in Britain in the Industrial Revolution*. London.

Wilsher, Peter (1970). *The Pound in Your Pocket 1870–1970*. London.

Wee, H. van der (1963). *The Growth of the Antwerp Market and the European Economy*. The Hague.

Wilson, T. (1925). *Discourse upon Usury* (ed. R. H. Tawney). London.

Woodward, D. (ed.) (1984). *The Farming and Memoranda Books of Henry Best of Elmswell 1642*. New York.

Woolf, Virginia (1929). *A Room of One's Own*. London.

Wordie, J. R. (1997). "Deflationary Factors in the Tudor Price Rise," *Past and Present*, 151.

Index